"Hastings's descriptions of events on the ground in Iraq are flat and impartial, delivered in just-the-facts style. But that only heightens his complete candor about his soul-shattering loss from Andi's death in a Baghdad gun battle."

—Kimberly Johnson, *The Washington Post*

"Outstanding . . . The writing is exceptional. . . . Reminiscent of Michael Herr's *Dispatches,* possessing the same raw immediacy . . . A touching love story . . . The world Hastings describes is choked with the craziness that characterizes all great war books."

—Bruce Elder, *The Sydney Morning Herald*

"Hastings provides a remarkable inside look at life in Iraq. He makes no overt political statements, yet pulls no punches in describing how many Iraqis behave toward each other and toward the foreign troops."

—Al Hutchison, *The Tampa Tribune*

"A modern war story . . . a reality many young people will get . . . [about a] couple in love, but with the Iraq War as the backdrop it became a story about sacrifice and the true cost of war."

—Marisa Buchanan, *NBC Nightly News*

"[Hastings] has a keen eye for telling details and a firm command of reporting the issues . . . a brave but controversial book."

—Mark Miller, *Newsweek*

"Of all the places to be in love, Baghdad might be the worst. But that didn't stop Michael Hastings and his girlfriend . . . until he awoke to news that was worse than any horrific story he had covered."

—*GQ*

"[A] powerful debut . . . Hastings reports with insight and grim humor from the front lines. . . . Like Mariane Pearl's *A Mighty Heart,* this is a tragic love story with broad appeal married to an unflinching account of wartime violence and brutality."

—*Publishers Weekly* (starred review)

"Leaves you gasping for breath . . . stunning . . . [*I Lost My Love in Baghdad*] gives the reader a remarkable inside look at life in a strife-torn land."

—A. C. Hutchison, *The Barre-Montepelier Times Argus*

"Hastings describes how two young, almost hopelessly idealistic people try to nurture and maintain a relationship amid the daily carnage in Baghdad. This is no sappy love story . . . moving and deeply disturbing."

—*Booklist*

"An unflinching and important account of the war . . . Hasting is not only a talented reporter but he is also a gifted writer, and his book is an important account of the Iraq War that every American would do well to read."

—*PhillyBurbs.com*

"Bittersweet . . . This book was a gift to Andi."

—Ann Curry, *NBC News*

"Michael Hastings's pain was off the charts, but he manages to tell his story—and the tragic story of his girlfriend Andi—with dignity, humor, and grace. This is a searing personal drama and a raw, compelling account of the daily battle to cover the war in Iraq."

—Andrew Nagorski, author of *The Greatest Battle: Stalin, Hitler, and the Desperate Struggle for Moscow That Changed the Course of World War II*

"Love and war always make for a potent brew, and in Michael Hastings's new book they infuse the horror in Iraq with an immediacy and a poignant sense of loss that are light-years away from the numbingly remote headlines we've been reading. This is what really happens when love, youth, and innocence descend into the abyss of death and devastation that is Iraq."

—Craig Unger, author of *House of Bush, House of Saud* and *American Armageddon*

I Lost
My Love
in Baghdad

A MODERN WAR STORY

MICHAEL HASTINGS

SCRIBNER

New York London Toronto Sydney

SCRIBNER
A Division of Simon & Schuster, Inc.
1230 Avenue of the Americas
New York, NY 10020

First Scribner trade paperback edition February 2010

SCRIBNER and design are registered trademarks of The Gale Group, Inc.,
used under license by Simon & Schuster, Inc., the publisher of this work.

For information about special discounts for bulk purchases,
please contact Simon & Schuster Special Sales at
1-866-506-1949 or business@simonandschuster.com.

The Simon & Schuster Speakers Bureau can bring authors to your live event.
For more information or to book an event contact the Simon & Schuster Speakers Bureau
at 1-866-248-3049 or visit our website at www.simonspeakers.com.

Text set in Adobe Garamond

Manufactured in the United States of America

1   3   5   7   9   10   8   6   4   2

Library of Congress Control Number: 2007049806

ISBN 978-1-4165-6097-5
ISBN 978-1-4165-6098-2 (pbk)
ISBN 978-1-4165-6116-3 (ebook)

To
ASP
forever

Violence and progress coexist in Iraq.
—General George W. Casey, former U.S. commander
of Multi-National Forces Iraq

Me and you and you and me
No matter how they toss the dice, it had to be.
—"Happy Together," 1967

In such dangerous things as War, the errors which proceed
from a spirit of benevolence are the worst.
—Carl von Clausewitz, *On War*

Author's Note

This book is my own personal interpretation of events. Some names have been changed for security reasons, others for reasons of privacy. A full list of altered names is included at the end of the book, along with an explanation of my sources.

—MH

I Lost My Love in Baghdad

January 17, 2007

Andi wakes up Wednesday morning in Baghdad. She takes an hour to get ready. She showers, brushes her teeth, and thinks about placing a Crest whitening strip on her smile. She eats only a Zone bar, high nutrition, and drinks a bottle of Ocean Spray cranberry juice from her small refrigerator. Her room is in the Ramal Hotel off Karrada Street on the fourth floor. It is a two-star establishment pretending to be four-star. Lots of gold and dark reds. There is only a single bed in her double room; she asked for the second bed to be taken out to make space for her yoga mat. The drapes on her window overlooking the compound are always closed. She puts on her jeans, a long-sleeved white button-down shirt, and a navy blue blazer. She checks her email on a laptop with a wireless connection, sends a message to her friend in New York, giving advice on relationship troubles. She grabs her black bag and folder with pen and paper. She closes and locks the door.

Andi walks down the four floors, says good morning to the owner of the hotel, who stands behind the front desk in a suit. She waves at the boy who cleans her room and brings her room service, light meals of hummus and tea. She steps around the metal detector at the hotel entrance, checks to make sure she has her mobile phone, then steps out into the isolated world of her compound. It is a self-contained fortress: two barely functioning hotels facing each other across a narrow, closed-off street, an entire city block taken over by the organizations that live and work inside the compound.

There is sun today, a clear sky, but at this hour it is still chilly. Her office is inside the compound, protected from the main avenue by

1

checkpoints and tall concrete walls. It takes her only a minute to walk there. She passes about a dozen vehicles, some armored white SUVs, others armored sedans, parked underneath an awning. She arrives at her desk about 9 A.M. She has a trip planned for this morning, her first in her new job at the National Democratic Institute. Compound life can be stifling, and she is looking forward to getting out into the city. She sits down and calls her interpreter, who tells her the meeting is still on. The interpreter will meet her at the Iraqi Islamic Party headquarters in Yarmouk, a neighborhood on the other side of the city. She calls the head of security, telling him she'll be ready to go soon. The security team is waiting outside, four European private security guards and three Iraqi drivers.

Across the Tigris River, other men are preparing for her arrival. A few of them were up earlier, most likely for prayer. They have names, though most don't use them. They are cousins and brothers. They drink chai and start to move to their cars. They stash weapons—AK-47s, grenades, and a heavy machine gun—in the trunk of an orange and white Opel. They load up two more cars.

The leader's cell phone rings. The ring tone is an Islamic prayer he downloaded from the Internet. The rest of the men are used to it, they know it is his phone. He gets confirmation.

She is coming. She is blond, American. They even have a name.

Andi sends a few more emails from her desk, typing quickly. She takes off her blazer and leaves it on the back of a swivel chair. A coworker wishes her good luck. She turns, smiles, says thanks. She doesn't turn off her laptop and the screen saver kicks in a few minutes after she goes outside. Her private security guard opens the door of the BMW sedan. The sedan has B-6-level armor, which is supposed to stop bullets. She gets in the car, and they leave the compound, traveling quickly through the morning traffic. There is a tail car and a lead car, nothing unusual. The traffic circles are snarled. Iraqi police fire shots in the air instead of using their horns.

It takes her convoy twenty minutes to get to the headquarters of the Iraqi Islamic Party. It is now 10:30 A.M.

Another phone call to the leader from his contact. The same ring tone. She has arrived. The orange and white Opel heads toward Yarmouk.

The meeting is off to a slow start; her interpreter is running a little late. Andi jokes and talks about the weather, about a story in the *New York Times,* about how she isn't able to get out of her compound much. One of the men she is there to meet refuses to shake her hand because she is a woman. Two security guards are with her in the room. The others wait with the cars in the parking lot. Glasses of chai are served. The interpreter, a young Iraqi woman, finally arrives and apologizes for being late. She was held up at a checkpoint, she says, a bomb scare, the typical morning.

They get on with the meeting. The purpose is to discuss how the Iraqi Islamic Party can effectively get their message out to the media. They are an important political party in the new government; the head of the party is one of the country's three vice presidents. It's also a chance for Andi to meet the politicians she'll be working with over the coming month, part of a training program the National Democratic Institute has set up to assist the Iraqi government in building a functioning democracy.

It is now 11:30 A.M.

The street outside the headquarters begins to empty. Traffic disappears; shop owners decide it is time to take a break. The street kids are nowhere to be seen.

The men are now in position. A machine gun is set up on top of a building. The rest of the men, nearly thirty of them, all carrying weapons, hide in alleys and shops along the street.

12 P.M. The meeting ends, goodbyes are said, cards exchanged.

Andi walks out to the parking lot. The three cars have their engines running. Her security guard opens the door to the sedan, the second car, and she gets in.

12:07 P.M. The first car drives out of the Islamic Party's compound and heads down the street. The driver and guard don't notice anything wrong. The route looks clear. There is no traffic, no one in the streets.

Thirty seconds later, her car follows.

Andi is sitting in the backseat.

CHAPTER 1

August 14, 2005

BAGHDAD

"Mike, get down, mate."

I am lying in the backseat of a blue BMW. My view is the car's ashtray on the back of the center console. My legs are wedged between the seats, my torso twisted at an awkward angle. I am wearing blue jeans and a button-down long-sleeved shirt, a vest of body armor firmly Velcroed to protect my vital organs. I've been in Baghdad less than one hour and am now a passenger traveling down the road from the airport to the Green Zone.

"Mike, just try to keep your head below the windows, mate."

My security manager is Jack Tapes, an ex–Royal Marine, who flew in with me that morning from Amman, Jordan. Neither of us slept much the night before. We had first-class tickets, so we waited, chain-smoking, in the Royal Jordanian first-class lounge at the Queen Alia International Airport. The flight, one of the two scheduled daily commercial flights from Amman to Baghdad, was delayed for about an hour. The pilots were South African, working on contract because of their experience flying in and out of war zones. The plane was filled with contractors and mercenaries and overweight Iraqi businessmen and officials. The stewardesses, also South African, were very pretty; a slight blond girl with wild green eyes served me shrimp on a small slice of brown bread and a bottle of seltzer water. I suspected they chose the prettiest girls on purpose, to give the passengers a sense of calm, the flight a feeling of normalcy it shouldn't have had. The stewardess stood in the aisle to talk about seat

5

belts, emergency exits, overhead compartments, electronic devices off, and flotation devices under the seats, a highly improbable safety feature considering we were flying over four hundred miles of desert. The "corkscrew landing"—the phrase used to describe the now legendary descent for civilians coming into Baghdad—was uneventful. The plane angled down, a sharp diagonal cut across the sky, the wings dipping in ways the wings of passenger planes aren't supposed to dip. I looked out the window at the sunlight bouncing off miniature homes and cars, a series of tiny sparkles, wondering if they were flashes of gunfire. The fear was more existential than physical. We were floating, circling, a big fat target over the dull brown landscape below. I remembered the warning on the State Department's website: "Civilian aircraft flying into the Baghdad Airport are regularly targeted for rocket and small arms fire." The travel advisory strongly recommended Americans not to visit Iraq. When the plane touched down, the stewardess's voice came over the intercom to give us the local time, one hour ahead of Amman, and then said, "Thank you for flying Royal Jordanian. We hope you have pleasant stay."

The day before, Tapes had briefed me on the pickup from the airport—what was supposed to happen, what car we would get into, what to do if we got hit, if there was "contact," as Tapes put it. We would be traveling in a Mercedes sedan. "B-6 armor," he explained, "the highest level available, made to stop 7.62mm rounds." In addition to me and Tapes, there would be a driver and an Iraqi guard in the Merc. Three other Iraqi guards with AK-47s would be in the tail or "follow car," a gray Chevrolet. Tapes diagrammed the whole thing out in the lobby of the InterContinental Hotel in Amman. "We'll drive through any contact," he said. First priority: keep going. "The Iraqi guards are okay," he told me, "but they're really 'shit shields'"—bodies to be shot before I got shot. Our biggest threat would be from American military convoys. "When they go out, they stop traffic for miles," Tapes said. "You get stuck behind one of those, and if a car bomb is aiming for them, you can get caught up in it. It's what happened to that Marla girl"—Marla Ruzicka, the twenty-eight-year-old American aid worker who was killed in April by a car bomb on Airport Road.

The plan seemed straightforward enough, and Tapes seemed reasonable enough at the time. He'd been working in Iraq for two years. He'd been involved in gunrunning in Fallujah and Baghdad, transporting and selling arms to other security companies. He liked to say that the best time to be in a war is right at the beginning, when you can do whatever you want, before people get their shit together and start making rules. Drive any which way, shoot any which way. The golden age to work in Iraq, he told me, had passed. "It's just no fun anymore," he said.

We stepped off the plane onto the tarmac. Private security guards from Latin America in floppy recon hats stood guard with M-16s. Military cargo planes landed on the U.S. side of the facility. Sad-looking planes with green IRAQI AIRWAYS decals sat on the runway. Slightly bombed-out hangars lined the landing area. The heat was intense, 45 degrees Celsius, 113 degrees Fahrenheit. According to the CNN weather report I'd watched the night before, Baghdad was the hottest place listed on the map.

A rickety fume-spewing bus, standing room only, brought us to the terminal at the Baghdad International Airport. I kept my bags close to me. The other passengers filed in, no smiles, the scent of body odor in the air reminding me that I had now entered the birthplace of civilization. The Fertile Crescent. Mesopotamia. Iraq.

We passed through customs and picked our luggage up off the baggage carousel. I'd brought two extra duffel bags filled with supplies for the bureau—one packed with Western food, Skippy peanut butter, Cap'n Crunch, and strawberry Pop-Tarts, the other with new DVDs and PlayStation 2 games. Our Iraqi security team waited in the arrivals section. They helped with my bags, and we walked at a brisk pace out to the parking garage. Tapes said we would wait a few minutes for all the VIP convoys—groups of SUVs with tinted windows and tail gunners—to leave first, on the theory that they were the "bullet magnets."

But something else wasn't right. Tapes was getting nervous, jumpy.

"Where the fuck are the guns?" he asked.

He was speaking to Massen, our Jordanian driver. Massen lived in Amman and was at the moment under some suspicion. A few days earlier, he'd claimed his SUV was stolen, along with eight hundred dollars, while he was trying to make the drive from Amman to Baghdad on what was called the Mad Max Highway, a straight five-hundred-mile dash across the desert that was now considered too dangerous for Westerners to take. According to Massen, gunmen stopped him and stole the car and he had to walk through the desert after spending a night out in the cold. He was demanding that *Newsweek,* or Tapes, reimburse him for the lost car and the airline ticket he'd had to buy to get back into Iraq. There was a question as to whether he had actually been ambushed, or if he and his friends in Amman had just decided to steal the car. Massen was going to be my driver.

"What the fuck do you mean, you didn't bring any guns?"

Standing in the parking garage, I noticed for the first time that none of my guards were carrying weapons. I also noticed that contrary to what I was promised—the heavily armored black Mercedes—I was going to be traveling in a smaller blue BMW.

"We didn't have the key to the gun locker," Massen explained.

"How didn't you have the key to the gun locker?"

"The *L.A. Times* took the key to the gun locker."

The *Los Angeles Times* and the *Wall Street Journal* shared the house in the Green Zone with *Newsweek,* a way to ease the pain of paying upward of $16,000 a month for rent.

"You're fucking kidding me, mate."

Massen shrugged. "I have a 9mm pistol," he said.

"One fucking pistol on Airport fucking Road? Christ. And where's the fucking Mercedes?"

"We didn't want to take the Mercedes today."

"You didn't what?"

Tapes's thick British accent grew thicker the more he swore. He took the 9mm pistol from Massen.

"And if we get fucking hit today, Massen, if we get fucking hit today, what do you think *Newsweek* in New York is going to say? They're going to say why the fuck did we spend 130 grand on an armored fucking Mercedes when you shits decided to drive in a fucking Beamer? They're going to say why the fuck wasn't Mike in the fucking Mercedes?"

Luggage loaded in the trunk, I got in the backseat of the BMW. Tapes sat next to me. He was highly agitated. "Once we leave the airport," he said, "you lie down."

Twisted down on the backseat, I can feel sunlight on the top of my head, on my hair, and I wonder if that means I am exposed and should try to wriggle down lower. It is very sunny, very hot, the air conditioner in the car doesn't work, and we can't roll the windows down because if a bullet gets into an armored car, it bounces around until it hits something, or more likely someone. I'm smiling. There is no fear; there is adrenaline. I know things aren't going according to plan. I know that there are no guns and I am in the wrong car and there was a serious breakdown in communication somewhere along the way. I think to myself: I guess this is to be expected in a conflict environment when you are dealing with former gunrunners and possibly criminal Iraqi men. I'm not going to say anything. I just got here, I'm new, I guess this is how it works.

Tapes is on the handheld Motorola radio used to communicate between the cars. He's telling the drivers to slow down, speed up, don't hold the radio too high above the window (if insurgents see a radio, they'll know you're guarding someone), avoid that bump, stay away from that car. He's looking out the back window, out the front window. I stay quiet, though I do want a cigarette, staring at the ashtray in front of me.

"You got to be fucking kidding me."

The car is stopped. A convoy. We are stuck in traffic. Twenty minutes pass before the car starts moving again.

"You got to be fucking kidding me, mate."

Another American convoy, another twenty minutes. The car is getting hotter, Tapes is keeping up a steady rhythm of fucks and shits. I am sweating and I remember this thing I read a year ago by Ryszard Kapuściński, the Polish journalist, about a trip he took to Azerbaijan. "Once you are in this kind of situation, you are in this kind of situation." Or something like that.

This is what I signed up for. Fucking Baghdad. I am finally here.

In January 1992, when the U.S. went to war with Iraq for the first time, I sat with my father in the kitchen of our childhood home in

Malone, New York, and watched the bombs fall on CNN. I was in fifth grade when the three-day ground war started, and I asked to be excused from phys ed class so I could see General Norman Schwarzkopf, Stormin' Norman, give a live press conference from Riyadh. I asked my teacher, Sister Marilyn, to bring a television into the classroom so I could watch. I took notes on a small pad with a pencil.

I've always been obsessed with the news. When I was six years old, I would wake up early before school to watch the newly founded CNN. But Iraq's invasion of Kuwait was news that went beyond the television. When the gulf war started, everyone in my class wore yellow ribbons and we all sang that song—I'm proud to be an American, because at least I know I'm free, and I won't forget the men who died who gave that right to me. It was a very small Catholic school in a very small town. During recess, I talked about the war with my friends, the few kids who'd been as glued to the TV as I was.

One day that winter, there was a special assembly in the gymnasium. A local actor was brought in as part of an educational initiative to explain the war to elementary school students. He got up on stage, carrying two rubber Halloween masks, one of President George Herbert Walker Bush and one of President Saddam Hussein al-Tikriti. He played each role, switching back and forth behind a folding screen on stage, explaining American foreign policy in simple terms, bad guys versus good guys. It was entertaining. I remember raising my hand and asking, why don't we just kill Saddam Hussein? The actor, prepared to improvise, put on the Bush mask and said something like: "Would you like it if they killed me, your president?" And I remember thinking, perhaps precociously, or perhaps I'd heard it somewhere, that the cost of one life is nothing if it could save so many others.

Months later, there was another assembly. The war was over, and this time we listened to a returning veteran who couldn't have been older than twenty. I raised my hand and asked him: Did you carry an M-16, and does an M-16 have automatic and semiautomatic fire? And if so, is there a switch on the gun? (Yes, it has both, and there is a switch.) He described trying to dig a foxhole in the desert, and how he went on a mission for two days, observing the enemy from a distance. I was riveted. It was like being in the presence of a celebrity—better, even, because this celebrity had been to war. I'd always been fascinated by the military. Throughout grade school, my favorite game involved hiding in the woods with cap guns and camouflage uniforms. Every month, I would ask my father to bring me to a nearby army/navy surplus store. When I was nine, he bought me a real Vietnam-era flak jacket that I had wanted.

Throughout the nineties, I stayed focused on the news about Iraq. I read about the economic sanctions, how human rights groups estimated that over half a million Iraqi children had died due to the restrictions on imports, about the allegations of WMDs and the U.N. deployment of weapons inspectors, then Clinton's bombing of over one hundred targets in Iraq in December 1998. I watched David O. Russell's gulf war adventure film *Three Kings* twice in the theaters and many more times on DVD. Saddam even made a cameo in *The Big Lebowski,* another of my favorite movies, popping up in a dream sequence at a bowling alley.

I moved to New York City to finish college in September 2000, taking classes in English literature and media studies at night and working part-time jobs during the day. It was an election year in which George W. Bush promised that America would do no more "nation-building." The song "Bombs Over Baghdad" by Outkast became a hit. On September 11, 2001, my father called and woke me up and told me to turn on the TV. I headed downtown, under the blue skies, making it to Houston Street before being turned back at the first police barricade. I watched the towers burn from the roof of a friend's apartment in the East Village. I turned twenty-two the next year, graduated, and got a summer internship at *Newsweek.* I started to report and write for the international edition of the magazine. I was hired at the end of the summer.

That August, I listened to Vice President Cheney say we were going after Saddam. I remember my initial response was, what a crazy idea. What a crazy, crazy idea, flying thousands of miles with an invading army to topple a government. But as the debate began, I started to think, well, democracy, freedom, 9-11, WMDs, maybe it's not such a bad idea. Being a contrarian, I argued with my antiwar colleagues, taking on the neoconservative talking points just to see how they felt, even though the talk of mobile weapons labs all seemed like complete bullshit to me, like whoever drew up the diagrams of mobile weapons labs had watched too much G.I. Joe as a child and could only imagine some kind of fantastic weapon that C.O.B.R.A (the evil terrorist organization fighting to rule the world, as the theme song pointed out) used to attack the real American heroes. On February 5, 2003, Colin Powell posed on 1st Avenue in New York City with a vial of fake anthrax. On March 20, 2003, the war started. For the next forty-eight hours, I watched TV, nonstop it seemed, switching between live coverage of the invasion and Adult Videos on Demand, alone in my New York apartment, thinking, I want to be over there, I want to be in Iraq.

Two years later here I am.

The BMW is moving at a crawl. My body feels each bump in the road. My sweat has soaked through my shirt.

"Okay, mate, you can get up now."

The car stops again. We are at the first checkpoint to enter the Green Zone. There are two lanes, divided by fifteen-foot-high concrete walls erected to contain the damage of suicide car bombs. One lane is "high priority"; only American military personnel and Defense Department contractors allowed. The other is for Iraqis and foreigners without proper identification. A sign in front reads DEADLY FORCE AUTHORIZED, in both English and Arabic. Follow the soldiers' instructions or you will be shot, it advises. Cell phones must be turned off; no photos allowed, either. I take it all in after seeing nothing but the car floor and the ashtray for the last forty-five minutes on what should have been a ten-minute drive.

There are palm trees. There are blast walls. A Bradley tank rolls past. Iraqi Army and American soldiers stand guard in front of a shack protected by sandbags. Water bottles and empty soda cans litter the ground. Dozens of beat-up cars are queued up, waiting in the sun to be searched. Their hoods and trunks are popped to check for explosives. A young American soldier watches from the shade of a blast wall as an Iraqi soldier lazily pats down the passengers in the car in front of us. The American spits chewing tobacco into an empty Gatorade bottle.

Nothing seems to fit. I don't know what it is. It may be the heat or it may be lack of sleep. Or it could just be the adrenaline coming down. I have this sensation that I am seeing too many parts that don't quite go together—randomly scattered signs of America in this completely un-American place, sun-blasted and slow-moving. I take it all in.

My first real look at Baghdad, and I remember my thought to the word.

What the fuck were we thinking?

CHAPTER 2

August-October 2005

BAGHDAD

Scott Johnson was sitting behind his desk on the second floor of the *Newsweek* bureau, a two-floor home inside the Green Zone, abandoned by its Iraqi owners and now rented to us. I walked into the office. He looked up and smiled.

"I brought a bunch of new DVDs," I said.

"Cool, we'll check them out later. Let's go get your badges."

Badges, I would learn, were the key to the Green Zone. I needed two of them—one military press ID and another called the International Zone (the official name for the Green Zone, usually just called "the IZ") badge. The IZ badges were color coded—red was the lowest (for most Iraqis), purple being the highest (for high-level government officials). The right badge could get you into the U.S. embassy; the right badge allowed you to walk freely in the IZ without an escort, got you priority access to the checkpoints outside the IZ. The right badge allowed you to carry firearms and not get searched.

We walked outside the bureau. The house had a small lawn and garden out front, surrounded by a six-foot-high white wall. It was located on a quiet street guarded at both ends by a private security company called Edinburgh Risk.

Scott got behind the wheel of the Mercedes. At thirty-one years old, he was the magazine's youngest Baghdad bureau chief. In a few short years he'd gone from reporting in Paris to covering the war in Afghanistan, then to Iraq and from there to become the bureau chief in Mexico City. Now he was back in Baghdad with the top job. He backed out of the driveway, explaining the rules for moving around the IZ as he drove.

Rule 1: Stay away from American, Iraqi, and private security convoys. They are authorized to shoot anyone who comes within one hundred meters of their cars.

Rule 2: Stop at all checkpoints, whether on foot or in the car. Turn on your hazard lights and the inside car light at night. If you don't turn the lights on, they might shoot you.

That was basically it.

I sat shotgun, cracking the three-inch-thick bulletproof window to smoke. The extra weight from the armor on the Mercedes made the car drive like a boat.

We were on our way to the Iraqi parliament building, or the Convention Center, a five-minute drive from the house, where I could fill out all the necessary paperwork. At the first checkpoint, Scott made sure to hold his badge up against the windshield so the Iraqi guards working for Edinburgh Risk could see it. We then took a left, drove around the July 14th traffic circle—a dangerous intersection, Scott pointed out, because American patrols and private security convoys often came flying over the July 14th Bridge, returning from the city, still hyped up on adrenaline and more prone to shoot. The traffic circle flowed onto a wide four-lane road, with deep potholes and without lane markings, where no speed limit applied. After another traffic circle, we passed an area that was once the crown jewel of Baghdad's government, well-manicured parks surrounding the massive seashell-like Tomb of the Unknown Soldier. The parks were now off-limits and overgrown; across from the tomb stood the complex of Iraqi government buildings, including the prime minister's office. The wide road narrowed down to two lanes, funneled in between blast walls, and abruptly ended in a parking lot for the Convention Center. At the end of the parking lot, there were twenty-foot-high barriers separating the Green Zone from the rest of Iraq.

As we stepped out of the car, the sun pressed down on us, a dry heat so severe that it took a few seconds for my body to understand how hot it was. I inhaled and it felt like breathing the crisp air inside an oven. We walked down a palatial white sidewalk to the first checkpoint outside the Convention Center and Scott showed his badge to Georgian soldiers who guarded it. They were part of the Coalition of the Willing, and their job was to guard key installations inside the Green Zone, despite their inability to speak English or Arabic. On the roof of the Rasheed Hotel, across from the Convention Center, snipers watched over the area. The next checkpoint was manned by Gurkhas, private security guards from Nepal. One hundred and fifty feet beyond them was another one before the steps of the Convention Center, manned by Iraqi police officers sitting in a wooden guard box that looked like a telephone booth. At the top of the steps, we were searched individually by an Iraqi security guard in plainclothes before we emptied our pockets and proceeded through a metal detector and X-ray machine. Finally, we were in the Convention Center, a multifloored complex that resembled any oversized venue for corporate summits. There were rooms for press conferences, government offices, and on the second floor an open-air cafeteria for Iraqi parliament members and the assembly hall for the Iraqi government. We walked upstairs to the second floor, where the military's public affairs offices were located, the Combined Press Information Center, or CPIC. Another Gurkha waiting in the hall checked our IDs again. I filled out the paperwork, handed to me by a sergeant working in public affairs, and grinned for the picture to get my ID. We left and drove back to the bureau. My first day in Iraq was over.

I'd arrived two years, five months, and twenty-five days after the war started, and Baghdad was under siege. Gone were the days of journalists traveling freely throughout the country. The stories I'd hear of the wild parties at the Hamra Hotel ("You know her, from Egypt, she swam in her underwear!"), the morning drives to Ramadi and Fallujah, casually searching for stories on the streets of Sadr City, moving without two carloads of armed guards—all of that had disappeared. Now about half our time was spent moving from one protected compound to the next, reporting by phone and email, conducting interviews with Iraqis who were willing to come see us. The other half was spent out on embeds with the U.S. military.

Most Westerners agreed that the good times ended in the spring of 2004. That April, the bodies of four Blackwater employees were strung up on a bridge in Fallujah. The next month Nicholas Berg, an American contractor, was beheaded on video, and the video was shown throughout the world. It was the month after that, they said, you could feel the change in the air. Things were going to get much worse. The war settled into a new pace. Brutality that had once captured headlines—three car bombs, over 115 dead—was now standard. The armed killers became better organized; there were more guns on the streets, more explosives, more suicide bombings. There were more suicide bombings in Iraq from 2003 to 2006 than in the entire world during the previous two decades. The improvised explosive device, or IED, evolved into a significantly more sophisticated and powerful weapon, the thing U.S. soldiers feared more than anything else. Death squads that had formed under the new Iraqi government, which was being propped up by the Americans, began launching a campaign of ethnic cleansing. By the summer of '05, many of the correspondents who had been covering the war from the beginning were leaving. A second and third wave of reporters was getting their chance at the story, but it was a much different story now, a much different time. Personally, I was just happy to be there. When I'd share my enthusiasm with the veteran correspondents, they'd tell me, "Just wait until you've been here a few times, you'll see."

It was much quieter in the Green Zone than in the rest of Baghdad. Americans jogged on the streets; soldiers in PT gear rode bicycles with rifles slung across their shoulders. Men and women from Alabama and Arkansas drove shuttle buses filled with Filipino and Iraqi day laborers from one side of the zone to the other. Americans lived in trailer parks, and dressed as if they were going to a NASCAR race: tattoos, tank tops, goatees, bellies hanging out over their too tight Levi's. Young black men wore baggy jeans, sported gold teeth and chains. Middle-aged white women with weathered faces wore push-up bras and cheap, stretchy, form-fitting pants. At any given time, some three thousand Americans and other foreigners resided in this ten-square-kilometer chunk of Baghdad, along with a few thousand Iraqis. It was the clearinghouse for the hundreds of millions of dollars in defense contracts, the Mecca of funds for "capacity building." There were street addresses, but places were known by their compound's corporate sponsor—the Lincoln Group house, the RTI compound, Fleur, DynCorp, CRG Logistics, and the biggest of them all, KBR, or Kellogg Brown and Root, the Halliburton subsidiary and civilian backbone for the American mission. The highest-ranking Iraqi leaders lived in a neighborhood of mansions called "Little Venice." There was a bastardized Disneyland quality about the whole place—a destination vacation for careers, an escape for those whose real lives back home were falling apart. There were even tourist attractions, like Saddam's Crossed Swords, the war monument with four giant sabers on a concrete parade ground, and the bombed-out Ministry of Information building.

The Green Zone had its own mixed-up culture. It started with those who protected it. The guards, for the most part, were neither American nor Iraqi. There was the battalion of Georgian soldiers, peasants from the outskirts of Tbilisi, given the task of manning checkpoints inside the zone. They had the manners of East European pillagers, and I would often see them speeding around helmetless in their Humvees, apparently drunk on the vodka they scammed from stores inside the IZ. No one seemed to know why the Georgians had this particular mission—a fairly important one, protecting the home of the new Iraqi government—but everyone agreed they aggravated more than helped, the way they crudely eyed Iraqi and Western women and spoke only in grunts.

Then there were the Gurkhas, Nepalese men with guns who spoke some English, having been trained in the Queen's Army. The squat brown-faced fighters—tough and extremely well trained—reminded me of Willy Wonka's Oompa Loompahs, snatched from a far-off land to go serve in a magical palace of the white man's eccentricity. After a private security contract changed hands, checkpoints and key installations in the Green Zone started to be manned by Peruvians and others from Latin America. They were barely literate, spoke only Spanish, seemed fairly incompetent. Yet they were given the important task of guarding the U.S. embassy. They worked for a company called Triple Canopy, which, like

Blackwater, was cashing in on the private security boom. These companies played a large part in the culture of the Green Zone, each of them employing groups of armed men, drawn from the ranks of retired soldiers across the world, though there was not much quality control. (Blackwater and Triple Canopy both had nicknames—Bongwater and Triple Comedy.) Along with the Nepalese and the Peruvians, the ranks of these companies included Americans, Britons, Frenchmen, Ecuadorians, Australians, Croatians, Fijians, and Senegalese, among others. An estimated twenty to thirty thousand private security guards—sometimes referred to as PSDs, for private security details, but also just called mercenaries—operated in Iraq. They held the jobs that the U.S. didn't have the manpower or expertise to perform. (The American ambassador, for instance, was guarded by a Blackwater detail, and Senegalese guards manned checkpoints inside an American base near the airport.)

The U.S. embassy was in Saddam's old palace, an imposing feat of architecture that showed off the vicious dictator's poor taste. It was now the brain center for the American occupation. Bureaucrats from every federal agency with an acronym (CIA, DIA, ATF, FBI, NSA, DOS, DOD, DOT, DOC, USAID, etc.) set up shop on the extravagant marble floors and relieved themselves in the palatial bathroom stalls that had been retrofitted by the Americans to include stand-up porcelain urinals. It was rare to see an Iraqi inside the embassy. The ambassador and the military commander of U.S forces in Iraq had their offices on the top floor. There was something telling and obscene about our being there. The gold fixtures and ostentatious chandeliers were the tacky choices of a brutal ruler flaunting his power, and it seemed even tackier for us to rule over the country from his former confines.

Not that I didn't like going to the place. It had a great, spacious lounge area, a former hall for imperial receptions where they had the best coffee shop in Iraq, the Green Bean, a Starbucks clone that served double lattes and vanilla smoothies twenty-four hours a day. The embassy also had a pool, where signs warned that no weapons were allowed while drinking. The American officials at the embassy worked in the palace, though they didn't live there. At the end of the day, they all went home to the KBR trailer parks and slept under flimsy ceilings that would do nothing against a direct hit from the regular insurgent attacks. (A new U.S. embassy is currently under construction in the Green Zone. The cost is an estimated $2 billion, and when complete, it will be the largest U.S. embassy in the world, about the size of the Vatican.)

To walk around the Green Zone, or even to get in, was impossible for most Iraqis—you needed that special IZ badge. Applying for a badge was a time-consuming, frustrating process that could take months. And once you received the badge, there was a chance the rules for badge applications would have changed, and you'd have to apply again. The badges became a fashion accessory displayed in pouches that everyone wore around their necks—they came in desert khaki, black, camouflage, and had embroidered inscriptions like OPERATION IRAQI FREEDOM and U.S. EMBASSY BAGHDAD. According to the legend I heard, the first person to sell badge holders was Crazy Tony the German. Tony drove down to Baghdad from Europe in a minibus shortly after the invasion, and set up shop on the American bases, selling souvenirs and badge holders. (His most popular souvenir, which got banned by the Americans, was a coffee mug with Kenny from *South Park*. The *South Park* catchphrase—"You killed Kenny, you bastards!"—was altered to "You sent me to Iraq, you bastards!" Kenny was pictured with a bullet hole in his head.) Tony was known for driving a moped around town when most wouldn't trust an armored car. He was also a source of cash for Westerners. The cash was generated from his souvenir and badge holder sales, which were huge. He could drop off tens of thousands of dollars in brown shopping bags in exchange for wire transfers to an account he kept in Croatia.

Newsweek had decided to move its bureau into the Green Zone in early 2005. The decision wasn't made lightly. The previous year a car bomb had exploded down the street from the *Newsweek* house in the neighborhood of Mansour, killing eighteen, shattering the windows of the house, strewing body parts on the road and scrap metal across the lawn. The next temporary bureau was in the Rasheed Hotel, and then finally we rented the house on the street guarded by Edinburgh Risk, sharing the house with the *L.A. Times* and the *Wall Street Journal*. (Despite the popular myth, most news organizations aren't in the Green Zone. The three news organizations also had bureaus at the Hamra Hotel, a popular location for journalists just over the Tigris from the IZ. The *Journal*'s office there was damaged in a double car bombing in November 2005.)

I was given a bedroom on the bottom floor. There was not much natural light in the house. There were notices up all over the place—fire plans, radio plans, advisories, labels on each piece of equipment, and rules governing the use of every room in the house. The rules were introduced by a veteran war correspondent who, after spending over twenty years in conflict zones, tried to control his environment as best he could. He had written a seven-page single-spaced introductory manual for Baghdad correspondents to read. It included directions to the house, its GPS coordinates, what you should carry when leaving the house (keys, radio, cell phone), what bedrooms belonged to each news agency, and a strong recommendation for visiting correspondents to clean up after themselves.

It was a way to mitigate the chaos and the chance of violent death that was always present, everywhere, at all times. You are standing next to a car bomb, and boom; you are sitting drinking a cup of tea and a piece of shrapnel from a rocket landing three doors down hits you in the brain; you are waiting outside smoking a cigarette, not under hard cover, and a bullet, shot in the air in celebration, lands on top of your skull; your Humvee flips over and you're crushed; a sniper in the distance, who could have picked anyone, picks you; your helicopter crashes; you're on the commercial jet that gets shot down. Wrong place, wrong time, bad luck.

We changed bureaus in January 2006. The new one was a much nicer house, and I would eventually consider it my home. It was where I got my mail, where most of my clothes were stored, where the bedroom had a shelf full of my books. It was a three-story seventies-era home with a clumsy layout; an excess of doors; and wiring that was totally fried (each room had at least half a dozen light switches). Half the time, the house ran off a large yellow power generator outside. There were six bedrooms, four bathrooms, a large kitchen, a nice lawn. It was once the home of an upper-class Iraqi family; that family was now long gone. We rented from a man who claimed to be the original owner. He now made his living leasing his four houses to foreigners. The owner didn't live in Iraq anymore, either. There were sandbags on the front office window and a guard shack outside. Thick black Kevlar blast blankets hung on the windows along with old curtains made from an odd-feeling brownish fabric. I slept in the downstairs bedroom, next to the living room, which was connected to the office (which was converted from a dining room). Our downtime was spent on one of the two couches in the living room, watching bootleg copies of TV series and movies. That was basically the only recreational activity; it was common to blow through an entire twelve-hour season in three days or less, depending on the news. *Rome, 24, Deadwood, The Sopranos, Lost, Battlestar Galactica, Firefly, Extras, The Office* (both British and American versions), *Seinfeld, Curb Your Enthusiasm, Desperate Housewives,* and *The Wire.*

But living in the Green Zone raised a difficult reporting question: How well could you cover Iraq if you weren't experiencing the real Iraq? Did working out of the Green Zone put too much distance between us and the Iraqi people? Were you by definition part of the occupation if you were in the IZ? There were advantages, for sure. We saved money on security costs. We had the best access to American and Iraqi officials. We rarely had to risk getting blown up at an IZ checkpoint in order to see an American diplomat or go to the generally worthless press events. We just had to roll out of bed. And from a more cynical perspective, American readers didn't seem to care too much about the lives of average Iraqis. They cared about American decisions, and American decisions were made, for better or worse, but mostly worse, in the Green Zone. There were drawbacks, though. The Green Zone was a constant target for rocket attacks and shelling, and our Iraqi staff was at a high risk to get kidnapped every time they left the IZ gates, which insurgents kept under close surveillance.

The question for journalists was always: How do you get closest to the story without getting killed? Not easy, when all Westerners are targets, and when your very presence endangers the lives of the people you are interviewing and working with. We constantly asked each other, How often are you getting out? Where are you going? What neighborhoods are still safe? No one I knew fell in love with Baghdad in the way journalists had with Saigon—there was no exotic intoxication or mystique. There was only a deep, unhealthy attachment.

Scott explained the rules of reporting. In terms of going out in the Red Zone it was a simple calculation of risk versus reward. If it was a story that would get in the magazine, perhaps you go to the scene, or maybe you set up a meeting in Baghdad at a family's home. But we weren't chasing bombs anymore, he made clear. A year ago, when seventy people were killed in a bombing, that was a cover story; now it's not even an item in Periscope—the two-hundred-word news briefs at the front of the magazine. We don't go out wandering around the streets looking for stories; it's too dangerous, and you can't stay in one place for more than an hour; the risk increases exponentially. There are exceptions—if the story is exclusive, or if it's an important interview—sometimes it's worth taking a risky trip. But normally you have two options—you can set up interviews in secure locations, like the Hamra Hotel or the Rasheed or the Iraqi parliament, or you can go out on embeds with the military. The third way, the thing most integral to the success or failure of reporting in Baghdad, is to rely on your Iraqi staff to get the story.

Our Iraqi staff was composed of four interpreters and an office manager, all fluent in English, all of whom also worked as reporters. There was Ahmer, Omar, Mohanid, Mohammed; later Ali and Hussam. There were ten drivers and guards, too. They were from Iraq's two largest religious groups, the two dominant sects of Islam, Sunni and Shia. (The Sunnis made up the minority of Iraq's population, roughly 30 percent; the Shiites the majority, close to 60 percent. Historically, there were tensions between the two groups—not unlike Catholics versus Protestants, and under Saddam's regime, the Sunnis ran the country, while many Shiites were brutally persecuted. The U.S. invasion switched the power dynamic, so now the Shiites were in charge.)

We had three Sunni staffers, who were brothers from a prominent Sunni tribe. In their past lives, before the war, they had been good citizens in the regime. Ahmer worked at the Ministry of Information as an interpreter; Omar studied to be a dentist; Mohanid was a nuclear engineer. Mohammed, our Shiite staff member, was also a former engineer.

The staff worked out of a safe house that was set up to look like an electronics shop. We never visited the safe house, and the location was known only to them. We communicated with them by phone many times each day, or over Skype, the instant-messaging service; they would come into the bureau a few times a week. In contrast to other parts of the world where I have worked with fixers, the majority of Iraqi journalists I knew were more passive. If you asked them to do an interview, you had to send a detailed list of questions and follow-ups. If you said, please ask if his brother was killed, and the person said yes, they would not instinctually ask, why was he killed? Who do you think killed him? What day was he killed? In Iraq, cell phone signals were often disrupted, and the people they were supposed to be calling turned off their cell phones. The staff would make one call, and then not try again. They were too ready to take no for an answer. Also, they were inclined to view events with a conspiratorial eye, bringing with them their own cultural bias: They seemed to think Jews and Kurds were behind everything.

This lackluster attitude wasn't true in all cases, of course, and in their defense, when I met our staff they were already three years into the war—three years of no electricity and the threat of death; three years of worrying their children were going to get killed on the way to school; three years with no end in sight. Of the more than 110 journalists killed since the war began, over 90 were Iraqis. And on a very basic level, I sensed they were not comfortable with us. We were friends, close friends, even, but the entire enterprise was too colonial to feel right. They had to go home to terrorized families at the end of the day; we could kick back and watch a DVD. No matter how well we treated them, or that we were paying them better money than they'd ever made before, we were Americans. We were responsible for their new and difficult lives.

One morning in October, I helped myself to a bowl of Frosted Flakes and sat down at a table in the living room. I was in a good mood. I had gotten my first byline from Iraq in the American edition of *Newsweek*, having obtained an exclusive document from the United Nations. An Iraqi staffer from the *Wall Street Journal*, Hakki, sat down across from me.

I could tell Hakki was agitated. His pale, doughy face and goatee were damp with sweat.

"Do you know what happened to me on the way here today?" he asked.

"No, what happened?"

"One of the PSDs waved his gun at me. Outside of my own home this American man waves a gun at me, threatens to shoot me. And for what? What had I done? I had crossed the street, that's what I did. And he points a gun at me?"

I nodded.

"You know," Hakki went on, "I cheer when Americans are killed. Not you, you are the journalists, you are okay, we are friends. But when these soldiers get killed I am happy."

He told me that a friend of his, the owner of a cell phone shop next to his own electronics shop, had been murdered recently. He explained that in "Saddam's time," if the secret police asked you for information, you gave it to them. It was how the system worked and how you survived. "Yes he was a dictator, but if you stayed out of politics, there was no problem. Now I cannot go outside. I have moved back home with my mother. This is freedom?"

I listened, thinking it was best not to tell him that my younger brother was in the 10th Mountain Division, scheduled to deploy to Iraq soon.

"Do you understand?" he asked. "Do you understand why I am angry?"

I finished up my Frosted Flakes and excused myself. I walked up to the roof to smoke a cigarette. I could see all of the Green Zone from up there, a suburb within a city of squat tan houses and sagging palm trees and government buildings. I could see part of Baghdad's skyline past the boundaries: a few high-rise buildings, an oil refinery, minarets, plumes of smoke of unknown origin. Bombs? Fires? Burning trash? The only sounds from the city to reach me were sirens.

What Hakki said had disturbed me. But I'd gotten my first Iraq byline in the magazine, and I was proud and happy and excited to be where I was.

I thought about calling Andi to tell her to go pick up a copy of the magazine from the newsstands on Broadway, but I didn't want to wake her up.

CHAPTER 3

June–August 2005

NEW YORK CITY

I met Andi two days before I found out I was going to Iraq. For more than a year, I'd been asking my editors to send me. At first, they laughed—literally. The former chief of correspondents, Marcus Mabry, whose laugh is legendary at the magazine, guffawed all the way down the hall. The foreign editor joked about me being "cannon fodder." But I persisted, and finally Marcus said if I was serious, he would send me to get the required security training. Three months later, in May 2005, I completed a training course in rural Virginia, run by a private security company called AKE.

There were about fifteen other journalists in the weeklong course. Most news organizations now required these classes before a staffer was allowed to cover a conflict. The highlights I remember: The thing to do if you accidentally entered a minefield was to yell "Stop, mines!" then freeze, then get on your knees, and using your pen, or a stick if it was handy, crawl forward or retrace your steps back, lightly digging into the ground in front of you. Another thing to note: Don't get kidnapped, but if you do, keep a positive attitude. We watched a video of a man in Chechnya whose fingers were cut off one by one and sent to his family in the mail. He wasn't able to maintain his positive attitude, and was later killed, fingerless. Also, as a general tip, the best way to stop massive blood loss was to tie a tourniquet—and your belt could work as one—very tight.

Despite the training course, I still didn't know if the magazine was serious about sending me to Iraq. So I was doing some freelance work to get other kinds of reporting experience, writing under a pseudonym for a website that traffics in New York gossip. My freelance assignment on June 1 was to interview Jerry Springer. The editor had called me in the afternoon to see if I'd like to go to a party hosted by Air America Radio for the launch of Springer's new radio show. I didn't really want to go, but I said I would. I took the F train up to 57th Street and walked to Rosa Mexicano, the restaurant where the event was being held. Andi was one of Air America's two publicists, and she was in charge of hosting and organizing the event. She and her colleagues had flirted with the idea of disinviting me—they didn't know if it was a good idea for the gossip website to cover the launch after all—but decided that protesting had the potential to make the situation worse.

The minute I walked in, an intern who had been assigned to keep a lookout for me went up to Andi and told her, "Michael Hastings is here."

Andi approached while I stood at a table that was serving nachos and guacamole. I told her who I was, that I was there to interview Springer. I remember thinking right then how cute she was.

Andi introduced me to Springer. I asked him about five questions. To my disappointment, he didn't say a single controversial or outrageous thing.

After the interview, I spoke with Andi for about fifteen more minutes. Her coworkers watched in horror as she talked to "the gossip guy." I made sure to mention that I was really a *Newsweek* guy, and that this gossip thing was just for fun. "Real news only," I told her. "Most of the time, at least."

"That's quite a notebook you're carrying," she said.

It was a classic reporter's notebook, spiral bound, sticking out of my back pocket.

"Do you think you're covering World War II or something? I mean, it's like you think you're in the movie, Newsie. Did you leave your fedora at home?"

There was an edge to the flirting. I could tell she thought I was full of myself, and she wanted to take me down a peg.

I looked at her face, at her blond hair falling below her chin, her turned-up nose and blue eyes, and near freckles. I thought, Here is a girl who would make a great girlfriend. That's how she looked to me, instantly.

I asked her for her card. She said she didn't have one—a lie—because she didn't want her name to show up on the gossip website. Before leaving, I tried to impress her by mentioning I was headed to a going-away party for a friend whom I'd gone to security training with, who was on her way to Iraq.

I transcribed the Springer interview and sent in the piece. There wasn't much to work with, and beyond that I was no longer in the mood for the casual pettiness the gossip site required. I'd been working with them for a few months, and I'd lost interest in writing about topics that I felt were essentially meaningless. The Springer interview was probably the most boring and harmless item the website ever published. Maybe it was intentional, maybe it was by accident, but her colleagues at Air America would say that it was a "Valentine to Andi."

I got an email from Andi the day the Springer piece ran, saying she was glad to meet me. I responded with a question: What, no comment on the Springer story? She accused me of fishing for compliments. I said she was right, and that we should have lunch.

The day before our first date, I got a phone call from Scott Johnson in Baghdad.

"Hi, Mike, this is Scott."

"Hey, Scott, how's it going?"

There was a time lag, partly due to the satellite phone connection, partly due to the fact that Scott always spoke so laid-back and slow.

"Did you get my email?"

"What email?"

"Are you free to come to Baghdad this summer?"

I tried to sound as relaxed about it as he did.

"Sure, I can do that, no problem."

I hung up the phone in disbelief. It was happening. I needed to say it out loud. I got up from my cubicle and walked into my friend Jack's office. "Dude, they're sending me to Iraq."

I call it our first date, but it was always debatable—I had asked Andi to come up for lunch at the Brooklyn Diner, across from *Newsweek,* to discuss Air America. She finally agreed, thinking it was work related, though I had very little intention of discussing business. In fact, I'd already eaten lunch that day.

She was coming out the door of the diner when I arrived.

"Sorry, I'm running late."

"I was just about to leave."

We sat in the corner booth. I told Andi I'd already eaten lunch, and she looked at me like I was an idiot. "Who goes to lunch after they've already eaten lunch?" I didn't have a good answer, so I told her the milk-shakes were really good. I ordered a vanilla shake, she ordered chocolate. I told myself to play it cool, to not tell her I was going to Baghdad until at least midway through the lunch.

About five seconds later, I said, "I'm going to Baghdad."

She didn't seem particularly impressed. Next month, she said, she was going to a concert in England, Live 8. "You don't know what Live 8 is, do you?"

"Of course I do," I lied.

She listed the bands that would be there: Coldplay, Snow Patrol, U2.

"Snow Patrol," I said, "the Irish indie band." I knew this only because a stringer had pitched an item about them for the international magazine a few weeks earlier.

"They're not Irish. They're Scottish."

"I bet you they're Irish."

We shook on the bet.

Lunch lasted about two hours, and in that time I managed to invite myself to her birthday party, which, coincidentally, happened to be right down the street from my apartment on the Lower East Side. I learned she was raised in Perry, Ohio, home to a nuclear power plant that Andi claimed made the whole town sick, though she had no hard evidence. I guessed she was a middle child—yes, she said, so she knew injustice well—and then I somehow guessed, on my second try, that her middle name was Suzanne. I learned she hated George W. Bush with an impressive passion and had a soft spot for conspiracies. "Bush went to Iraq to get revenge for his father," she said, fully convinced. I nodded sympathetically; her convictions were strong, but her politics were a little simplistic. In her world there was good and evil, the corrupt and the pure, and her role, she believed, was to be an advocate for the good.

She asked me who I voted for.

"Me? To quote Canadian Prime Minister Diefenbaker, 'Dear sir, what I do in the ballot box is between myself and my god.'"

"Oh, God. Are you a Republican?" she asked. "Who did you vote for in 2004 when Bush, yet again, stole the election? He stole it in Ohio, you know."

She reported back to her friends, I reported back to mine. One of her friends said: "Oh, don't let him pull that 'Pearl Harbor I'm going off to war' stuff on you."

There are two pictures from her birthday party. One, she called the Vader picture—I'm smirking in it, as if the darker side of my personality is winning out. In the other she has her arms wrapped around me, her head on my shoulder. Another guy at the party asked me if she was my girlfriend. I told him no. "She acts like it," he said.

I called her the next day and asked her when we were going to have dinner.

"Dinner?"

"You promised me a dinner at your birthday party."

"I did?"

"Yes, you don't remember? You did have a lot to drink, and I know you rarely drink." (There was never any mention of dinner, but I had figured her memory wouldn't be a hundred percent, and gambled that a promised-dinner gambit might work.)

We had dinner on Sunday night on the Lower East Side. The restaurant was Alias, on the corner of Clinton and Rivington. When we got inside, she immediately said:

"This is your date restaurant, isn't it? This is where you bring all the girls?"

"What girls? Of course not."

She was right, though. I'd brought three previous dates there.

The Lower East Side in those days was becoming gentrified, overrun with hipster bars and nightlife lasting until 5 A.M. After midnight, the streets outside my apartment on Allen Street were always loud with breaking glass and drunken yells and crowds of men and women in tight black jeans and stylishly mussed hair, doing drugs, drinking, and doing more drugs.

I convinced her to go back to my place after dinner. The NBA Finals were on, and I knew she liked sports. I told her I'd been dabbling in online sports gambling, and that I was down about two hundred bucks. She followed me to my apartment. I had a futon bed, and a table piled with junk mail and change, my computer, one other chair, and a wide-screen television. I turned on one of the floor lamps, partly dimmed, and I lit a scented candle, then I turned on the game. She looked at me, perplexed.

"You can sit on the futon," I said. I sat on the futon.

She didn't move.

"Come here, you can sit next to me."

She stepped toward me, hesitating. She sat down on the bed. I attempted to reach my arm around her shoulder.

She jumped up from the bed.

"What are you doing?"

"Uh, I'm trying to kiss you. What do you think I'm doing?"

"You think you can just kiss me?"

"You came back to my apartment."

"You said we were going to watch the game."

"Fine, watch the game."

"No, I'm leaving right now."

"You're leaving? Jesus Christ. So you come to my apartment, I try to kiss you, and you're shocked?"

"It's not appropriate."

"Whatever. Leave, then."

"Is this what you do? You bring girls back here, and they just start making out with you?"

"Yeah, that's the idea of a date, you know."

I was pissed off and embarrassed. I expected to hook up, and her virtuousness made me somewhat ashamed. I felt stupid, so I covered it up with swagger.

"So you're rejecting me? You better leave then."

She sat down on the futon.

"This is the first date. Who does this on the first date?"

"Well, it's more like the third date—we got milkshakes, your birthday party."

"This is the first date."

"I thought you were leaving?"

"You want me to leave?"

"Do what you want. But obviously I don't want you to leave."

The game was on.

"I think I'm going to lose another twenty bucks," I said.

She looked at me.

Eventually, our emotions settled. I started saying things, talking in a soothing prattle, finally moving next to her on the futon. I rubbed her hand and spoke softly, and told her that if she was uncomfortable, I wouldn't be angry if she left, that I understood wanting to take things slow, so please, if you don't want to be here, I understand.

Then I leaned over and kissed her. She kissed me back.

CHAPTER 4

June-August 2005

NEW YORK CITY

We were in love before we said it; we said it only after we were far apart, when I was six thousand miles away and eight hours ahead. Later, she would ask me, "When was the moment, when was the moment *you knew?*" I'd say, "When I saw your face at the Jerry Springer party I knew." Or, "When we went out to dinner at Shelley's on 57th, when I convinced you to try an oyster, which you had refused to try in the previous twenty-six years of your life, that face you made, I knew then." On a night in July in my bed, I told her I loved her. I whispered it. I don't know if she heard. I was worried she might have heard. It just slipped out, in passion, and then I rolled over on the futon, the bed she made me get rid of, and wondered if she heard and if she loved me back.

Andi would say she hugged me at her birthday party for a reason. She would say she really knew, yes, at Shelley's, when we looked at each other across the table. When she went to London for the Live 8 concert, she did not stop thinking about me, she said. She lost interest in the guy she was supposed to visit, standing in a crowd of two hundred thousand at Hyde Park, when Snow Patrol came onstage; she thought of me. They told the crowd they were from Ireland. I'd won the bet and she wanted to call me up right then and tell me, but didn't. She told me she was certain when we went to the double feature of *Wedding Crashers* and *Willy Wonka and the Chocolate Factory*, and I bought her popcorn and peanut M&M's, and kept feeding them to her until she started slightly choking, then spit up a piece in my hand. She knew when she was supposed to fly home to Ohio, and her plane kept getting delayed because of the weather, so instead she came to my apartment, and we made a weekend out of it, getting left field seats that Saturday at a Mets game. She knew from the moment she refused to give me her business card.

Neither of us let on, though. All our friends were advising us to stay away—it doesn't make any sense, so went the counsel. He's going to Baghdad in two months. How is that going to work?

It didn't make sense to us, either, really. Why would she choose to get involved with a man who, by the nature of his profession, was always leaving? But my deployment to Baghdad gave urgency to our relationship. Every night, every dinner, was one day closer to the day I was leaving.

On the night we first made love, we ate dinner at a Greek restaurant in midtown. It was a Saturday evening. I was coming from work. We sat down at the table, and she told me my apartment was making her sick.

"I have a fever. I'm in a daze."

"You've only been there once," I said. "And look, I'm fine."

"No, I think it's your apartment. There's some kind of superflu virus breeding in there."

She looked at the menu and frowned. "There's a lot of lamb," she said.

She didn't touch her food; I ate an appetizer, an entrée, and had a coffee.

"It's good you're enjoying the meal," she said.

I'd assumed we would go to her place after dinner. She lived on Central Park West, about five blocks away. She told me that was out of the question; she had a roommate and it wouldn't be appropriate. She said she would go downtown, despite the health hazards of my studio. We argued about it. I told her I would have gotten a voucher for a *Newsweek* car service, if I'd known, and now we had to flag down a cab, and that was such a hassle around here.

"We should have just gone to your place," I said.

"Why are you freaking out? You okay? You're going a bit odd on the voucher."

Finally, I waved down a cab, and we went to my apartment.

"When was the last time you cleaned your sheets?" she asked.

The minute we were alone, though, the argument over the voucher seemed ridiculous. I asked her how she was feeling. "Better," she said, "but you really need to clean your apartment." I kissed her. She was so soft, her head resting on my old pillow with its *Return of the Jedi* pillow-case. We fell asleep. But when I awoke in the middle of the night, she was putting her clothes on. "What are you doing?" I asked. "I'm leaving," she said, "I need to get home." "Don't leave—there's no need." "No, I don't want to stay," she said. If she left, she would explain to me later, she couldn't get hurt. She'd be leaving me before I could leave her.

Toward the end of July, Andi helped me shop for Iraq. She also gave me a gift basket of gum and other travel items, souvenirs, and books to remember her by. On my last night in New York, we went back to Alias, where we had gone on our first official date. In every way, it was more awkward than that first night. We fought; there were too many feelings to do otherwise. I said I'd like to stay longer in Iraq than the two months I was scheduled. This hurt her feelings. She said she was convinced I wouldn't come back. Our conversation was so intense, the negative vibe so palpable, that the waitress didn't even ask us if we wanted dessert—she just brought us the check as soon as she could to get us out of the restaurant. By the time we got back to my apartment, there was too lit-tle time left to stay angry. We forgave each other and made promises—we would stay together.

I gave her a book, Hunter S. Thompson's *Rum Diary.*

"Where did you get this book?" she asked.

"Oh, I bought it."

"You bought it? Isn't this the book that has been on your floor for the last month?"

"Yes, it is."

"So when did you buy this gift for me?"

"Well, I think I bought that book a couple of years ago."

"So, you're giving me something you found on your floor?"

"If you put it like that, it sounds bad, sure. But I'm giving it to you. Just read what it says."

On the inside flap, I'd written: *I don't miss, but I'll miss you, mh.*

The next morning, a Saturday, I lugged my bags down the stairs and flagged a cab. I had to go in to work for the day. I would leave from the office to the airport in the afternoon. We both got out on 57th Street. She held in her feelings when we said goodbye. I tried to kiss her, but she pulled away and walked around the corner. That evening, I got on an eleven-hour direct flight from JFK to Amman. For a while, I wondered if Andi and I would actually be able to make it. Would she wait for me? Was I capable of keeping my commitment to her? And then I started thinking about Iraq.

CHAPTER 5

August–September 2005

BAGHDAD, AL KARMA, CAMP FALLUJAH

American soldiers usually asked me the same three questions during an embed.

Question 1: Do you carry a gun, sir?

No, no, I don't.

That's fucked up. I wouldn't go anywhere in this country without a gun.

Question 2: So you must get paid a lot of money to be here?

Not really, not as much as you think.

Question 3: Why don't you reporters ever report the good news?

I learned not to answer this one honestly—saying I hadn't found any good news didn't win friends.

Fuck it. You gonna put me on the cover of your magazine?

I went on four embeds on my first trip to Iraq. To spend time with American soldiers was to experience Iraq framed by the square bulletproof Humvee windows and behind "combat locked" doors; Iraq from three thousand feet in a Black Hawk helicopter; Iraq through the scope of an M-4 rifle. It was a world with its own language and geography. Divisions, brigades, battalions, companies, platoons. 4th ID, 3rd ID, 10th Mountain, Two-One Marines, Three Fourteen, 256th Field Artillery Regiment, First Cav. Roger. Outstanding. What the fuck over. It was a world that could be described almost entirely by acronyms. MNFI, MNSTICI, MEF, TOC, AWOC, DFAC, TCPs, OPs, TTPs, HMWWW, CHUs, MiTTs, SPITTs, BEPs, MEPs, PFCs, LTs, PAX, PX, LZ, CPATT,

MSRs, IBAs, AOs, LN, TCNs, BOLO, AIF, LSAs EJKs, GOI, SPs. Multi-National Force Iraq is MNFI. A TOC is a tactical operations center. An LSA is a life support area or a logistics support area. AIF stands for Anti-Iraqi Forces, the enemy. LN is a local national, an Iraqi. GOI is government of Iraq. Iraqi street names were usually irrelevant; routes were named after things soldiers could easily remember. Route Green Bay, Route Wolverine, Route Blue, Route Orange County, Main Supply Route (or MSR) Tampa. Each AO, or area of operations, had its own hotspots: RPG Alley, IED Alley. Iraqi town names were interchangeable with the military bases that were now located near them, the forward operating bases. FOB Justice, FOB Duke, FOB Prosperity, FOB Victory, Liberty, Slayer, Striker.

Someone who never left the FOB, who never "goes over the wire" (the wire being the perimeter that separates the American bases from the rest of Iraq) was a "FOBBIT," like a Hobbit. A subspecies of the Fobbit was the TOCroach—someone who doesn't even leave the headquarters. It was the latest version of slurs from previous conflicts, like REMF (rear echelon motherfucker), or POGUEs (people other than grunts), meant to underscore the difference between those who fight the war, the troops who are killing or at risk of regularly being killed, and those who generally stay out of harm's way and support those who fight the war. There were names for Iraqis, too. Vietnam had gooks and Somalia skinnies. In Iraq, the military had depersonalized the lingo—sometimes Iraqis were Hajis (each base had a market run by Iraqis called "the Haji shop"), but more often they were merely "local nationals," or "AIF," or just "bad guys" and "terrorists."

If you wanted to relate to the soldiers or marines (never refer to a marine as a "soldier" in print, I was warned; marines are marines; use "troops" if you need to generalize between the services), you had to understand their acronym-laced dialogue.

"The BUB's at 1630 in the TOC, and Delta's CO is going, but the BC's not going to be there so the S-3's running it." Translation: The daily battle update brief is at 4:30 P.M. in the headquarters, and the commanding officer of Delta company will attend. The battalion commander won't, so the battalion's operations officer will be in charge. "Our ROE is fucking retarded." The rules of engagement, under Multi-National Force Iraq, are unsatisfactory. "Three AIF detained, seven AIF KIA. Two LNs WIA and one TCN WIA requesting MEDVAC, nine-line to follow." Three insurgents captured and seven killed; two Iraqi civilians and one third-country national (meaning a civilian who is not Iraqi or American) need to be brought to the hospital.

Roger. Outstanding. What the fuck over.

IED was the deadliest abbreviation. The improvised explosive device. The roadside bomb. The cause of over 60 percent of American casualties. I wanted to understand the IED—the Eye-E-Dee in Eye-Rack—so I put in requests to embed with the guys who go looking for them.

Scott Johnson and Jack Tapes helped me pack for my first embed. I looked through the equipment we had in the bureau: a collection of helmets, eye protection, and body armor that had piled up in the house since the war started. There was a heavy blue vest that had a high collar to protect the neck and a piece of material that hung down to protect the groin. It came with a Velcro sticker that announced PRESS across the chest. Tapes told me that the neck collar and groin cover probably wouldn't actually stop any shrapnel. He also pointed out that there was no need anymore to announce you were press, as that wouldn't prevent anyone from shooting you. He recommended a new set, which we had in brown and blue, that was about four or five pounds lighter. It had two ceramic plates, one in front and one in back, that could stop an AK-47 round. It also had thin material on the sides that could stop 9mm bullets. I chose the brown one. Tapes took a piece of silver electrical tape, wrote my blood type on it (O POS), and stuck it on the front of the vest. Then I chose a large black helmet, Wiley X eye protection, and loaded my Sony Vaio laptop with software for the BGAN, a satellite modem that looked like a small gray box and could get a high-speed Internet connection from almost anywhere, as long as there was nothing obstructing the signal. I brought my phones: an Iraqna, a small gray Nokia that worked only on the local network; my T-Mobile, which worked internationally; my BlackBerry, which also worked internationally; a reliable Thuraya satellite phone for a backup. I brought my Sony digital tape recorder, my seven megapixel digital camera, five notebooks, and a half-dozen pens. I threw in two pairs of jeans and two pairs of Old Navy khaki cargo pants that I'd bought with Andi in New York, five white T-shirts, a towel, four pairs of hiking socks, four pairs of boxers, three long-sleeved button-down shirts, a pair of shoes, and a pair of lightweight hiking boots. I found a silver sleeping bag. I packed the electronics, along with chargers for all of them, into a black Victorinox laptop bag, and stuffed the rest of my gear into a purple North Face bag.

I tried it out to see how it felt. Wearing the body armor and helmet, with the North Face pack on my back, and the laptop bag slung over my shoulder, I could barely move.

Scott took one look at me and said, "Dude, you're bringing way too much stuff."

Tapes gave me a smaller backpack that he'd used in the Royal Marines. It was black, compact, and looked much cooler than my purple North Face rack. I got rid of a bunch of my extra clothes, my pair of shoes, and a medical kit (it took up space, and I figured I'd be with military guys who would have that). Tapes helped me jam everything else into his pack.

The next night, eleven days after I'd arrived in Iraq, I was riding in a Buffalo on my first combat patrol. I was with the Desert Rogues, of the 1st Battalion 64th Armor Regiment, out of FOB Rustamiyah in southeastern Baghdad. The Buffalo is a massive armored vehicle, built originally for minesweeping. It weighs more than forty thousand pounds and has an excess of video cameras and mechanical arms, traveling on six giant tires. To get in, you climb up a ladder on the back, then step through a small door into a passenger compartment about ten feet above the ground. There was allegedly air-conditioning, but the whole cabin was hot air and steam and my eye protection fogged up. My body armor and helmet were soaking with sweat. The point of the trip was to find bombs, or as one officer described it: "You'll be driving around at five miles per hour looking at trash."

Trash is everywhere in Iraq. It is the most distinguishing feature of the landscape. The trash defies description. There are huge piles of it outside homes, on doorsteps, in street corners, filling any vacant lot. No triple-canopy jungle or endless dunes, just pile upon pile of twisted and discarded junk, plastic, scrap metal, empty bottles, tin cans, cardboard boxes, gasoline containers, decaying fruit, a stunning collection of random shit. It is mind-boggling, as if every family in Iraq decided to toss their garbage cans out the front door at the same time, and when they figured out that no one was going to come pick it up, just proceeded to cover the trash with more trash.

In all that trash the insurgents hide their deadliest weapons, the IEDs. The IEDs are camouflaged as trash. They look like almost everything else on the ground. Very clever, very scary, very hard to see.

"What are the chances of finding bombs?" I asked the driver.

He looked at me. "We've been doing daily sweeps since April," he said. "So far, we haven't found a single bomb."

"Oh, okay. Why is that?"

"The Buffalo makes a lot of noise. The fucking insurgents can hear it coming a mile away and take their bombs someplace else."

"Oh, okay."

The patrol inched along. I tried to take notes, capture some dialogue. We were the middle vehicle, sandwiched between a tank and a couple of Humvees.

There was a flash a few hundred yards back. I didn't hear any noise. A call came over the radio—a local national had driven too close to the convoy, so the machine gunner opened up. The LN was apparently drunk and had driven in by mistake. The bullet had hit him in the leg, and the car went off the road into a ditch. The Iraqi police would bring him to the hospital. The machine gunner was twenty-one years old. One of the soldiers in the Buffalo with me said, "He'll be saying he's sorry now, but I bet he'll fucking brag about shooting the guy later."

The patrol continued, on to Sadr City and back for about four hours. Iraqi families stared up at the colossal machine as we passed. We did not find any bombs. The captain who was running the patrol confronted me afterward. He was worried I was going to write about the shooting.

"This is a twenty-one-year-old kid. Are you going to ruin his life?"

I hadn't planned to write about the shooting, figuring it wasn't really news. An American accidentally shooting an Iraqi was a common occurrence, and the story on how the military didn't release statistics on the frequency of accidental shootings had already been told.

"I was praying," the captain continued. "I thought when that car went off the road it was going to blow up." He leaned closer to me to make his point. "These kids," said the twenty-five-year-old captain, "are making split-second decisions to save our lives."

I didn't disagree. Any driver of any car on the street, any asshole with a bulky sweater, could be a bad guy waiting to detonate. I took very few notes that night. It was too overwhelming. If I'd had more experience, I probably would have written a piece about the shooting. It was one of those things that happen in war, and would've made a great on-scene story for the *Newsweek* website.

With all the threats, all the varieties of bombs, shooting first made sense. You or them? Kill an innocent by accident, or risk letting someone blow up you and your buddies?

In addition to the IED, there was the VBIED, or vehicle-borne improvised explosive device, the car bomb (pronounced Vee-Bid). There was also the SVBIED, the suicide vehicle-borne improvised explosive device, or suicide car bomb. (Es-Vee-Bid.) The troop favorite was the DBIED, the donkey-borne improvised explosive device, the Dee-Bid, which was rumored to have been witnessed more than once. The EFP, or explosively formed projectile or penetrator, also known as the shape charge, was a particularly deadly bomb that could rip through the thickest armor. The U.S. military officials claimed the EFPs were being imported from Iran. (The commander of the Desert Rogues showed me a photograph of the damage from an EFP detonation. He kept the photo on his laptop. The metal charge had gone through the driver's window and killed one of his soldiers. "See the brains on the steering wheel," he said.)

The afternoon following the patrol, I spoke to an intel officer named Matt about a recent Es-Vee-Bid experience. Matt was six one, with blue eyes and reddish hair. We'd been talking for a while, sitting under the shade of a makeshift gazebo outside headquarters, when he got around to telling me what was on his mind.

He'd been out on patrol, one of those getting-to-know-the-neighborhoods, win-hearts-and-minds kind of thing. The soldiers were giving out candy to the kids. One of the soldiers was swarmed by children, jumping, smiling, standing in the middle of the street.

Matt was walking around the corner to the next street when he heard the loud explosion and ducked. He got a look in his eye as he told the story. His hand shook slightly.

"I ran around the corner," he said. "I saw things, little body parts, children. Tiny pieces of children." He looked at me like he needed to apologize for what he was saying. "You know, I know this sounds cheesy," he said, and then, "Things you're not ever supposed to see. Arms. Legs. Of children."

One American and at least fifteen Iraqi children killed. Matt's eyes drifted. He told me there'd been a counseling session afterward, set up by the army's mental health unit to deal with post-traumatic stress after incidents like this. Matt said he attended the meeting, but didn't think it helped very much. I told him I would email him to follow up and do a story. I was interested in how the army was handling combat stress. He never responded to my emails.

The Desert Rogues took me in a convoy across the city, from FOB Rustamiyah on the east side of the Tigris to Camp Victory on the west, to drop me off for my next embed. Camp Victory, one of the bases surrounding the Baghdad Airport, was home to an army EOD company. Explosives ordnance disposal. The Baghdad Bomb Squad.

The bomb squad had a small shack and yard, "the Bomb Garden," decorated with explosives; rows of grenades and mortar shells (30mm, 60mm, 120mm, that's a big one), Iranian grenades, Italian grenades, American grenades, Russian-made rockets, mortar tubes, all manner of land mines. Next to the Bomb Garden was the Garden of Shame, where they kept the objects that soldiers had thought were IEDs but turned out to be false alarms. There was a tea kettle, an extension cord, a piece of cable, a brake drum. The bomb squad had responded to these calls, spent hours preparing to defuse them, only to find out that they had wasted their time.

I arrived and heard I had just missed a big one. Danny, a bomb squad tech from Tennessee, jumped out of a Humvee and rushed up onto the wooden porch of the shack, his face red beneath a do-rag, pumped on adrenaline, carrying a long sliver of metal. He'd just detonated the big IED. Ka-boom.

"Take a look at this shrapnel," he said. "Big as a lawn mower blade. Touch the edge."

I touched the edge; it was sharp.

"Imagine that flying through the air. That's sharp enough to kill you," he said, then added the shrapnel to the collection in the Bomb Garden.

The twenty-one-man bomb squad worked in twenty-four-hour shifts, responding to calls from units all over the city. When patrols spotted an IED, they called in the bomb squad to get rid of it. The unit was led by Captain Gregory Hirschey, an all-American blond who carried around a large mug of Seattle-made coffee and a frozen bottle of Gatorade. To relax, Hirschey's soldiers spent most of their time playing Halo 2, the multiplayer video game, where futuristic warriors tried to kill each other. It got their minds off the war. Every time they went out, they knew there was a chance they'd be blown up. They were always going straight to the bombs. IEDs ranged from the simple and inexpensive to the complex and hi-tech. They could be triggered with infrared sensors, motorcycle alarms, trip wires, detonation cords. They could be pressure activated; they could be "daisy-chained," to set off a series of explosions. There also were "second and tertiary devices," bombs set up to kill units responding to an IED; bombs set up to kill the bomb squad. The guys in the bomb squad sometimes wore 120-pound protective suits that made them look like giant green marshmallow men. Often they'd deploy robots to defuse the IEDs, which they controlled remotely with a joystick and video monitor. Hirschey said that his best robot operators were also the unit's "kick-ass Halo players."

I went out for four or five calls, and watched them detonate UXO (unexploded ordnance), of which there was plenty lying around Iraq. According to the State Department, even before the war there were 10 to 15 million land mines across the country left over from World War II, Iraq's eight-year war with Iran, and Desert Storm, making it one of the most heavily mined countries in the world. Hundreds of thousands of mortars, grenades, and other munitions from Saddam's army also were not secured during the U.S. invasion, which gave the insurgent bomb makers plenty of material to make their IEDs.

Hirschey was a father of three and didn't think he was going to make it out alive. He told his wife that he'd had a premonition of his death. "If you're going to die, why not die for your country," he told me, trying to laugh it off. By the time they'd completed their seven-month tour, his unit had responded to 2,178 incidents. During the last month, one of his soldiers lost an arm to an IED. With only two weeks left before his sched-uled return, Staff Sergeant Johnny Mason, a close friend of Hirschey's, was disarming one bomb when a second IED was detonated, killing him instantly. Hirschey told me he'd become numb to the threat. "After a while you quit looking," he said. "I don't know what it is. You almost feel like you're part of the walking dead."

My bomb squad story didn't run for a few months. It was overtaken by an event back in the United States, Hurricane Katrina.

I was sitting in the mess hall at Camp Victory, eating dinner with Cap-tain Hirschey and the first sergeant of the bomb squad on the day Katrina hit New Orleans. There were wide-screen TVs in each corner of the mess hall, and all were turned to the Fox News Channel. At the end of dinner, the first sergeant pointed to three men watching intently at the table across the room. "There's your story," he said. "Those guys are from the Louisiana National Guard."

I changed tables and asked if they'd be willing to be interviewed. "The eye of the storm went over my parish," one of the soldiers told me. On screen a white steeple seemed to emerge from dark water. "It's passing over the hospital where my mom works. She's a nurse." The news reported there was no power at the hospital. Another soldier said: "I had to get emergency leave on the last squall to go home and fix the flooding in the basement. I can't imagine what this is going to do." A third soldier leaned back in his chair. "People back home constantly worry about us," he said. "Now we get a chance to worry about them." The three soldiers were members of the 141st Field Artillery Unit in the 256th Brigade of the Louisiana National Guard. They had been in Iraq almost a year. They had eight days left on their tours before they were scheduled to leave. They told me banners for their homecoming had already been put up, and were now washed away.

The captain and the first sergeant had left the mess hall by the time I was finished talking to the Louisianan soldiers. It was up to me to find my way back to the bomb squad headquarters. It was dark, about 9:00 P.M., and all the huts and tents and trailers looked the same. At night, the base was an endless field of gravel, passing trucks kicking up a spectral fog of dirt particles. I felt like I was walking around the grounds of a county fair after the lights had been shut off and the gates closed. I soon realized I was lost. I walked off the main road and approached a building that looked familiar. When I got closer, I saw that it wasn't familiar at all. But painted on the building was the name of the 141st Field Artillery, with their nickname underneath, the Baghdad Headhunters. I had somehow, through no design of my own, stumbled upon the rest of the Louisiana contingent. About a dozen soldiers were sitting at a picnic table behind their headquarters. I introduced myself. "I'm a reporter for *Newsweek*," I said. "I just spoke to some guys at the mess hall, and I was wondering if you mind if I hang out for a while." They didn't ask anyone for permission. They gave me their names and started to tell their stories. They had one cell phone to share and were trying to get through to their families. They were depressed. After surviving a year in Iraq, after losing soldiers to this country, they'd just learned the city where they grew up and were on the verge of going home to was destroyed.

The cell phone rang.

"Hi, Mama," said Specialist Jason Ragas.

The men quieted down.

"What side of the levee? The north side or the south side? Ten-plus foot of water throughout the parish? Where are you getting this? Nola.com? Can we get Nola.com?"

The men moved inside to the Internet to check the website. Fifty percent of homes in St. Bernard's Parish, where three men lived, were now gone. "I got a fifty-fifty chance my home is destroyed," Ragas said.

"The roof of the civic auditorium was blown off," one soldier said, scrolling the webpage.

"That's right by my parents' house," said another.

The soldiers continued to look online, doing a neighborhood-by-neighborhood assessment. At one point Sergeant Robert Pettingkill said, "That's it, all my possessions, gone."

Sergeant Jeff Bohne, thirty, told me he hadn't heard from his "hard-headed wife," who had decided to ride out the storm in New Orleans with his eleven-month-old son, Jacob. Because of the deployment, he guessed he'd seen Jacob for a total of about thirty days. He was also supposed to close on a new home soon. "I don't care about the house, it's my son. I can't get through to them." He tried to call again on a cell phone, and got the message: "Due to a hurricane in your area, this call cannot be completed."

The feeling that they all shared: We should be in New Orleans, protecting our families and homes. We are the National Guard. That's what we signed up for, not Iraq. Many of them had been out sandbagging and distributing water in previous natural disasters. One of them said his wife even got a call this morning from the National Guard with a message for him to "show up at Jackson Barracks at eight o'clock. No shit."

I went back to where I was sleeping—a two-bed trailer behind the bomb squad shack. I set up the satellite phone, balancing the BGAN modem on top of a Hesco barrier, a thick, five-foot-high cement container filled with dirt to protect the trailers from mortar attacks. I hooked up the Ethernet cable and sat on the steps of the trailer, the Sony Vaio on my lap. I dashed off an email advisory about the Louisiana National Guard and Katrina. The editors responded quickly. I passed out for about four hours, woke up, and started writing. The story hit the Web immediately—the first piece of reporting for *Newsweek* on Katrina, as the domestic correspondents had yet to get down to Louisiana and the scope of the disaster was just becoming apparent.

Later that week, President George W. Bush posed for a photo op in *Air Force One*. He didn't land in New Orleans to see the devastation first-hand, he flew above. A photographer snapped a picture of him looking out the window.

Everything looks peaceful from thirty thousand feet, even New Orleans after the storm, even Iraq.

My next request was to go to Fallujah, the site of the worst battle of the war in November 2004, less than a year earlier. Though the U.S. military claimed after the fight, which cost the lives of 273 Americans and over three thousand Iraqis, that they had "broken the back of the insurgency," insurgent attacks in the city hadn't stopped. Both sides had become entrenched throughout Anbar Province, with Sunni insurgents and Al Qaeda fighters moving to areas surrounding Fallujah, and to the nearby city of Ramadi. My email to the military said simply: "I want to spend time with the Marines taking the fight to the terrorists," a sentiment I figured would get me access.

I flew to Fallujah in mid-September on a CH-146 Marine Corps helicopter. It was a troop and cargo transport craft, with space inside for at least thirty men. It moved slowly through the air, the twin rotor blades on top—one in front and one in back—keeping it stable, and it felt like you were sitting on a floating platform. It was a forty-five-minute flight at night—they tried to fly the troops in after midnight to lessen the chance of getting shot down. When I landed at Camp Fallujah, no one had heard of me. A reporter? Hunh. Maybe you should go to the Embark tent. I didn't know what or where the Embark tent was. I hopped on a shuttle bus, and the driver told me he was going near there. I was joined in the bus by a platoon full of marines who had just arrived in Iraq. For the first time, I was the veteran, with a whole month of experience under my belt.

At headquarters, no one had heard of me, either. Not so unusual. They told me to spend the night in the Embark tent until the public affairs officer woke up in the morning. They explained the Embark tent (for disembark) was where all new arrivals were kept until they were assigned permanent barracks. Rows of green cots stretched back into darkness. I lay down, but knew I wasn't going to sleep. Marines came in and out, quick bursts of flashlights pointing at the wooden floor. There were fits of coughing, endless snaps of rucksacks being opened and closed, thuds of men searching for boots. Wristwatches beeped on the hour, and the occasional digital alarm clock went off accidentally. Four air conditioners were on full blast. I'd made the mistake of taking a shower the day before, and bringing my damp towel with me. I didn't want to take out my sleeping bag, as it was already 4 A.M. and I would have to roll it up again in two hours. So I just covered myself with the towel, damper than I expected. This was a mistake. I was freezing. I went outside and smoked and talked with two marines who had arrived that night for their first tour. They couldn't sleep, either; both had a look of shock on their faces. The reality of their situation had started to register—they were actually in Iraq, sitting on a base called Camp fucking Fallujah—and they would be here for at least a year.

The next day the public affairs officer found me. He was a weird dude, a gangly forty-something man with acne scars who told me he considered himself something of a journalist, having worked for an army paper on Okinawa, and that he missed his wife, who was from some South Pacific island. He told me to speak to another public affairs officer, a young female marine lieutenant who had arranged my embed. We tried her office, and were told, since it was Sunday, she was probably at mass. We finally tracked her down in the mess hall. I sat down across from her. A marine officer sat down next to me; she introduced him as her husband. They said a prayer, which caught me off guard—I'd never seen anyone pray over KBR food. We chatted briefly about being married in a war zone; they both expressed gratitude that they were able to deploy at the same place, at the same time. Then she told me what my schedule looked like. I'd be with the 2-2 Marines, who would soon be going out to patrol a main supply road heading into Fallujah. I got a lift across Camp Fallujah in an SUV to meet them.

Four Humvees were waiting for me, the marines milling about the trucks.

Lance Corporal Robert Freeman was my driver. He told me to call him "Freebase." I asked Lance Corporal Freebase what was on the itinerary for today.

"Drive around and don't get blown up," he said.

I wrote this down.

"You gonna put that in your magazine? Make sure you say it's from Freebase."

Lance Corporal Freebase had just turned nineteen, he said. He smiled and gave me a Marlboro Red. Lance corporals, he informed me, had the lowest life expectancy of any Americans in Iraq.

We spent the afternoon patrolling up and down a two-lane highway, pounding Mountain Dews for caffeine, kicking back a Red Bull, smoking Marb Reds in the Humvee, stopping to take a piss out in the middle of the desert. Up and down the road, thirty miles an hour, so hot your brain gets tired. It was the platoon's usual patrol for "route security," making sure it was clear of bombs. They did it six times a week for eight to ten hours a day. There was not much to look at—rough sand flattening out under a blue sky. I dozed off a few times, lulled by the weight of my helmet, the heat, and the slow rhythm of the Humvee.

We stopped to move gas cans away from the road.

"They make great fireballs with the IEDs," explained Lieutenant James Martin, who used to work in financial services in New York City before 9-11. After 9-11 he joined the Marine Corps. "I hate to do it, because that's how those Iraqis make a living, selling the gas in those containers. But we have to."

There was a tree branch in the middle of the road—another possible IED. Martin approached on foot, poked at it with his boot, then dragged the branch to the side of the road. An hour later, we came upon a half-open cardboard box. Martin stepped out, raised his rifle, and gave the box a kick. Nothing. Out in the field, troops often didn't wait for the EOD units; they preferred to walk up to suspected IEDs and check them out for themselves.

Martin told me he once kicked a car tire inner tube, and all he heard was a thud—a 155mm mortar shell made in South Africa was on the inside. "I confirmed it was an IED." He laughed.

A little later, the Humvee's radio sounded off. Another platoon on patrol from the 2-2 had gotten hit with a bomb. No one was killed, but the machine gunner on the Humvee had been hit with shrapnel. The gunner in my Humvee, hearing the news, peeked down inside the truck to get clarification.

"What got hit?" the gunner asked.

"The right side of his face," one marine answered. "Don't worry about it. You don't need the right side of your face, do you?"

Lance Corporal Freebase, still driving, remarked over his shoulder to me, "I told you, drive around and don't get blown up."

Martin's platoon dropped me off at another, smaller outpost near Karma. Karma was like a suburb of Fallujah, a rural town of a few thousand people about fifty miles west of Baghdad. Karma had become a Sunni insurgent and Al Qaeda hotspot.

The marines in Karma wanted to take me on a foot patrol the next day. They told me to wear fatigues when I went out with them. I was uncomfortable with this—journalists aren't supposed to dress like marines. If a sniper sees me in civilian clothes, they said, I'd be the first one shot. I wore the fatigues. They also told me to shave, because a beard would make me look like an Iraqi interpreter, or "turp." Insurgents liked to shoot and kill Iraqis who work with Americans, the marines explained. But I didn't shave. I wanted to have my beard once the embed was over, to look as much as possible like an Iraqi. There were obvious limits—I was still a white boy with blue eyes. But, at least in theory, I tried to blend into the culture as much as I could.

My anxiety the night before the foot patrol wasn't a fear of death or dismemberment. It was that the last thing Scott had said to me before I headed off to Fallujah: "Don't go on any random patrols. Just report the video-game story." (A story I was working on about how soldiers spent their free time. The editors in New York thought we'd been doing too many embed stories lately, and they were pressuring Scott to not put his correspondents at risk for stories that might or might not run.) And here I was, not twenty-four hours into my trip, going out on a random patrol. But what else was I going to do? Sit around the base and chat? I was worried, though. If I get hurt, I thought, Scott's going to be really pissed off at me. It's going to seem like I fucked up, like I couldn't follow a simple instruction—don't go on a random patrol.

It was night on the small outpost. I called Andi to check in. I was wearing my helmet and body armor with boxers and flip-flops, as you weren't allowed out in the open without full protection. Andi was going to a wedding in Boston with her friend Keri. All the guys are going to hit on you, I told her, so be careful. I felt a little insecure from this far away. I didn't like the thought of her going to a wedding without me. Make sure you tell everyone you have a boyfriend, I said.

The next morning, I drove in an open-back Humvee to OP2, or Outpost 2. I was surprised that the marines were still traveling around in the backs of trucks without armor, as exposed as they would be if they were lounging in the back of a pickup truck. The marines told me that they never got the good equipment; their battalion didn't have enough of the newer "up-armored" Humvees to go around. They dropped me off at OP2. OP1 had been truck-bombed a few weeks earlier, injuring four marines, so they'd moved OP2 farther back from the main road leading into Karma. It was a shitty house, concrete and no glass, with two floors and part of the roof missing. About twenty marines lived there in the most spartan conditions.

The 2-2 Marines walked the streets of Karma every day "engaging the local population" and "showing their presence," a strategy to let them know who runs the place.

Karma was hostile. The locals didn't wave.

Corporal Khalid Aziz, a twenty-four-year-old veteran on his second tour, led the patrol. He explained what to watch out for: "If it's too quiet, you know something is up, because all these motherfuckers know when something is going to happen." A Moroccan by birth, though raised in Baltimore, Khalid was the rare marine who spoke Arabic, a fact he tried to hide, because once the locals knew they directed all their complaints at him. And there was plenty to complain about. Earlier in the month, two men, two women, and two children in a car failed to stop at the extensive barriers and warning signs near OP2. A marine standing guard fired at the car. He shot the tires out. The car kept coming forward. He kept firing. The two women were killed, one of them the mother of the children in the backseat.

Why didn't they stop?

Bad driving, dusty windshield, human error, stupid fucking Iraqis, who knows.

The Rules of Engagement hadn't saved the family. The ROEs were always a popular topic. The fact that they weren't allowed to shoot to kill right away irritated the marines. The enemy always had the advantage—they could shoot first. As Khalid told me, "You're supposed to wave, throw a flashbang, say hi, make a baloney-and-cheese sandwich, shoot in front, shoot the tire, shoot the other tire, have some tea, shoot the engine, and *then* shoot the windshield."

We started out on the patrol. There were four marines and five Iraqi Army soldiers on foot. I had on a Camelback, a water bottle you strapped onto your back so you could drink with your hands free. I carried a notebook. The morning patrol wasn't too eventful—a stroll past a school where insurgents frequently launched ambushes, then on to a mosque where Khalid told me they hid all their weapons but which was nonetheless off-limits to search; then to a cemetery, again off-limits, where the insurgents stored more weapons. We went into a house for an activity called the "Yellow Pages" or the "knock and talk." The purpose was to take photos and record the names of the men in the household and to poke around and see what there was to see. The men in this particular house did not look happy at the intrusion. We took a break, and the family offered us water. I sat down on a couch next to a marine and smoked a cigarette.

It was a little tense. An Iraqi man, one of the family's sons in his twenties, glared at each of the Americans, including me. I asked the marine sitting next to me if this was the usual reaction.

"This is nothing," he said. "One time, we went into a house to do the knock and talk. One of our guys went up on the roof. The lieutenant was talking to the head of the household in the kitchen. All the women were waiting outside. We heard this sound, like it was raining, and then a woman screaming and we could hear her vomiting. The woman comes running into the kitchen in tears. She's pregnant. The marine on the roof had decided to relieve himself. He pissed all over this guy's pregnant wife."

"Winning the hearts and minds, right?"

The marine shrugged. "Yeah, we apologized," he said.

At a traffic intersection known as the Lolly Pop because of a large white circular sign, Khalid asked me if I had ever seen a flashbang. A flashbang is a grenade that just makes a really loud noise. "WHA-WHOOM," he said. "Watch this." He threw the flashbang in front of an eighteen-wheeler. It went off. The Iraqis standing in the street flinched and looked startled. The eighteen-wheeler slammed on its brakes. "That's the flashbang," Khalid said and smiled.

That afternoon, I went out on a second foot patrol. This time we walked down the main street, a passage cramped with market stalls, shops, people, and cars. Most of the traffic stopped when the drivers saw the marines on foot, except for a yellow car that kept inching forward. A marine fired his rifle at the ground in front of the car, two quick shots. Pop, pop. The car slammed on its brakes. The marine approached the car. When he got to the window, an Iraqi man sitting in the backseat vomited. "Probably because he's scared," the marine told me. Toward the end of the patrol, we heard a loud explosion about three kilometers away. The radio came to life: Another platoon had been hit. Four casualties. A gray plume of smoke appeared on the horizon. "That's from the IED," a marine pointed out to me.

We walked back. As we passed by the school, I was about to step on what looked like a pothole in the pavement. The staff sergeant walking behind me casually said, "Sir, you may want to stay away from that, that's a spot where they've blown up IEDs." I moved across the street.

We'd been on patrol for two hours. I was tired and dehydrated and wondered how anybody did this every day over the course of a seven-month combat tour. What were the odds that you'd survive this shit? There were roughly 210 days of patrolling on a tour. About three quarters of those days, you're out on three patrols a day. That means some 472 extremely dangerous missions, invariably carried out while sleep-deprived and drenched in sweat and carrying at least thirty pounds of armor and equipment. The story I wrote for the *Newsweek* website was headlined "A Daily Dance With Death." The odds of becoming a casualty were significantly higher than the Pentagon made it sound. Yes, there were more than a hundred thousand troops in Iraq, with an average of two being killed a day; but the vast majority were support troops, those who never left the bases. Military officials estimated that only about 20 percent of the troops regularly left the FOBs. If you took that into account, then if you were on the front lines, your odds of being killed became more like one in ten thousand. One in ten thousand, 472 times.

It's a cliché at this point to talk about the honor of the troops, how warm and fuzzy and patriotic they can make us feel. But I was amazed at the bravery of these kids. They'd signed on the dotted line in the recruiter's office because they felt an intense need to serve their country, or they were looking for action and adventure, or they were struggling and wanted to make something out of their lives. They were between eighteen and twenty-eight, they chewed tobacco and had had juvenile records and tattoos and three kids before the age of twenty-two. They were poor kids from South Carolina and middle-class kids from Wisconsin and Hispanics from California. They were calm in the face of deadening fear and boredom. I liked them. They were living in a world where a fuckup could get them killed, or their friend killed, or maybe they would kill someone by mistake. And even if they didn't fuck up, they could still get killed. The pressure was enormous. Theirs was a world I looked upon with awe sometimes and as total bullshit other times. It was odd to see them here, so flawed and scared and macho and young, and to think of them as an applause line in a politician's stump speech. But they were also killers. They were highly trained in the art of eliminating other human beings.

After the two patrols, half a dozen of the marines sat with me outside the decaying outpost. We talked in the glow of green neon lights as it grew darker. I sat on a canvas tailgating chair; the marines sprawled out on water coolers, foldout metal chairs, or on the ground. They had their concerns. One explained that he had been asked to come to his high school to speak to the students. A student asked him if he would kill an eight-year-old if the eight-year-old was pointing a gun at him. "If the eight-year-old had a gun," said the marine, "I'd kill the eight-year-old." He said the crowd back home gasped, but here the circle of marines laughed at the story. They were not baby killers, though a baby might die every once in a while.

Lance Corporal Andrew Gladue, twenty-two, from Georgia, was on his second tour in Iraq. He had a slight mustache and short black hair matted on his forehead. He inhaled a Marlboro and asked me if I could answer something.

"Sure," I said.

"Back home, do they think we're fighting a war?"

"I don't know how much time people really spend thinking about—"

"We think we're fighting a war," he said.

The next morning I went back to Camp Fallujah, arriving at 4 A.M. and going to the Media Tent, a dusty beige canvas quarters with a plywood floor and rickety iron bunk beds with stained mattresses. Only one air conditioner worked. I passed out quickly, and slept well until my T-Mobile woke me up. It was Andi.

"Hi, baby," I said, stumbling out of the tent to get better reception. "How are you?"

"I'm good, I'm leaving the wedding and I was thinking of you."

"That's good."

"Some guys asked us to go out to a bar, but we didn't."

"That's good."

A pause.

"How are you?" she said. "Is there anything you want to tell me? My third eye senses something is wrong."

"Well, I'm tired right now. I just got back from these patrols, but yeah, I guess I wanted to let you know that I am going to be here for two more weeks, which means I won't get home until like October fifteenth."

Silence.

I explained it wasn't a big deal, just two more weeks. Scott had asked me if I wanted to stay longer, and I didn't want to pass up the opportunity. The more time I could spend on the ground there, the better, I explained.

"You're not coming home, are you? You're going to stay there."

"I am coming home, and I still want to be with you."

She told me she had to go and hung up. I called back, but she didn't answer.

Fuck. Didn't she understand that I'd just come back from a fucking stressful two days?

That night, I took a helicopter back to Baghdad. Andi wasn't answering my calls, and I was worried and annoyed. If she couldn't handle this kind of minor setback, I thought, what chance did we have?

I finally got through to her when I was back at the *Newsweek* bureau. We talked for three hours. She told me that at the wedding, all she thought about was me. But she also told me that a guy there tried to kiss her.

"What? He tried to kiss you?"

"I ducked! I didn't kiss him."

"What the fuck? Didn't you tell him you had a boyfriend?"

"I did. He asked if I loved you."

"Who is this guy? What's he do?"

"He's an accountant in Boston."

"An accountant? Jesus Christ, didn't you tell him you're dating a fucking war correspondent?"

She told me that she wasn't interested in him at all. She wanted to be with me, but she really was worried that I wasn't going to come back. I'm coming back, I said, in two weeks. I promise. And if that fucking accountant emails you, don't email him back.

Something about Fallujah, something about the Boston wedding, it all had a clarifying effect on our relationship. The day after our three-hour conversation, we instant-messaged with each other over Skype.

Andiparhamovich: It's hard for me to say it you know
Andiparhamovich: But I think I love you
Michaelmhastings: I think I love you too

CHAPTER 6

October 15-19, 2005

BAGHDAD, DUBAI, NEW YORK

I am trying to leave Iraq, waiting nervously in the Baghdad International Airport, in another fucking line, my passport in hand. I slept two hours last night. It's a Monday, and there's a sandstorm.

I've spent the last two weeks in Mosul, the country's third-largest city, two hundred miles north of Baghdad. I was embedded with the 172nd Stryker Brigade, a three-thousand-man unit from Alaska that fought in a new kind of armored vehicle called the Stryker. It looked like something out of *Star Wars*—four massive wheels, its body painted metallic green. The Stryker could reach speeds up to seventy miles an hour, and had room inside for a squad of soldiers. The driver, crammed in the nose of the vehicle, used video screens to see the road. I was in Mosul to cover Iraq's constitutional referendum. The Iraqi government had finally agreed on a new constitution; now it was up to the citizens to vote. The Stryker Brigade's mission was to make the vote run smoothly—securing the polling stations, transporting ballot boxes and election officials around the city.

There were a few issues. Copies of the constitution weren't distributed properly across the country, so few voters actually had read it. That didn't stop them from voting. The referendum was on Saturday. That afternoon, I rode around on the roof of the Stryker, lying down next to a bag of soccer balls the soldiers were handing out, snapping photos and taking notes as I watched Iraqis come out by the thousands to cast their ballots. I wrote my story, just making deadline, saying the vote was a success—in that it actually happened, and there was not much violence.

On Sunday, I caught a flight in a C-130 cargo plane from Mosul to Camp Victory in Baghdad, got a ride in an SUV from an Estonian public affairs officer to a helicopter pad on the other side of the camp, where a pilot offered me a lift to the Green Zone. The trip took four hours and was amazingly smooth for military travel. On Monday, I drove to the Baghdad Airport. That's when things stopped going smoothly.

Besides the sandstorm, there is a bureaucratic problem—I don't have an exit visa. To leave Iraq as an American citizen not working for the government, you need the Iraqi government's permission. To get the exit visa, you pay a bribe ranging from $50 to $150 to an Iraqi official, which gets you a stamp on the passport allowing you to leave. Sometimes you can get by without it, but sometimes you can't. This is one of those times. At the first immigration check, the immigration official, a pudgy fellow with a mustache, hands my passport back to me.

"Why no stamp?" he says.

"The office to get the stamp has been closed for the last five days," I tell him. "And the stamp is only good for five days, so I couldn't get it, and the flight was supposed to leave early this morning, so if I wanted to make my flight . . ."

Not even a shrug from the official. He doesn't like me.

"Why no stamp."

I need to get permission to leave. My flight has already been canceled because of the sandstorm, so it looks like I'll have a few hours to try to work something out. I'm with my driver, who speaks English, and my Iraqi security guard, Uday. I send my driver to meet our office manager outside the first airport checkpoint. He has printed out a letter saying I am authorized to leave. It looks like an official letter—it's written on *Newsweek* letterhead. I give it to the customs official. He shakes his head and doesn't give me the letter back.

I ask my driver to try to bribe the official. That doesn't work, either, and the customs man dislikes me even more now.

I confer with my driver on what to do next. "Do you think we can get the visa stamped today?"

"Enshallah," he says, "enshallah."

God willing. I don't need God, I think, just get the stamp on the damn passport.

It looks like the flights to Amman are all going to be canceled, so there's a chance I might get stuck overnight at the airport. (It will be safer for me to stay at the airport for the night than to go up and down Airport Road again.) I give my passport to my driver, and he goes into downtown Baghdad to get the passport stamped with an exit visa.

I wait. I'm letting my nerves show. Now I don't even have a passport with me. I want to get out now. I want to leave. I want to see Andi. I promised her I would be home on Tuesday. I smoke freely, though the Muslim holiday of Ramadan has begun and smoking in public is forbidden and offensive to believers. I'm being culturally insensitive, but I don't really give a shit. I justify my smoking by telling myself the airport is basically American soil now anyway.

An announcement crackles in Arabic saying that all flights to Amman are canceled. I start to listen for other flights that might be leaving, flights going anywhere. Beirut, Damascus, Cairo, Erbil, wherever, it doesn't matter. After keeping my shit together since I arrived in Baghdad in August, I feel like I'm about to lose it.

It's getting late in the afternoon; there are no civilian flights once the sun sets.

My driver returns with the exit visa stamp on the passport. A crowd has gathered at the immigration counter, pushing and shouting. A sweaty fat man stands there, calling out a destination. "Dubai," he says, "Dubai."

Unlike most airports in the world, where there is a generally organized schedule, the Baghdad Airport is a permanent clusterfuck. Little is computerized or modern despite the more than $150 million investment to refurbish the place. There is no working flight board listing arrivals and departures; there are about seven security checkpoints to get on a plane. Stranded passengers sometimes sleep in the terminal for days before their flights leave. Flight times are vague estimates at best; when you ask about a departure or arrival time, the answer from the airport staff is: It will fly when it flies, maybe in an hour, maybe in five hours, maybe tomorrow, enshallah.

The sweaty fat gentleman calling out Dubai works with a charter company.

"Ask him if there are still seats free to Dubai," I tell my driver.

My driver asks.

"Yes, there are, but the flight is leaving now, four hundred dollars for a ticket."

"Get me a ticket," I say.

The sandstorm hasn't cleared; I look out the large glass windows in the terminal at the dull beige color in the air.

The fat man escorts me through the first customs and ticket check. I triumphantly show my exit visa to the customs official who hadn't let me through earlier.

I am screened again by a metal detector. A South African private security guard from a company called Global Security stops the fat man.

"You can't just keep bringing people on once the flight has been called."

I look at the South African. "Dude, I need to get on this flight."

He lets us through.

At an unmarked ticket counter, I pay a man $400. I search my pockets for the cash. I've divided up $1,000 in three different spots, including a roll of hundreds in my sock, and my hand is shaking as I pull out the notes.

There is no time to check baggage. I hurry through the terminal, past another metal detector, down a flight of stairs where a bus is waiting to take me out to the plane. I carry a large duffel bag, my large North Face backpack, and my laptop bag. I walk up the steps to the jet. I am the last one on. My bags bang against everyone as I walk down the narrow aisle. I hear shouts in Arabic directed at me, which I believe mean, "Watch your fucking bags, white boy," but I don't care. I am happy. I am on the runway. I am going to see Andi.

The plane says Hungarian Airlines, flying under the name of the charter company, Jupiter Air. The flight staff is Hungarian, and the stewardess with her blond hair and heavy makeup looks like she could pass for a prostitute in her spare time. The flight is only half full.

I sit down and put on my iPod, a 1 gig Shuffle Andi gave me in July. She'd loaded up the songs, too, including "This Modern Love" from the soundtrack to *Wedding Crashers,* a movie we saw together three weeks before I left for Iraq.

I lean back in my seat.

The flight starts to take off. There is a draft coming from somewhere. The 737 is shaking more than it should. The wheels lift off the ground. I don't hear any loud noises. The music in my headphones plays. I smile. I smile in a way I haven't since the days before I got sober seven years ago. The addict in me is alive again and oh what a feeling. I survived. I made it. I didn't fuck up. Bliss.

I know now what they are talking about when they say "war junkies," now I understand exactly what they mean. I've felt it before. I know the pull, the intoxication, the life-affirming chemicals released after seeing the abyss and coming back from it. When I was a teenager I used to snort cocaine and smoke crack and party all night and booze for months because I wanted to know what it was like to hit those highs and to feel those highs when they all came crashing down.

It feels good to live after death. It feels good to not be dead. It feels so good to find myself alive and flying home. The music plays in my ears and I float further and further away from the war. Fucking Baghdad.

Two hours after takeoff, Dubai appears, and the feeling does not go away. The city's skyline is lit up, excessive amounts of electricity surging up skyscrapers, large ships rocking in the ports on the Persian Gulf. The airplane door opens, and I am out and then onto a pristinely clean bus that runs silently, almost magically fume-free, its temperature-controlled air so refreshing and cool. I had forgotten the finer things in life. I'd gotten used to a stew and rice for dinner, to mosquitoes and flies and bats and lizards, to nothing ever working right. Dubai is the opposite, a return to civilization, it is the Hong Kong of the Middle East, Las Vegas meets Islam, no open gambling but plenty of money laundering, row after row of towering buildings, an indoor ski hill, the only seven-star hotel in the world, a man-made island shaped like a palm tree.

Through the terminal—a giant duty-free shopping complex disguised as an airport—and into a taxi in under fifteen minutes. The cab is no smoking. I check in at the Hyatt Regency. Five Russian prostitutes hang out in the lobby, young girls, barely eighteen if that. I have dinner on the twenty-fifth floor, a revolving glass-windowed restaurant with a buffet of smoked salmon, shrimp, lobster tail, lo mein, steak, everything refrigerated and fresh.

The next day, I'm on an Emirates flight direct to New York, with a choice of movies from an entertainment console hidden in the armrest. The flight goes over the mountains of Iran, up toward Russia, and I follow it on the map on the color monitor, traveling over countries that I haven't yet set foot in, wondering what the future has in store. Flying through the night to see Andi, texting back and forth the entire way. I watch *Batman Begins,* and seeing Katie Holmes as the tough district attorney reminds me of Andi. Everything reminds me of her and that I haven't been with her in two and a half months. She would tell me later that she loved that movie, too, because at its heart it was about understanding evil and then fighting it.

Andi meets me at JFK. It is awkward at first. The car she has come out in can't find me. It's a cold October night, and I wait on the sidewalk until finally she pulls up. I jump in the backseat and grab her hand. The first thing she notices is that I've lost weight, the result of my last embed sitting inside armored vehicles for hours on end, sweating, sweating, sweating. She can see my bones, she tells me later. She could never be with someone skinnier than she is, she jokes. We go straight to my studio apartment on the Lower East Side. I don't remember now what we talked about. I remember her sitting next to me in the backseat, I remember holding her hand, driving over the bridge toward the Manhattan skyline at 10 P.M. I remember the return to my apartment, dragging my bags up two flights of stairs, searching for my keys, finding them, opening the door then locking it behind us, click, then making love, and then her cell phone is ringing and the cab driver is saying we forgot to sign the credit card receipt. I go back out to the street, to New York in the fall, sign the receipt, and then I return to her.

CHAPTER 7

October 17-December 27, 2005

NEW YORK, OHIO, VERMONT

Two months. We had just over two months—October 17 to December 27—before I was scheduled to go back to Baghdad. Two months of the holiday season, two months of dinners every night and double features every weekend in New York. Of doing all the romantic and maybe corny things people do in the city, inspired by the images from our movie-watching childhoods—late autumn walks in Central Park, the lighting of the tree at Rockefeller Center, and Macy's Christmas window displays. I was keenly aware of our time together, the self-consciousness of our romance, as if we were living on film, playing the roles of a correspondent back from the front, his beautiful love at home waiting for him.

There's so little time. If we only have two months, we can't go our separate ways for the holidays. We have exactly sixty-seven days. That's practically no time at all. You must come to Ohio to meet my parents. You have to come to Vermont to meet my family. We can do it all, no problem—the first weekend to Cleveland, back to work for a few days, then a JetBlue flight to Burlington with a day or two to spare for shopping on Church Street. My parents even say they'll wait to decorate the tree.

But first we had to last to the holidays, first we had to survive getting to know each other again. All the worries and concerns we'd suppressed over the phone calls and instant messages resurfaced. And this was when I made a mistake. There are events in any relationship you regret, things you wish you could take back, and for me, it was a dinner with a female friend that I didn't tell Andi about. I was just going to have dinner and go back to my apartment, and that would be it. I was going to be faithful. I was just going to enjoy the attention, share my war stories, an ego thing. Didn't I deserve a little glory?

Andi called right before I was about to leave for dinner. It was the first night since I'd returned that we hadn't been together. She was in a good mood. I told her I was going to dinner with a friend; she said it's not So and So, is it? No, I said, it's not. It's Such and Such.

The dinner was uneventful, no big deal, harmless.

The next week, Andi wanted to put her work number in my cell phone, using her initials, ASP. I told her she couldn't look at my phone, that it was private—which screamed guilt—and within moments she was looking at the text messages, the one from So and So, saying she would meet me for dinner soon. It took Andi a few minutes to put the dates together, but when she did, the rest of the night was spent in repairing damage—her in tears, me begging and apologizing. The next day I sent flowers and asked for forgiveness, saying I wouldn't do it again. The days that followed were efforts to overcome our insecurities, push-me-pull-me, cautiously letting our guards down, then putting them up again, then easing them back down. And like all of our emotions, our fights and reconciliations were magnified by the ticking clock, and the knowledge that we were together now but Iraq was closer each day.

We spent Thanksgiving together at her Upper West Side apartment, still struggling to get past the bad vibes. Anything could trigger them (on that day it was the fire alarm I accidentally set off after a mishap cooking pancakes at breakfast; I'd put too much butter on the pan). But we finally pulled it together and went downstairs to watch the Macy's parade. That night, we ate at Tavern on the Green, the landmark restaurant on the west side of Central Park. I hadn't eaten there since I visited New York as a kid. Andi chose the place, having never been there. We sat at a table under the glass ceiling and white lights of the garden. I pointed out where Louis in *Ghostbusters,* played by Rick Moranis, was consumed by a devil hound; he presses up against the tavern's window, screaming for help, amusingly ignored by the diners inside. I called over the house photographer and he took a photo, making us stand to pose. I knew she had some anxiety about making a scene in public, and I asked the photographer over just to get a rise out of her, but at least now we had a picture, one that she said showed off her "big eye"—a left eye she insisted was larger than the right, though it was imperceptible to almost all other humans.

With each day, the deadline approached and the sense of urgency increased. The visit to her family, the visit to mine, then it's done, I'm back to Baghdad. As much as I tried to push it out of my mind, Iraq had changed something in me. I wanted to keep covering the war. I liked it. And I wasn't sure how to respond when Andi kept bringing up how she would feel once I left. I preferred not to worry about how I'd feel until I was already gone.

Andi's home was Perry, Ohio, a forty-minute drive along Lake Erie from Cleveland, population 1,195. She'd left five years ago. Her father, Andre, was a schoolteacher and football coach. Her mother, Vicki, was a nurse at a Cleveland hospital. Always working, always paying bills. Her older sister Marci got married at twenty-four and moved down the street to her husband's childhood home. She had two daughters, Kayla and Abby. Andi hoped to mold her nieces in her own image. She bought the girls the "Presidential Barbie"—why can't a woman be president?—and filled their heads with feminist ideas and liberal talking points. She also filled their stomachs and bloodstream with candy and chocolates, a cocktail of hyperactivity. She was cool Aunt Andi from New York, sending packages purchased from the Toys "R" Us in Times Square, hundreds of dollars' worth of the newest toys.

Then there were her two younger brothers—the Twins, Cory and Chris—who she insisted took all the attention away from her when they came along. "I was eleven years old!" she would say. "The middle child. I had to fight for attention. I was a straight-A student, and look at the Twins—they got in trouble all the time! I've never even smoked a cigarette!"

"Why are there no baby pictures of me," she would demand. "Just pictures of the Twins! I'm adopted, I'm almost positive I'm adopted."

"I've seen pictures of your family, you look like them . . ."

"No, I'm adopted!"

She left for Cleveland on Friday. I was going to meet her there on Saturday. I had postponed my flight until later because I had to work longer than I expected that day. She told me to forget it, don't come, you're too busy. I said, no, I'm coming, I'll be there, don't worry about it. She said no, don't come. I said I'm coming, baby, and I hope you're there to pick me up at the airport.

She was there. We drove through Cleveland, where I'd never been, and she gave me the tour—the Jake, or Jacob's Field, where she went to Indian games with her dad, the Key Bank building, the hospital where her mom gave birth to the twins. We stopped at the Outback Steakhouse in Mentor for dinner (pronounced "Mentir," she corrected me). We arrived at her sister's home at 11 P.M.

"Marci, can you please get rid of those cats," Andi announced as we walked through the door. Marci and her husband and the girls lived in a two-story white home on the grounds of a tree farm. Rows of baby pine trees stretched in all directions around the house.

Andi introduced me to Marci. "Beautiful Christmas tree," I said, looking at the tree in front of the picture window, its white lights casting a holiday glow on the peaceful and quiet living room.

"Marci, why aren't there any baby pictures of me?"

Marci shook her head. "Oh, Andi."

We slept on the two couches in the living room. Around 4 A.M., I awoke to coughing—heavy, constant coughing that sounded like it was coming from a radio.

"What's that?" I asked in a daze.

"The baby monitor."

"The baby monitor? For who?"

"Kayla . . ."

"Should someone do something? I mean, she sounds sick . . ."

"She is sick. I think it's the nuclear plant."

"Can't we change the channel to get the other kid?"

We fell back asleep.

In the morning, we were greeted by the nieces, Kayla, a feisty blond four-year-old, who looked like a miniature Andi, and Abby, who at age six was already Andi's political protégée.

That afternoon we took the kids to a movie, *The Chronicles of Narnia* (I fell asleep during the film, much to Abby's astonishment) and Andi gave me a tour of Perry.

She wasn't joking about the nuclear plant. It didn't fit with the flat, rural landscape. The steam it was billowing came out in large white clouds and seemed to drift over the town. The scene reminded me of the opening credits of *The Simpsons*. I began to think she might have a point about the possible high rate of cancer in her town. (Admittedly, she had only anecdotal evidence: Her father had recently recovered from leukemia, miraculously keeping his full head of hair, a Parhamovich trait.)

The weekend was a milestone for Andi. She was twenty-seven years old and had never brought a boy home for Christmas. But this was only the second serious relationship she had ever been in.

Months after we started dating, she told me about the first guy. She had lived with him briefly during her early twenties after she moved to Boston, where she worked for Jane Swift, the governor of Massachusetts. He could be abusive, she said. He hurt her so badly, she told me, that one day when he was out at work she found the strength to leave. She packed up all her things and never told him where she went. Soon after that she left Boston and moved to New York.

After that, she said, she put up walls. She wouldn't let anyone get close. She did not date anyone for almost three years, until the summer we met, when she was finally starting to think that life held possibilities, perhaps even the possibility of love, though this was a shocking notion to her. She told me that I had broken through the walls. Her parents had a saying: "God help the man who loves Andi Parhamovich." After spending the afternoon in a local shopping mall, where Andi did not find anything she wanted, I grabbed her hand and said, "That man, God help me, is me."

That night, Marci cooked a Christmas dinner for us. Andi's parents, Vicki and Andre, came over.

"So you write for *Newsweek*," her father stated.

"Yes, I do."

"I have to be honest, I don't read *Newsweek* very much. I like the *Sporting News*, though."

"The *Sporting News* is a good publication," I said.

Andre told his favorite Andi stories. When she was in second grade, there was a competition to see who could read the most books in a month. The winner would get a certificate for a Personal Pan Pizza at Pizza Hut and a private dinner with the teacher, Ms. Barth. On the first weekend of the competition, Andi's parents wondered where she was; she had disappeared. Her dad peered in her room and saw her reading next to a stack of books. At midnight he woke up, not sleeping well, and checked in on his daughter again. She was still awake. "Don't bother me, Dad, go away, I have sixty-two more books to read before Monday." She was determined to win. By Monday, she had somehow read all eighty books on the list, sealing her victory, and claiming the Pizza Hut certificate and the dinner with Ms. Barth.

Other stories her family told: the cats! Andi claimed she was allergic to cats; she accused her parents and siblings of not taking her allergy seriously, despite, as she remembered it, nearly being hospitalized after a visit with Andre to her grandmother's house, a house with closed windows and at least three felines. Andi also boycotted a field trip to Washington, D.C., held during the girls' softball season, saying that it was an equal rights issue. The school would never have scheduled the trip during the boys' baseball season. She boycotted the senior prom; sexist, silly. At the age of fifteen, she refused to wear a red dress in her sister Marci's wedding because she didn't want to condone such a patriarchal and antiquated institution. (Finally, protesting the whole way, she put on the red dress and walked down the aisle for her sister.)

Injustice. Her entire life she couldn't tolerate injustice.

The pre-Christmas dinner was a success; I bonded with Andre, with Vicki, with Marci, even with the Twins. Andi joked that finally Joe, Marci's husband, would have an ally to ward off the crazy Parhamovich clan. On Monday morning, Vicki dropped us off at the airport and we flew back to New York. Five years earlier, when she left Perry for Boston, Andre and Vicki had followed her (she was driving with her soon to be roommate) to the Massachusetts state line, eight hours from Perry. Then they turned around and drove back. As we were sitting on the runway, heading back to New York early Monday morning, I realized I was glad to have met them—thinking what kind people they were and how deeply they loved their daughter.

We arrived in Vermont two days before Christmas, five days before I was scheduled to return to Iraq. We shopped at the last minute on Church Street and bought presents. A popcorn maker for my parents, books and DVDs for my brothers. (She had already given me three framed prints from photographer Ropert Capa: one of Israel's 1948 war, another of bombers in the air taken in 1944 on June 16 [her birthday], and another from the landing on D-Day.)

I had given her a digital camera. Andi napped on the couch while my brothers and I played the board game Heroscape. She wrapped presents in the guest bedroom while I talked about life in Iraq with my younger brother, Jeff, who had just completed Ranger school training and was scheduled to deploy to Iraq the following August. Jeff joined the army as an officer in November 2004. Our grandfather had served in the Pacific theater in World War II; our father spent eight years as a doctor in the Army Reserves and the National Guard. Jeff is the youngest of three boys, and I felt he wanted to distinguish himself from his older brothers—I was the writer, and our oldest brother Jon was always the intellectual, the vale-dictorian. Jeff was the athlete, a member of a fraternity at college. He didn't want to waste his postcollege years working at video stores; he wanted to test himself, be a patriot, and see history firsthand. Our parents, both physicians, had raised us to be independent thinkers, to pur-sue the careers we wanted. That's what we were doing, and that had brought us both on a path to Baghdad.

On Christmas morning, Andi handed out presents to us, an excessive amount of gifts piled around the tree, sliding smoothly into the ritual, one to Jeff, one to Jon, one to Brent, one to Molly, one to Grandma Ruth, one to me, and repeat, until the baked stuffed French toast and oyster stew were ready. For some reason my dad put on Mariah Carey's Christmas album and we all laughed at him, but no one turned it off. We played board games late into the evening, then we went to the guest bed-room (though for reasons of decorum I pretended to sleep on the living room couch), where Andi rested her head on my shoulder and I felt my white undershirt start to get wet.

"Baby, uh, are you crying?"

"No," she said, sniffling.

"Why are you crying?"

No answer, but my shirt was getting wetter.

"Baby, you're ruining my shirt."

"You're not very good at consoling."

"Oh, look at your baby tears."

"Baby tears," she said. "Baby, baby tears."

"There's no need to cry. I'm not leaving yet."

"You're leaving in two days."

"Exactly. We have two more days together. No need to get upset now."

"You don't get it!"

"Get what?"

"You're leaving."

"It's my job. It's what I do."

She didn't say don't go, she didn't ask any questions. She told me that the last time I left she cried, too, but she hid it from me. This time she isn't hiding it. This time it was much more serious. We've met each other's parents, we've made plans for vacation in March.

"It's just two months," I said. "Then we'll see each other."

"You're not very good at consoling," she repeated.

"I'm trying, I'm trying."

I held her tight, and she held me, and we slept until the alarm on her BlackBerry beeped at 4:45 A.M. and I sneaked back to the couch and pretended to wake up there, in time for our flight back to New York.

Forty-eight hours later I was in Amman.

CHAPTER 8

December 28-30, 2005

EMAILS

To: andi parhamovich

From: mhastings@gmail.com

Sent: dec 28, 2005, 4:11 A.M.

Subject: letter from amman en route to baghdad

Dear Andi:

It's 3:20 am in Amman, Jordan, and I'm jetlagged. I woke up after five hours of sleep. The window of the hotel room is open so I can hear the cars on the highway. The noise reminds me of New York. Otherwise it would be too quiet. I tried to go back to sleep. It didn't work. I closed eyes for an hour. I thought of you, and what I wanted to write.

You have blonde hair, fine and real. You glow. It's your face that does it; partial dimples and October eyes, ethereal, angelic. Your body is perfect. Your skin is flawless, and for some reason your stomach always looks tan. Your figure is warm, soft, and when you wrap your legs around my chest like a lemur and rest your head on my collarbone, what we call the nook, there is perfection. It reminds me of the other day, during the game of Heroscape, and you were napping on the couch in Vermont while my army attacked its enemies. When the dog jumped up on you, and pressed against your legs, you looked so comfortable, and I was amazed at how well you fit in the living room, looking so pretty and peaceful and cute. You are funny and so extremely bright, too.

What about us, what about the last two months? The last seven months. I've told you that if I fail at loving you, I will have failed at love. I have had no reservations about our love, and this is a first for me. I am away again, and I realize that it's not easy. It's not easy, this love thing, and we both have dark corners in our hearts. Yours is dark in the places where you have been betrayed and abused; mine is cloudy and bruised near the left ventricle; self-destruction does haunt me, an old and nasty friend, a habit, because there was a long time in my life where I thought the only thing to do with my self was to destroy it. We are both guarded against happiness, and that's what we have found in each other. Like the Keymaster and the Gatekeeper from Ghostbusters, we keep waiting for the Stay Puft Marshmallow Man to appear and step on everything we have. Worse still is the pressure that comes from seeing our future; what it could be, how it could be. How we want it to be.

The crazy thing about us is that we fit. I want the best for you; I want to see your dreams work; I want to bring out the best in you; I want to do all this.

I Lost My Love in Baghdad

There's me in Iraq, and that's interesting, as I say. I have never written to anyone about the danger and fear of this enterprise. The life and death of it. The fact that there were times, perhaps one or two, when we were lying in your bed or on the cloud, and it was again late at night and I opened my eyes and thought what the fuck am I thinking going and risking getting killed when everything here is so good. And my heart would start to beat a little faster and my thoughts move quicker and I would say, jesus, what if. Perhaps I'm being overdramatic. I don't want you to worry.

Part II

Again it's 3:20, this time twenty-four hours later. The above is crude and not my best writing, it's a deadline situation though, and I wanted you to know that you can have faith in me. I want you to put your concerns about such and such out of your mind. I am stupid, very stupid, but not that stupid. I am interested in you, singular. Your love is startling, like when I am overwhelmed by your cuteness. Everything will be okay; we can work. There is no need to fight. We are difficult, but what's the point of life, in general, if there is no challenge.

So—

I'm getting on a plane in seven hours to go back to the country that has been with us since milkshakes. I want your support; i love your support. Cuddle bear! Pocket Sized! My little refugee, hair twirled just so, sleeping, awake, crying "fan," peekaboo face peering up from the pillow. You are strong, beautiful, strong; independent too, otherwise this wouldn't have a chance. This is now much more than a chance; it is very real and I want it, and I want you.

—MH

p.s. if this letter is not satisfactory, I will try again.

To Michael Hastings

From andi parhamovich

Subject: re: a letter from amman en route to Baghdad

Sent: 12/31/05

Dear Newsie:

It's Friday, Dec. 30 , the first Friday you haven't been with me, and my
heart hurts and my mind is scrambling from all of the "thinking." I keep
rereading the letter you wrote me—my Hemingway letter—and I can't
seem to get a grip on my emotions. I keep thinking about the nights we
missed. You will probably think this is crazy, but I can remember the 12
or so days we didn't spend together these past few months. I remember them now because at the time I was thinking "I should be with him
now, he will be gone soon." I kept thinking I needed to soak up every
minute—every spore—of our time together because when you are gone
there is this void.

I wonder if you realize how much you have changed my life and how
much I love you. I wonder if you realize that before you, I was strong
but emotionally weak. I was independent but hoping for something
more. I was always around people but always alone. And then you came
along. I can still remember you charging into the room head first with
your notepad in your back pocket. Your entrance was duly noted by
about four or five interns, and I recall looking for an enemy and only
finding a cute reporter with a Cheshire-cat smile. No one wanted me to
talk to you that night and yet no one could pull me away from you.
Even now, when I first see you, whether it's early in the morning after a
6 AM flight or late at night after we've both worked all day, there are
times when I have to take a moment to catch my breath because I can't
believe how much I love you and how deeply I love you.

I Lost My Love in Baghdad

I remember you telling me during milkshakes that you were going to Iraq and, at the time, I would have never guessed how much that country would play a role in our relationship. In some ways, it is the country that has kept us together and in other ways it is what has almost torn us apart. After reading your letter, I didn't think it was fair to have you put all that emotion out there without anything in return from me. So, this is my Hemingway letter to you.

I've learned that it is hard to live in the present when you have been abused in the past and the future is the light at the end of the tunnel. For awhile there, I blocked out what was happening to me in life, but then you came along and made me want to embrace the present, which is not an easy task when the past is so powerful. There were times I had to sleep with the light on for fear of what would happen, there were some nights I didn't sleep at all and locked myself in my room . . .

I can remember I had to lie to all of my friends and family to cover up the shame I had for allowing this to happen to me. It's hard for me to write this even now because I never thought I would find any kind of happiness as I was sitting there in that room with my books and hoping that tonight would be a "quiet night." But finally, thankfully, one day I woke up, and I got my courage back and I left. It's true that I have many bruises from that time in my life that may never fully heal, but they have a shot at fading. I know that sometimes those bruises can make dealing with me difficult, but I want you to know, baby, that you, your loving me, has helped them fade, and I thank you for that.

You mentioned in your letter that we are both afraid of happiness. We both have demons to battle. There have been times when I've picked fights with you for no reason except that you were making me happy. Why do I do that? Why do I have to push away the one person who has shown me unequivocal love and happiness? I'm tired of the pushing. I'm ready to stop pushing.

I want you to know that I trust you, and I have faith in you. We've both been through traumatic experiences, but I believe we are each other's reward for overcoming them, and we have each other to help battle them in the future. I guess my point of this whole letter is that we don't have to go it alone anymore, and that feels good, and I love you.

I am so incredibly proud of you, baby, I really am.

I'm glad you're the one I get to leave the parties with.

Miss you. Hug.

asp

ps—I'm not a writer

CHAPTER 9

January–February 2006

BAGHDAD, NAJAF

I am flying on a Black Hawk helicopter in the middle of the night, en route to Najaf with my translator, Mohammed. We're sitting on jump seats facing the tail rotor. My helmet is strapped tightly to my chin, my camera hangs around my neck, my hands are jammed into my jacket pockets against the cold. Suddenly there's a bright flash, a golden burst I catch out of the corner of my eye, and I immediately think: Fuck me, the son of a bitch was right. We are going to crash.

I am surprisingly calm for the moment.

I've known Mohammed for six months. We've worked on half a dozen stories together and I've gotten to know him better than the other translators. I asked him to go with me to Najaf, the holy Shiite city in southern Iraq. I wanted to do a story on the fledgling Iraqi Army. Training and equipping a new Iraqi security force was the cornerstone of the U.S. military strategy. (The old Iraqi Army was disbanded by the United States after the invasion, and the unemployed soldiers almost immediately organized and joined the insurgency.) Once the new Iraqi Army was up on its feet—once it could restore stability to the country without American assistance—then the Americans could withdraw. A handover process would occur: Iraqis stand up, America stands down. Or so went the talking point. But the training had been slow and unsuccessful. Absentee rates for Iraqi Army units regularly ran as high as 50 percent; reports of Iraqi soldiers fleeing rather than fighting were still common. American troops talked of the "death blossom"—how under sudden attack an Iraqi soldier will open fire in every direction, spraying lethal petals of lead. It was now January 2006, almost three years in. According to the military only one Iraqi battalion of around 750 men out of the 130,000-strong Iraqi Army could operate without U.S. assistance. At least $3 billion had been spent on the training. I wanted to see how the American policy was progressing in southern Iraq, a more peaceful part of the country.

Mohammed doesn't trust American policies on Iraq. He has two kids; he doesn't tell them he works for *Newsweek*. Only his wife knows; his friends and extended family believe he is still working as an engineer, repairing air conditioners. It is a danger if even the children know, he once explained to me. His son came home from school one day, excited that his classmate had an American pen. An American pen? Yes, his son told him, his father works for the Americans. "I was glad then that my son did not know I worked for the *Newsweek*," he says. Mohammed knew that if the wrong people had that information, his son's classmate's father could be killed. He makes the comparison to Saddam's day when children were taught to inform on their parents.

Mohammed is overweight, with a silver mustache and gray-streaked black hair that he parts carefully. He is pushing thirty-six. He has been my resource for most of my information about Iraq. He is not just a translator, but a cultural interpreter, bringing me to some kind of limited understanding of the country.

I'd done the required reading—*Understanding Iraq, The Arab Mind, Guest of the Sheik*—but a single conversation with him was more enlightening. He explained the complex history of Iraq's political parties, what life was like for Iraqis during the sanctions of the nineties, how if you were young and wore a suit and tie, Iraqis were more likely to take you seriously. He told me what I couldn't see. After interviews with Iraqis, he would always say, "What he really meant was . . ." His view of the war was a mixture of disappointment and disbelief, and now a rapidly diminishing hope. Did the Americans mean for this to happen? How could they not have a plan? He didn't care for the new line coming from Washington, which was basically: If Iraq is fucked, it's not America's fault.

We gave them freedom, we toppled a dictator. The ball is in their court. They must stand up before we stand down.

"It's your country, my friend."

Mohammed and I find that it makes for a hilarious punch line.

Accidentally blow up a house and kill four children?

"It's your country, my friend."

Oops, we ended up arming Shiite death squads?

"Sorry, your country, my friend."

Toppled a dictator?

"That's for you, my friend."

Search your house, men over there, women over there, children crying, oh you say you're innocent, shut up, shut the fuck up, we're occupying you for your own good, lying motherfuckers, stand over there and shut the fuck up.

"It's your country, my friend. Democracy is on the march!"

Our journey to Najaf began early in the morning at LZ Washington in the Green Zone. Just across the street from the U.S. embassy, Landing Zone Washington looked like a concrete soccer field, a gray rectangle surrounded by high blast walls. We checked in for our flight at a trailer where the helicopter ground crew worked behind a wooden desk, marking down passenger names and Social Security numbers on clipboards with the flight manifests. We were "manifested" for a flight arriving sometime around 0800—exact times were never given out for security reasons—with our "show time," as the military called it, 0700. That meant we had to be there by 7 A.M. to get on a flight that would probably arrive around eight o'clock. Each flight had a mission name; we were supposed to be on the "Warhorse Express."

A young black woman, rank of specialist, announced that the Warhorse Express was en route. About eight passengers gathered around her. She told us to follow her walking single file to the far end of the landing zone where the Black Hawks were touching down, their rotor blades kicking up dust. A Black Hawk crew member came out to meet her; she pointed at her clipboard and screamed into his ear. The helicopter blades were too noisy to hear their conversation, but she conveyed the result of the discussion by yelling, "There's no room on this flight for you."

Mohammed and I walked back to the trailer.

There were three more false alarms throughout the day—three times we trudged out to the helicopters only to be turned away.

We passed the time inside the trailer on one of the two fake leather couches, keeping company with passed-out soldiers, their body armor and helmets sprawled on the floor. We watched the television set in the corner of the trailer—playing the Armed Forces Network—and one of the soldiers put on the *Team America* DVD by the creators of *South Park*. A sign taped up next to the television set said that if you were offended by anything playing on the TV because of its obscene nature you could complain to the desk. *Team America* certainly qualified—there was an explicit sex scene with puppets—but no one complained.

I napped on the couch, falling in and out of consciousness. Mohammed was too nervous to sleep. Today was the first time he had ever seen a helicopter up close. He believed they were dangerous. In fact, our entire Iraqi staff had told him he was crazy to go with me. It took some convincing.

"Those helicopters crash," he told me. "Look, four of them crashed in the past two weeks."

"Mohammed, we aren't going to crash. The helicopters are perfectly safe. The odds are very much with us. There are hundreds of flights a day, thousands a month, all across Iraq."

Mohammed looked at me skeptically.

"We're not going to crash," I said again. "The only reason for the crashes is the weather. More helicopters always go down in the winter in Iraq, those are the statistics.

"It will be fun," I assured him. "Something you can someday tell the grandkids about."

The last Warhorse Express for the day arrived at 8 P.M. Finally, it seemed that we were going to get on it. I helped Mohammed get his body armor on, pulling the Velcro snap around his large waist to get it tight. It was the first time in his life he had worn that kind of equipment. We trudged out to the helicopters and climbed in the side, one large step up, difficult to do with armor and a backpack on. Mohammed stumbled and I gave him a push to help him up into the helicopter.

I smiled.

"See, isn't this fun," I say, as we lift upward into the sky.

The Black Hawk is full. There's a passenger in each seat: three rows of four metal and canvas seats, one row in the front and two rows in the back facing across from each other. Behind the cockpit, two machine gunners in flight helmets, heavy gloves, and jumpsuits watch the ground, one on the left, the other on the right. It's dark inside, but there's just enough yellowish light for me to see the face of the man sitting across from me. He is an American contractor in his sixties wearing fatigues and a soft cap. He looks old; he closes his eyes. Green duffel bags are piled on the floor up to our knees. The few soldiers on the flight hold their rifles with the barrels pointed down for safety reasons. I squeeze my laptop bag between my legs, paranoid that if I let the pressure off it will go flying out the open door.

Mohammed sits next to me. It's darker outside as we move away from Baghdad, and I feel safer flying in the night—harder to see, harder to shoot—sailing above the twinkling generator-powered lights of Iraq, heading south.

We are buckled in, the three straps that meet at the middle of the chest clasped into a scratched buckle, pulled tightly. The two pieces of yellow foam in my ears—protection handed out by the flight crew to all passengers—dull the noise of the blades and the wind.

I am admiring the view, relieved to finally be on our way. It does all look peaceful at night from above.

Then there is the flash, a ball of fire only fifteen feet away.

My stomach jolts, my nerves freeze up, and then a moment later my mind clears.

We are going to crash. Mohammed was right.

There is a split second when my brain seems to take me somewhere else; a clear sensation of the unbelievable—falling from the sky when you aren't supposed to be falling from the sky—becoming believable.

And then I realize the helicopter is still moving normally. We are in fact not falling from the sky. Another part of my brain kicks in to interpret the flash—it is just the helicopter shooting off a flare.

I've see them shoot off flares all the time at night, sometimes red, sometimes green, sometimes golden. They shoot them off for kicks, for illumination, out of caution because the helicopter sensors think they are being shot at. From below you watch the flares float down through the sky, slowly, sometimes setting things on fire on the ground.

I turn to Mohammed, he turns to me. We both had freaked out. I feel silly that I even thought I was going to crash. We start to laugh. I pat him on the shoulder.

"Fun, see?"

We got off at Forward Operating Base Kalsu, halfway between Najaf and Baghdad. We spent the night in a tent for transients near the FOB's landing zone. The next morning, we caught another flight to FOB Duke, the base twenty miles outside of Najaf. We were greeted by Lieutenant Colonel John McCarthy, the head of the American MiTT unit we were going to embed with. MiTT stands for military transition team; they are the units of American soldiers assigned to train the Iraqi Army and police. The program started in 2005. Lieutenant Colonel John McCarthy's unit was given to the Iraqi Army's Eighth Brigade, which was commanded by an Iraqi colonel named Saadi al-Maliki.

The MiTTs were supposed to serve as "training wheels," to use the metaphor American officers favored. Colonel al-Maliki's training wheels were slowly coming off. He had just taken over a base that Americans used to occupy, called FOB Hotel, a few minutes outside of downtown Najaf. How were the Iraqis handling the new responsibility? The precedent wasn't promising: At the violent northern city of Tikrit, in the days after the Americans handed over a base in November 2005, the Iraqis had trashed it, according to a story in the *Washington Post*, looting the base of everything valuable.

McCarthy brought us to FOB Hotel to meet Colonel al-Maliki. We were pleasantly surprised. The base seemed to be fully functioning and clean, with laundry services, smart uniforms (a change from the usual rag-tag outfits found on the Iraqi soldiers), a medical clinic, and a dirt soccer field. It wasn't the fucked-up mess I was expecting. Al-Maliki, too, appeared competent and professional. I worried that I didn't have a story—I was hoping for that fucked-up mess. It would have been great for me, if not for Iraq. But I started to see another story, perhaps one that would make it into the magazine because it was against the trend: Al-Maliki's unit looked like it was actually pretty good. I knew my editors in New York were also sick of the weekly "Iraq is going to shit" piece; they advised that I be on the lookout for new angles (like a story on American soldiers playing video games, or Iraqi artists) to give our readers a change of pace from the unrelenting bad news. Maybe this could be one of those stories; maybe Mohammed and I had stumbled on a good news story that had a chance to make it into the magazine.

Al-Maliki was very sure of his soldiers, and of the job he was doing to protect Najaf. He offered to take me on a tour of the town in his SUV. He was in charge of guarding the Imman Ali Mosque, one of Shia Islam's holiest shrines. I hopped in his Toyota Landcruiser, no body armor on (I didn't want to insult him), windows rolled down, and we drove down to the mosque. Two and a half years earlier, in September 2003, a bombing at the mosque had killed at least 125 people, including an influential Shiite leader. In August 2004, Moqtada al-Sadr's militia holed up in the mosque and fought U.S. forces until the Iraqi government brokered a last-minute ceasefire. Now it is safe, said al-Maliki, no problems except for the Iraqi police. They are infiltrated by militias, he explained, and can't be trusted. We drove past the largest cemetery in Iraq—not surprisingly, a Shiite cemetery. (The Shiite religion embraced death and martyrdom and had done so since A.D. 680 when Hussein—the son of Ali who was the son-in-law of the prophet Mohammed—was killed along with seventy-two of his followers by the Sunnis.) "Take your pictures," al-Maliki told me. "If you come back dressed like an Arab, you can walk around here safely."

"Tomorrow morning," al-Maliki said, "you will be able to watch my men in action." He and McCarthy had planned two simultaneous raids to capture insurgents—one raid in the center of Najaf, the other in Al Hayderiah, a rural area outside of the city. Al-Maliki claimed the insurgents were suspected members of the Mehdi Army—Shiites, in other words, who had been making IEDs to attack both the Americans and the Iraqi Army. Mohammed and I agreed to go along. We spent the night at FOB Hotel, where we were given a large room with at least ten beds. We had it all to ourselves. The room was decorated in bright colors, and the bed sheets were pink and blue.

Mohammed and I discussed al-Maliki in our private barracks.

"Mike, I am impressed," Mohammed confided in me. "This is impressive, seeing this."

We leave for the raid before dawn. Lieutenant Colonel McCarthy and al-Maliki stay behind at FOB Hotel to command the operation.

Mohammed and I are in a Humvee commanded by a young captain named Andrew Card, who is on his second tour in Iraq. He likes to keep up a steady chatter of humor over the intercom—"Fish heads fish heads, roly-poly fish heads, fish heads, fish heads, eat them up, yum . . ." To keep his men on their toes, he calls out, "Intelligence check," and asks them a trivia question. He sends a text message to base over his FBCB2 onboard computer, spicing up the dull military language: 3 HMMWVs AND 15 PAX ENROUTE FROM FOB HOTEL, LOVE WAR HORSE 5.

It's raining and the sun isn't up. There are three Humvees—HMMWVs, High Mobility Multipurpose Wheeled Vehicles—in our convoy along with a pack of Iraqi Army vehicles, five or so olive-green Nissan pickup trucks with plates of armor on the back and light machine guns bolted to the floor. We are in the countryside, and high grass and weeds are on both sides of a narrow dirt road. The road has steep banks, dropping off into marshlands. We park about a kilometer from the target houses, small farms hidden behind a row of trees.

The gunshots off in the distance start as soon as Captain Card steps out of the Humvee. There is a light fog and drizzle. I try to take pictures but all that comes up on the screen are faceless images and out-of-focus bodies. The road is muddy, sucking my boots in deep on each step. Mohammed is wearing sandals and is having a more difficult time.

We head toward the houses. Mohammed is falling behind. Card tells me we are going to meet up with the raiding party, one American platoon and a platoon of Iraqi Army soldiers. We can see them down the road, in front of a small boxlike farmhouse.

There are more gunshots.

This time, I can see them, the red tracers flashing a few hundred meters away and sailing overhead, coming from a small farmhouse.

I stop. "Mohammed, you probably should stay back here. Interview some of the Iraqi soldiers. There's no need for you to come up any farther."

He says, "No, it's okay."

The next shots sound closer.

"Look, there's no point in you going up here, I don't need a translator for this kind of stuff."

He smiles; those last shots were pretty close. "I'll stay back," he says.

Card keeps moving. "It's like rural Georgia," he says. "Once the natives see a trespasser, they start shooting, then all the neighbors join in. They're not shooting at us, they're shooting above our heads."

We meet up with the raiding party. An American major has ducked behind a Humvee, yelling into the radio. He asks if the Iraqi soldiers have control of the situation and orders them to go to the house where the shots are coming from.

Captain Card recommends that I move behind the Humvee as well.

The firing increases in intensity.

A group of Iraqi soldiers appears from the fog. They are pushing a line of five men in sweatpants and sandals, stumbling, hands tied behind their backs. The prisoners are not intimidating. They are all men, ranging from teenagers to a gray-haired and frail-looking farmer.

The Iraqi soldiers have captured the insurgents.

The firing stops, though the Iraqi soldiers do not go look for the people who were doing the shooting. They already have their prisoners.

They're proud of their capture and they move around the prisoners, posing, but they don't look like professional soldiers and they are not wearing uniforms. One Iraqi soldier, a teenager, has on a black ski mask, a leather jacket, and carries a 9mm pistol. Another young man casually struts with a rocket-propelled grenade launcher over his shoulder.

I take pictures, but the images are still blurry.

"Have we searched all the houses?" the major asks.

The Iraqi patrol leader, a lieutenant, says, "Yes, all the houses are searched. We have the prisoners."

"That was quick," the major says. "Are you sure you searched all the houses?"

"Yes, yes, we have searched all the houses."

Without saying it, the Iraqi leader seems to suggest the mission is over. Let's go home and get out of the rain.

We walk back to the Humvees. I join up with Mohammed.

"How's it going?"

"Remember, Mike, last night, when I said I was impressed and things looked like they were going well?" he says. "I've changed my mind. This is why. How can a country have an army when its people can shoot at it and nothing happens to them? That is not authority. In Saddam's time, that would not have happened. People respected the army."

"Good point," I say. "But, you know . . ."

I pause and he looks at me and smiles.

"It's your country, my friend," we say.

I talk to the major, asking what he thought of the Iraqi Army's performance. "Good," he says, "but they had trouble reading maps."

Mohammed and I head back to FOB Duke. I interview another American officer about the Iraqi Army. He says he is worried that we will equip Iraqis whom we will later have to fight. He tells me he doesn't trust them, really. "We're not teaching them everything we know," he says. "Remember, it was U.S. forces that trained Adid in Somalia." He's referring to the warlord the U.S. soldiers had to fight in Mogadishu. This officer's fears are not unfounded: Since 2003, the Americans have given hundreds of thousands of weapons to the Iraqi forces, and according to a U.S. government report, 30 percent of those weapons are unaccounted for. Are they in the hands of the bad guys, Sunni insurgents or Shiite militias? Probably. No one knows for sure. They are lost.

Later that night, Mohammed and I go to the dining facility, the DFAC (pronounced Dee-fac). Mohammed is impressed at the setup. There is a sanitized hand-washing facility at the entrance, silver sinks and bright lights and antibacterial soap to wash away the germs. I point out the food options to Mohammed. It is a role reversal. For the first time, I understand the situation better than he does. We are in Iraq, but this is the American version. There is a Baskin Robbins ice cream bar, a taco bar, fried chicken, hamburgers, cheeseburgers, spaghetti, all the Gatorade and soda you can drink. The workers are Filipino and Indian, shipped in by KBR to feed the Americans. We fill up our plates and head back to our trailer to sleep on our two single beds, our firm mattresses and synthetic white pillows.

The next morning we wait for another helicopter to bring us back to Baghdad. Mohammed has gotten his first inside look at the American military occupation, and he is surprisingly not bitter. He sees goodness in the Americans, and what they are trying to do. He did hate Saddam, but he struggles with the question of whether it is better to live in a world of totalitarian repression or maddening anarchy. He started working for *USA Today* after the invasion, and we hired him in 2005. He did have fun on the trip, and in general, he's taken to journalism. He's making more money than he did during "Saddam time," as it's called. When he moved to a nicer house two years after the war started, the men he hired as movers were old Baathist officers whom Mohammed got to order around. But he found little pleasure in the irony.

The helicopter is late. We are both very tired, and we're running low on things to discuss.

"How did you sleep?" Mohammed asks.

"Okay," I say. "I had a weird dream."

I tell him about my dream: I am driving in Baghdad, showing an editor around—my boss, Fareed Zakaria. But Baghdad is a large glass mall, a cluster of pyramids connected by futuristic railway cars. Everywhere I bring him there are men with guns. They don't have feet, it appears, and they move too quickly, sliding on some preset pattern, leaving a vivid color trail like the motorcycles in the movie *Tron*.

"Ah, yes, insurgent dreams," says Mohammed. "I have those."

I don't think to ask him the obvious follow-up questions—what are insurgent dreams? What are his dreams?

Mohammed tells me he has never seen *Tron*, then he asks about other American movies. He asks about Tom Cruise. I tell him there's a rumor that Tom Cruise is gay. "Tom Cruise a gay? No, I don't believe it. A gay. Wow."

Mohammed is shocked when I tell him popcorn and a soda can cost ten dollars at an American movie theater, and that doesn't even include ticket price.

I should have asked him about his dreams, but it is only in the following year, long after our conversation, that I'll come to really understand what he meant by insurgent dreams. One night, I'll even dream of him and another translator, Ahmer, stuck on the side of a cliff in the middle of a blizzard. We were all at my old home in upstate New York sitting on snowmobiles, and then I send them out on a story without the proper clothing and with radios that are running low on batteries. The storm gets worse and the temperature drops quickly, and they freeze to death on the ledge of a mountain.

There are other dreams: My mother is in Baghdad, but this time Baghdad looks like a college town, and she's dropping me off to work at a twenty-four-hour convenience store. As we commute, I lie down in the backseat of the car (a '92 Buick Park Avenue, the car I crashed drunk when I was nineteen). In another dream, Baghdad appears as a campus on a hill. A group of us—reporters, I think—take a walk to some kind of cultural center. There are a series of checkpoints, but the grass is green and there are maple trees so we aren't worried. The insurgents don't show themselves in such nice weather and ideal surroundings. In another, I am in a car with Scott and it looks like the real Baghdad now. "Why are we going this way?" he asks. "We should turn back." And then I am driving a bus on a dirt road. A veteran correspondent, Rod Nordland, tells me to drive faster, there is a pickup truck following us. Head to the lake and the beach. I think the only safety is the lake. I jump in and start to swim. Insurgents can't swim, can they? Yes, they can, and one comes after me, splashing me as he gets closer and then he kills me. I wake up in my bedroom in Baghdad and stare at the clicking ceiling fan. Something profound has changed in my thinking. Never before had I died in a dream. I usually woke up first.

Mohammed and I take a flight back to Baghdad. I write the story of our Najaf trip at the bureau. I do a few follow-up interviews with other Iraqi Army officers. The story is headlined: "We Want Better Weapons." The subheading: "American relationship with Iraqis marked by mistrust." I was lucky the story made it into the magazine. I filed on a Saturday, the same day Vice President Cheney shot a man in the face with a shotgun. That news didn't break until Sunday afternoon, after the magazine closed.

CHAPTER 10

January 18, 2006

AN INSTANT-MESSAGE EXCHANGE OVER SKYPE

michaelmhastings 21:48:22
    baby
Andi: 21:48:33
    newsie
michaelmhastings: 21:48:43
    how are you?
Andi: 21:48:52
    i'm good babe—how are you?
michaelmhastings: 21:49:02
    very good
Andi: 21:49:03
    i just wrote you like 3 paragraphs
michaelmhastings: 21:49:05
    really?
Andi: 21:49:10
    when you emailed me
michaelmhastings: 21:49:11
    can you send them?
Andi: 21:49:12
    yeah
Andi: 21:49:14
    weird

Andi: 21:49:27
    send anyway?
michaelmhastings: 21:49:29
    well, we are in love
Andi: 21:49:38
    yes we are
Andi: 21:49:45
    but baby it was a diatribe
michaelmhastings: 21:49:52
    against me?
Andi: 21:49:56
    NO
michaelmhastings: 21:50:00
    ok, then send
Andi: 21:50:04
    cap punishment
Andi: 21:50:13
    about what you see over there
Andi: 21:50:34
    and how I wish I could know what you see

There was a new tension in our relationship—Andi wanted to understand what I was going through, and she wanted me to understand what it was like to be waiting on the other end.

A little under a month had passed since Christmas in Vermont. We sent each other long, serious emails—what she called "the Hemingway letter"—or rapid notes just to let each other know we were there, and we stayed in as constant contact as we could by instant messaging. IMs were the medium of choice in Baghdad. Everyone—soldiers, journalists, contractors, diplomats—communicated by instant message. Andi would be at her desk in New York at Air America, and I'd be in the bureau in Baghdad and we would fire off telegraphic descriptions of our days. She felt like she was missing out sometimes. She would make jokes at first. What if I came to Iraq, if you saw your love on Airport Road? Then you'd know how I feel. "You live such a different life," she would say. "How can I relate to that?" I protested. I want to hear about your days, your work, the crisis management you are constantly doing at Air America. She would tell me about those things, but our conversations usually turned back to Iraq.

michaelmhastings: 21:51:28
    so here's what happened—
Andi: 21:51:34
    ok
michaelmhastings: 21:52:20
    the baghdad central criminal court is this three floor complex, very futuristic looking, that straddles the green zone; one entrance is in the GZ, the other opens out onto a street in the red zone
michaelmhastings: 21:52:55
    i went back today with mohammed

The Central Criminal Court of Iraq, or the CCCI, or the Triple Cee Eye, was where Iraq's terrorism cases were being tried on an almost daily basis. Insurgents and murderers and criminals of all ages from across the country got their day in court at the CCCI. Some of the criminals were those that the Americans arrested; others the Iraqi forces had detained. It seemed like a good place to find stories, so I went there with Mohammed to watch the trials. I didn't expect to do a big story on the Iraqi justice system. After spending two days there I was left with a series of impressions about what was going on, if not a full understanding. You didn't have to be a constitutional scholar to figure out that the Iraqi justice system was deeply flawed.

It was bizarre: Iraqi lawyers, American soldiers, and Iraqi prisoners in orange jumpsuits thrown into the same space. In one room, there was a televideo conference display, where an American soldier in Germany was giving testimony about an Iraqi insurgent he had detained the previous year. The American had left the country; they weren't going to bring him back for a trial. So he stuttered out his testimony over a live video feed as military prosecutors and Iraqi lawyers huddled around a television screen, asking him questions over the linkup. ("Yes, sir, that's right, there was, uh, there were sixteen 60mm mortars and those mortars were, uh, two hundred meters from the farmhouse, and when the detainee was questioned he said those mortars belonged to his, uh, brother, who we could not find and he told us the brother was, uh, killed, so we think the mortars definitely belonged to the detainee. There were no other houses around that area.")

The courtroom itself was a carpeted space with wooden benches for the three judges and a docket for the prisoners. One Iraqi prisoner after another filed in. Each of them went through the same ordeal: questions from the chief judge and brief statements from the defense attorney, the prosecutor, and sometimes a witness.

One man, Omar Hamza, limped slowly in, his hands chained, his left leg dragging behind him.

"My fingernails were pulled," he told the judge. "Look, look at what they've done to me. I am not a terrorist. I am innocent."

The judge gave him three months.

Another prisoner stepped up.

"Yes, your honor, I have been tortured."

"Why didn't you file a medical report?"

The man smirked. "A medical report? To who? It was they who tortured me."

"But you have no evidence of the torture," the judge said.

"The evidence is on my body," the prisoner replied.

A five-minute deliberation.

"Guilty, life in prison," the judge said.

"I was hung up from my hands and beaten with cable wires," one prisoner claimed, "and I'm not even the right man."

"What do you mean?"

"The man who they claimed I killed is still alive. My cousin saw him yesterday."

"Do you have any evidence of that? That the man they say you killed is still alive?"

"I have a witness."

An older Iraqi woman, his mother, was called to the microphone to testify on his behalf. Yes, the man whom her son is accused of killing is in fact still alive, she said.

"But what about the four other men you are accused of killing?" the judge asked.

"I am not a killer."

The judge deliberated.

"Guilty, but we'll give you seven years."

And so on.

There was no DNA, no fingerprints, no CSI moments. The confession was the evidence. An American military lawyer told me that the actual trial wasn't important. The investigation before the trial was what counted. It was more like the French system, he told me, where prosecutors gathered the evidence and presented it to the judges before the trial actually went to the courtroom. There was no trial by jury. What mattered was whether the judge believed the detainee was guilty or innocent, based on the confession. And the confessions were coerced with torture. The Iraqi justice system seemed to have a flaw.

A recent U.N. report had called attention to the "widespread and systematic" human rights abuses taking place in Iraq. Those doing the abusing and the torturing were mostly in the Iraqi police, which was overseen by the Ministry of Interior, which was being propped up by us. The Iraqi security forces were being trained and funded by the Americans; officially, they were under the command of the top American general in Iraq, George Casey, though there was no real control. It was all completely screwed up. In November 2005, U.S. troops raided an Iraqi police base known as the Jadriya Bunker, where they found about eighty Sunnis who'd been detained by the Shiite police force. The detainees didn't look good. Three investigations were launched—one by the Americans and two by the Iraqi government. No results were ever made public. But the U.S. did say they were instituting new training procedures for the Iraqi police. From that point on, they'd receive thirty-two hours of classes on human rights and the rule of law.

That didn't seem to solve the problem.

I described all of this to Andi, including the strangest case I had watched.

michaelmhastings: 21:54:12
> then we go into the court room, where there is a buzz about two female detainees

michaelmhastings: 21:54:22
> turns out they are sisters, and the brother is also on trial
> so the three are standing there
> they are accused of killing two of their cousins, and trying to kill a third, the husband of one of the women

michaelmhastings: 21:55:47
> her name is Zeena

michaelmhastings: 21:56:38
> anyway—the prosecutor says—here is what they are accused of, but there is not enough evidence, as the confessions for the women were made after torture.

Andi: 21:56:47
> god

I lay it all out for her. There is one piece of physical evidence. Zeena gave a picture of her husband to a neighbor. The neighbor allegedly gave that picture to a group of terrorists, so they'd know who to kill. Zeena denies this. The prosecutor finishes presenting his case.

Zeena's defense attorney says, essentially: "This is all bullshit."

The three were all up for the death penalty. An Iraqi lawyer sitting next to me and watching the proceedings told me that the brother, Ziad, would get life in jail, and the two women would be let off.

I followed them outside the court and interviewed Zeena while the judges deliberated. She told me she was an American citizen, who had lived in Phoenix and San Diego.

"Why did you come back?"

"I came back in 2003 after the invasion. I have been locked up for nine months, and the conditions are terrible."

She told me she wanted to go back to the States. She had wanted a divorce, and her husband didn't. He took the children with him to Diwaniya. A few months passed, and the husband wanted to meet her in Baghdad to convince her not to divorce him. On the way to the meeting, her husband was ambushed by two carloads of men with AK-47s. Two cousins, also in his car, were killed. The husband was wounded but lived.

Zeena was arrested.

michaelmhastings: 22:03:57
    zeena is in the police station with her sister in west baghdad (the
    same neighborhood where the reporter was kidnapped last week)
michaelmhastings: 22:04:09
    the police threaten her
michaelmhastings: 22:04:20
    they bring her brother to the station
michaelmhastings: 22:04:24
    they say to her brother:
michaelmhastings: 22:04:33
    we will rape your sisters in front of you unless you confess
michaelmhastings: 22:04:44
    they start to take off the sisters' hijabs
Andi: 22:04:46
    jesus

The five-minute break was up. The judges called us back into the courtroom and began to read out the sentences. Zeena: not guilty. The other woman with Zeena: not guilty. The brother, Ziad: sentenced to death.

michaelmhastings: 22:07:41
    the courtroom gasps
michaelmhastings: 22:07:44
    like a movie
michaelmhastings: 22:07:50
    the two girls start screaming

michaelmhastings: 22:08:04

> the brother starts crying and they escort him out

michaelmhastings: 22:08:19

> the other sister won't let go of his wrist

Andi: 22:11:15

> god

Outside the courtroom, I had a chance to ask Zeena what she was feeling. She didn't answer. Her eyes were wide, her mouth opened and closed. Some kind of noise came out, a groan and then a scream.

And then they were all gone, the orange jumpsuits disappearing across the lobby. Mohammed looked at me. "Mike, I have never seen anything like this. This is all very emotional for me. To see my people tortured. To hear about the torture and the killing."

michaelmhastings: 22:28:37

> so that's the summary of it, basically

michaelmhastings: 22:28:44

> nothing big—no blood or guts

Andi: 22:28:45

> jesus

Andi: 22:28:59

> emotional blood and guts though

michaelmhastings: 22:29:07

> yeah—

Andi: 22:31:13

> it's an incredible story

Andi: 22:31:51

> I can't even fathom it

Andi: 22:35:45

> baby how are you though?

Andi: 22:36:00

> after seeing and hearing all that?

michaelmhastings: 22:36:03
    baby, i'm fine how are you?
Andi: 22:36:12
    ok ok
Andi: 22:36:16
    just making sure

Andi sent me this email shortly after our IM exchange ended:

That's why I can't imagine what you see every day; the level of
such extreme torture and gross indifference toward human life.
And that's why I worry about you and wonder if you are ok and
how you are holding up because it is a lot to take in and you are
such an empathic sponge. You absorb it all, and I know it weighs
heavy on your mind and heart even if you don't admit it. It's hard
to be a witness to human suffering and even harder to realize
there is no clear plan, or even hope, to put an end to it. Twain
once said trying to establish peace is nearly impossible because
you have to be able to tame the human race first, and history
seems to show that that cannot be done. And particularly, in this
war alone, it seems that that cannot be done.

My twenty-sixth birthday comes, January 28. Andi and I talk late into
the night about how we'll celebrate it when we see each other in Vienna
in March.

CHAPTER 11

March 2006

BAGHDAD

It's Thursday, March 2, 2006. Eleven days ago the Golden Mosque in Samarra was bombed, kicking off Iraq's civil war. Officially, the civil war is being denied by the Americans and most of the Iraqi government. Unofficially, and in real life, everything is rapidly going to shit.

I am pacing around the driveway at the *Newsweek* bureau, talking on my T-Mobile to Andi. I'm trying to save our vacation plans.

"There's a civil war," she says. "It's on Google News. I know the airport is closed. You won't be able to get out. I'm not coming."

"The airport will be open. I'll be there."

"No, and I can't rebook the ticket—I checked. It costs like three thousand extra."

"I'll pay for the ticket. Just come. I'll be there, I promise."

"You can't do anything about it. The airport is closed, there's a curfew. I get CNN here, you know."

"God, please, baby, I'll be in Vienna. I may be late a day, but I'll make it there. A car will pick you up at the airport and take you to the hotel."

"You don't understand—I can't imagine going to Vienna and you not being there. It would be too sad. You don't understand."

"This is crazy—I know what's going on here better than you. I'm telling you I'll make it out on time. And if I'm late, you can see Vienna. Go to a museum or something, it's a beautiful city. Plan our trip for the next day. Do whatever you need to do. I'm leaving tomorrow. I'm on the flight for tomorrow."

"That's what you said yesterday."

"Baby, it's a fluid situation."

"Yeah, right."

At the moment, I happen to be taking the government's tack and denying the civil war, too. It's not that bad, I've been telling Andi, my flight will be leaving on time. Civil war? What civil war? Everything is great here. The vacation will go on.

I am supposed to see Andi in Vienna on Saturday. I have two days to get there.

I walk inside to the office. Munib comes to talk to me.

Munib is twenty-six years old and works as our cook and houseboy. The previous bureau chief discovered him at a nearby chicken restaurant. He dresses much more stylishly than I do. I describe him to friends as an Iraqi metrosexual. He wears slick pointed-toe boots, knockoff designer T-shirts, and tight jeans flared at the bottom. His facial hair is always immaculately groomed and he likes more than one dab of cologne. He used to drive a cherry-red BMW, but because of a few recent incidents (he was chased by a local militia with his fiancée in the car) he is looking to trade in the car for something less conspicuous. No one really knows how he has the money for a Beamer, but he is such a likable kid we don't hold it against him.

Munib gets a kick out of working with us crazy foreigners. His view of our culture is amusingly distorted, but he gets the gist of America. His favorite movie is *Jackass*. We watched the DVD the other night, and we've been calling each other jackasses since. He once bought a pink flowered apron and wore it around the house while doing his chores. He was dead serious, figuring that Americans like those kind of things.

Since the mosque bombing, on February 22, Munib has been stuck inside the Green Zone with me and another *Newsweek* correspondent. When at the bureau, he lives in a small shack outside the house. He wanted to go home, but we said it wouldn't be safe. The Iraqi government had declared martial law, and it looked like the government might mean it. We figured there was a pretty decent chance that curfew violators would be shot or detained.

This didn't really bother Munib. On the day of the bombing, when the rest of the country was starting to kill each other (dozens of mosques were attacked; hundreds were reported dead) and when most other Iraqis dared not leave their homes, he decided he wanted to cook spaghetti Bolognese for us for dinner. It was one of his five rotating dishes, along with a baked eggplant dish, roasted chicken, a chicken curry with potatoes, and two variations of a thick beef stew. He didn't have the right ingredients for the spaghetti sauce, though, so he told us he had to go shopping in the city. He said he would take the *Newsweek* scooter, a black moped. We warned him against it, saying that there was a curfew and that we'd be happy with chicken curry instead, but he smiled and sped off down the road.

When we didn't hear from him for a few hours, we started to get worried. He wasn't answering his phone. That afternoon, he pulled back into the house, plastic grocery bag in hand.

"You're okay?" I asked.

"No problem," he said.

"How was it out there?"

"Okay, okay," he said.

"Did you have any trouble?"

"No," he said, pausing.

"No trouble at all?"

He smiled and shook his head.

"So no police or soldiers stopped you?"

"Yes," he said, his grin getting bigger. "The soldiers says, 'Stop. Where you go? We shoot.'"

"And what did you say?"

"I said, 'I go shop for spaghetti!'"

I pictured him giving the Iraqi soldiers a wave and not slowing down on his moped, with the red *Newsweek* sticker on its side, and the soldiers just shrugging rather than shooting as he rides off, laughing hysterically.

Today, Munib is smiling as he comes into the office, like he has this really great joke to tell. He knows I want to get out, bad, and that already my flight has been canceled for the last three days.

"On TV . . ."

"What?"

"Curfew tomorrow!" he taunts.

"Fuck! You bastard!"

"Mike is never go home. You stuck in Baghdad."

"Yeah, I'm stuck, but you're stuck, too—Munib curfew in the Green Zone. Munib never go home if Mike never go home!"

He laughs and backs out of the room.

"Jackass!" he yells at me.

"Jackass!" I yell back.

"Jackasssss!" he sings, closing the door.

It's a fluid situation.

I have to tell Andi this, but I wait. Perhaps the curfew will be lifted by morning. Perhaps I will be able to make it out anyway. And if there is a curfew, it doesn't necessarily mean that the airport will be closed. On other days when the government has declared a state of emergency and the U.S. military has instituted a "no roll" policy, as they call it when no cars are allowed on the streets, the airport has remained open. So there's still some chance that I might get out, and I discuss this possibility with Jack Tapes. Can I leave tomorrow if there is a curfew? Can we get to the airport?

Positives: There is likely to be little traffic, so you can drive fast and won't be a target. Negatives: There is likely to be little traffic, so you will be the only car on the road, an obvious target.

"And how do we find out if the airport is open?"

"Hard to say," Tapes says. "We'll have to wait until morning."

The signs had been appearing for at least eight months, probably longer. In July 2005, John Burns of the *New York Times* prophetically asked: Is Iraq in a civil war? At the same time, Ambassador Zalmay Khalilzad, as he was taking office, broached the subject, saying one of his goals was to prevent a slide into civil war. "Sectarian violence" was the new buzzword to describe the kind of attacks occurring in Iraq, the frequent fighting between Sunnis and Shiites. I started to hear stories from our Iraqi staff. Our Sunni office manager had to move out of his house to live with his parents because Shiite militias were targeting Sunnis in his neighborhood. Most of his Sunni neighbors were fleeing, too. Flyers containing death threats were posted on houses and littered on the street. Both Shiites and Sunni groups were doing it. An American officer showed me a flyer he'd found saying that if a Shiite family didn't leave their home, they'd soon be killed. Executions and kidnappings at illegal checkpoints were on the rise. There were now an estimated thirty kidnappings a day in Iraq. Our staff had taken to carrying two forms of identification, or *jinzya*. One ID had a Sunni family name, the other a Shiite family name. The purpose of the fake IDs was to increase their chances of survival at a checkpoint. You had to guess what group was doing the checking. Was this a Sunni or a Shiite roadblock? There were an estimated one thousand checkpoints in Baghdad alone.

In the media, we were trying to make sense of what we were seeing and hearing. I spoke to a U.N. official who in the early nineties had interviewed refugees from the Balkans. The stories she heard at the time seemed incredible; it was only in the years that followed that the scope of the massacre became clear, she said. She wondered if the same pattern was repeating itself in Iraq. Four months earlier, I had asked an analyst from a Washington think tank if he thought Iraq was in a civil war. He told me he preferred the term "low-intensity ethnic conflict." It reminded me of the semantic wrangling that had occurred during Rwanda—was this a genocide or just a lot of killing? In the months following the Samarra bombing, U.S. military officials twisted and turned to find their own definition of what was happening in Iraq without calling it a civil war. At one press conference in Baghdad, Major General William Caldwell, in response to repeated questions from CNN's Michael Ware, said Iraq wasn't in a civil war because "all the governmental functions are still functioning, and we don't see an organization out there that's trying to overthrow and assume control of the government." This was an odd definition. Most civil wars throughout history occurred while there was some kind of functioning government and to call the Iraqi government functional was itself kind of laughable. And, on top of that, there actually were a number of organizations trying to overthrow and destroy the government—Iraqi insurgents, Al Qaeda–linked terrorists, Shiite militias. The standard definition of civil war seemed to apply to Iraq: "war between opposing groups of citizens of the same country."

I wrote my first story about the civil war a week before the Samarra mosque bombing. An Iraqi police officer I interviewed described the torture that was going on at the prison he worked at, called Al-Hakimiya. The officer, who told me to refer to him in print as Mahmoud, said the Shiite police force was detaining and torturing its prisoners, mostly Sunnis. He said the jail was corrupt, nasty. Prisoners would have to pay a forty-dollar bribe to make a cell phone call; to get released, wealthy Sunnis would be charged $30,000 or $40,000. "I saw by my own eyes, cables to the ears and operating the electric shock equipment," Mahmoud told me. "I've seen prisoners without toes or fingernails." He said the guards would sell painkillers to the prisoners after they were done abusing them. He said he tried to tell American soldiers what was going on when they stopped by, but the response he got was, "We are only here to support you."

The accusations of one unnamed Iraqi police officer weren't strong enough to publish without corroboration. To back it up, I talked to four Iraqi defense lawyers who described similar abuses at Al-Hakimiya and other prisons run by the Ministry of Interior. Reports from the U.N. and other human rights groups depicted the same pattern: the Iraqi police illegally detaining and abusing men without cause. I called up the man in charge of Al-Hakimiya prison, Brigadier General Sadoon of the Iraqi police's Major Crimes Unit, to get a comment. Unsurprisingly, he denied the human rights violations.

"I've heard there is torture going on at your prison," I told him over the phone.

"Not at all," Brigadier General Sadoon responded. "Come see for yourself."

Sadoon gave me the number of his American military advisor, who agreed to pick me up in the Green Zone and take me on a tour of the prison so I could see for myself that there was no finger pulling or electric shock treatment at Al-Hakimiya. On a sunny day in early February, a convoy of Humvees picked me up and took me to the jail in Baghdad.

Al-Hakimiya was a dark gray five-story rectangular building that squatted, unassumingly, a hundred yards back from the city street. The prison was famous for its dark history. During Saddam's time, it was run by the mukhbarat, or secret police. Saddam's political enemies and other suspects of the regime were kept inside. Prisoners who survived their stay had a name for the interrogation cells—they called them "operating rooms."

We parked the Humvees in the large courtyard outside the jail. A few blue and white Iraqi police pickup trucks were parked by the entrance; other police officers watched the street from a machine gun tower.

As we walked up the front steps of the building, the American advisor looked at me and said: "Have you had all your shots?"

"Yes," I said.

"Good. The sewage isn't working in this place. It's dripping down from the top floor. It's the biggest shithole in Iraq," he said. "Literally."

I waited for Brigadier General Sadoon in a small room outside his office on the first floor. His personal assistant, a police detective, sat behind a desk. He looked like he was about six feet and 230 pounds. His black hair was buzz cut, the sides of his head bare, a small scar on his thick brown neck. I tried to ask him a few questions, using the Kuwaiti interpreter assigned to the American advisor, but the detective would not give his name; he would not say anything. He stared at me. His eyes had seen bad things; he had done bad things. Or so I imagined. The interpreter suggested he might not want to talk.

Brigadier General Sadoon was more personable. He had the look of a smooth undercover cop. He was a fit thirty-something and wore a mustache and lightly combed hair, dressed in plain clothes, and sported a brown leather jacket. He called us into his office and spoke at length about how there may have been past abuses at the prison, before he was in command, but he assured me that nothing like that was going on now. He showed me where he slept when he had to spend the night at his office—there was a bedroom attached to it, with a queen-sized bed

115

and television set. He told me I could interview as many prisoners as I wanted. He then introduced me to the warden, a short man with a large gut named Omar, who would take us on the tour.

The prisoners were kept on the fifth floor. We climbed up a damp stairwell that smelled of human waste. The fifth floor looked like an apocalyptic dormitory, a dark stone hallway with about five large rooms crammed with dozens of floor mats, bedrolls, and bunk beds. At the end of the hall, a door opened out onto a room with bars for a ceiling, an open-air cage with no windows, only sunlight pouring in from above. This was the room where the prisoners could get a breath of fresh air, which cost each prisoner, according to Mahmoud, fifteen dollars. It was packed with thirty black men who were sitting, standing, jostling for space. Omar explained that the men were Africans, from Sudan. He told me they were being kept on immigration violations, picked up during a raid on a Sudanese neighborhood in Baghdad. A few pleaded for my help. I gave out cigarettes as I asked questions and took down names. I tried not to make any promises. "I'm here to tell your stories, I'm here to tell your stories," I repeated.

The Sudanese prisoners told me they were being treated great.

Omar smiled. "See, they are all treated well here," he said.

I didn't know what to make of it. What were thirty Sudanese doing in an Iraqi jail?

We walked back down the hall. I stopped in the largest cell. The prisoners shouted out to me: "No torture," they said. "Not here." I didn't see any visible signs of abuse. But three prisoners told me they had been tortured at other prisons on the way to Al-Hakimiya. An older man from Mosul pointed at two teenagers—he said they were brothers, eighteen and nineteen years of age. In Mosul, he said, the police forced them to have sex with each other. Omar the warden warned me to not go too far into the room: "The prisoners could take you hostage." I looked in the next cell. A man with a sweaty face and deranged eyes pressed his face up to the small metal square in the door. I asked him what he was in for. He stared at my interpreter and responded: "Beheading Kuwaiti translators and killing journalists." My interpreter told me he was just fucking with us, but he wasn't stretching the truth too far. This prisoner was accused of kidnapping and murdering a European, Omar told me.

At the end of the hallway was another cell. A group of eighteen Iraqi police officers sat cross-legged behind black metal bars.

"Are these cops under arrest?" I asked.

Omar gave me the rundown.

"They had a confrontation with the Iraqi National Guard," he said. "The ING said they were doing work outside of their jurisdiction." The eighteen police were highway patrolmen who had been detained on January 20 when they were stopped at a checkpoint in Baghdad after arresting a prisoner of their own. The man the cops had detained, Omar said, had been wanted by the Americans. The ING wanted to impress their American colleagues, so they decided to take the suspect—and arrest all the cops.

One of the detained police officers stood up. Omar opened the gate to let him speak.

"They wanted our prisoner, and when we refused to give him to them right away, they arrested us," said the cop, Ma'an Hadi. "They took our five cars and they beat the crap out of us." Hadi said he and the other policemen were from the south, near Nassiriya.

Ten minutes later, back on the ground floor of the detention facility, the American advisor explained that the eighteen cops had been "doing what they shouldn't be doing."

I pressed him for details, but he told me there was an "ongoing investigation" and he didn't want to comment.

I honestly didn't know what to make of the entire scene. Thirty Sudanese, eighteen Iraqi police officers, possible torture, possible abuse. What else did I expect to find in an Iraqi jail besides the utterly bizarre? But where was the news here, where was the story?

Two weeks after my visit to the prison, the results of that "ongoing investigation" were published in an article in the *Chicago Tribune*. General Joseph Peterson said the U.S. had captured its first "death squad." This was the first time a high-ranking military official had used the term. According to the story, the arrest had occurred in January, and there had been twenty-two members of this death squad. Four of the death squad members were being detained by the Americans at Abu Ghraib, and the other eighteen were being held in Iraqi custody. All were members of the Iraqi police highway patrol.

Eighteen Iraqi police. Detained in January. Being held at an Iraqi jail. Hunh.

I had what looked like the first interview with an Iraqi death squad.

Those eighteen souls, who sat dejectedly on the stone floor, thin, ragged, mustached, in their sagging blue uniforms, those eighteen pathetic-looking people at Al-Hakimiya were a death squad. They didn't look like a death squad.

Startling revelation about war #1036: the sheer ordinariness of killers. Death squads are normal people. Death squads are neighbors. Death squads are regular guys who have been given a grim wartime label to describe what was becoming an all too common occurrence. Better to say "death squad" than to say "eighteen Iraqis holding regular jobs who go around in packs at night to kill other Iraqis who hold regular jobs."

After the *Tribune* broke the story, I told my editors that I had a story on death squads, an exclusive. "I think I talked to members in a death squad," I said, describing my day in Al-Hakimiya. The story ran with the headline "The Death Squad Wars." I wrote how death squads were now being used by both Sunnis and Shiites, a dirty war of execution lists and brutal interrogation rooms, a war being fought just out of view of the Americans.

The story came out on a Monday. On Wednesday, February 22, the Al-Askari Mosque in Samarra, also called the Golden Mosque, was bombed. The mosque was considered one of the most important shrines for Shiites in Iraq. Sunni insurgents, likely from Al Qaeda in Iraq, were believed to be behind the bombing. Though no one was killed in the bombing, the mosque's famous golden dome was completely wrecked. The country's still pent-up ethnic tensions were unleashed, causing the war to descend into a Hobbesian nightmare.

I rushed to get an embed to cover the widespread fighting. I hooked up with an infantry unit from the 10th Mountain Division who were stationed in Baghdad.

Their mission was to travel the city and take digital photographs of mosques in an attempt to confirm (or, ideally, deny) that mosques were being attacked. I saw the email with the soldiers' orders, which read: "Take digital photos of the mosques that were reported as damaged [and] positively confirm or deny the reports . . . Each picture must clearly show that the mosque has sustained damage or that there is clearly no damage to the structure. When possible pictures or videos should be taken from multiple angles . . . Do not enter mosques to take pictures." This was not a joke. Their mission was to take digital snapshots of mosques.

It was part of the military's larger strategy of the week. In the aftermath of the Samarra bombing, the media was reporting claims from Iraqi political parties saying that over two hundred mosques had been attacked and hundreds, if not thousands, of people had been killed. Since the Golden Mosque was a Shiite shrine attacked by Sunnis, the Shiites were now attacking Sunni shrines, a tit-for-tat battle targeting each other's places of worship. Despite what was obvious to me and other journalists on the ground, the military continued to counter the claims of civil war, announcing that the number of mosque attacks was being greatly exaggerated by Iraqi politicians. That was the official position, and that's why I found myself driving around Baghdad with Captain Greg Stone from Potsdam, New York, as he took pictures of mosques.

Captain Stone and I were both around the same age, and from the same region of New York—the North Country, the rural-poor part of the state only miles away from the Canadian border, a place that used to be built around farming but now depended on the growing prison industry. I grew up in Malone, New York, a thirty-minute drive from Potsdam. These shared biographical facts took on a strange significance for me. How could two guys from Malone and Potsdam become bit players in a drama unfolding in a hostile foreign capital? It definitely gave me a darkly comic feeling that somewhere along the way in arriving at this moment in history some very bad decisions must have been made by someone or something.

We went out on Saturday morning. Stone's patrol of three Humvees moved through the city, emptied of traffic. We started in the over-crowded Shiite slum of Shula. As we rolled down the narrow streets, the tall antennas on the Humvees hit the low-hanging power lines—in poor neighborhoods, the thin multicolored wires had been set up by the locals in a chaotic, jerry-rigged fashion to siphon electricity from the city's struggling power grid. Each snag, causing the wires to bounce like rub-ber bands in the convoy's wake, caught the attention of the Iraqis watch-ing us pass by: Would they be out of power, would they be able to fix their wires? Or would it survive the vehicles? The Humvees' loudspeak-ers blared a message, read by an Iraqi interpreter: "Attention, attention, the Iraqi government has a curfew for your safety until 4 P.M. . . . From four to eight, you may go to prayer . . . The president of Iraq urges calm. Thank you for your attention." We stopped to talk to an Iraqi soldier manning a checkpoint. He told us that two people in his area had been killed the night before, and four young men were kidnapped and exe-cuted "just thirty minutes ago." I took notes.

"In this neighborhood, that's a regular day," Captain Stone said.

By midafternoon, we got around to looking for mosques.

Captain Stone had a list of thirteen mosques he was supposed to inspect. Seven of the mosques were in his sector; the other six weren't. He had grid coordinates and names for some of them. The grids did not seem to match with names. The names did not seem to match with the mosques. We drove around the rest of the day, trying to find the right mosques. The soldiers in Captain Stone's patrol repeated a series of increasingly confused questions: Do we know what mosque this is? Are we sure it's in our sector? Is it a Sunni or Shia mosque? How can you tell again? A black banner means Shiite, right? Are you tracking?

They found a burning tire at a Sunni mosque. It had been thrown over the side of the courtyard wall by someone. "Does that count as a mosque attack?" a soldier asked. "I don't know, but let's get a picture of it," Cap-tain Stone replied.

How do we know when those bullet holes in the wall were made? How do we know the people we're talking to at the mosques are telling us the truth? That mosque looks okay, but are we really sure? What the fuck over.

We drove in circles. We got lost. We figured out where we were. We found mosques. Stone wasn't a hundred percent sure they were the right mosques, but in his sector seven mosques needed to be found and photographed and by the end of the day seven mosques had been found and photographed.

We drove back to Camp Victory. I sat down in my trailer and started to write. I needed to check the spelling of Captain Stone's first name— was it Greg or Gregory or did I totally misremember it and it was something else? I went into the 10th Mountain's TOC, the tactical operations center, and something was not right.

It was 2 A.M., and I sat in a small waiting area looking at a row of pictures of American men and women up on the wall, with the dates of when they were killed under their names, when I overheard a major on the phone saying, it wasn't good, that the IED had killed two, get the chaplain. His voice carried down the hall and the sound of it chilled me. Two Americans had been killed outside that mosque with the burning tire, where we had just been a few hours earlier. Two men whose names I didn't know, who died on a patrol I could have just as easily been on. The chaplain walked past me, a Korean-American man wearing PT gear, and I asked to talk to him. "Not now, now I need to go pray," he said. I walked down the hallway and found the office of the major whose voice I'd heard. His face was gray, so gray with the news that two of his boys had just been blown up, and that meant a ceremony and letters home and empty boots and two more pictures on the wall of the TOC. "It was bad," he told me. "It was a big one." Big enough to kill two, the shrapnel blowing the back of one of the soldiers' heads right off.

I went back to my trailer and filed the story about the outbreak of civil war, including a quote from an American State Department official I interviewed. It wasn't a civil war, the official said, but the Iraqis had "looked into the abyss" and recoiled in horror. It was the first time I had heard the abyss quote, but over the next few weeks it would be repeated by those in higher office, until it became a talking point a month later for President Bush—"They looked into the abyss and did not like what they saw." This Samarra bombing showed the Iraqis and their government what a civil war would look like, claimed the officials. Not that they are in one. But it would look like this. The Iraqis, the U.S. government claimed, were scared straight.

The abyss. They looked into the abyss and they learned a valuable lesson.

I am standing outside my trailer in Camp Victory. I haven't slept in twenty-four hours. It is approaching 4 A.M. I have a satellite phone in one hand and my T-Mobile in the other, my laptop is balanced on a concrete duck-and-cover bunker. I keep the thin white door to the trailer open a crack so the light from the stale room shines a few feet outside, allowing me to see what I am doing. I am waiting to check my email a final time to make sure the story closed with no errors. I am supposed to do a telephone interview with Fox News in an hour, *On the Record with Greta Van Susteren,* to discuss what is happening on the ground in Iraq. I am making phone calls back to the States.

Hi Mom, yeah it's late here. I'm waiting up for a TV interview. It was weird, two soldiers in the unit I was with were killed, but I don't say it was a matter of hours and a different patrol. I don't say it because I've learned it's better to keep scary things like that hidden sometimes because, after all, I'm the one who chose to be here.

Why hasn't Fox News called? They're supposed to call my T-Mobile or sat phone. That's why I am still awake at 5 A.M. and I'm standing outside my trailer in the dark to get clear reception for the TV spot and the power generators that keep Camp Victory going are humming loudly and I have to catch a helicopter in two hours because my embed is over and I don't really want to stay for the ceremony of the two dead soldiers and that's really unprofessional of Fox not to call and cancel the interview.

You look into the abyss, see your reflection. Lean closer.

But Fox doesn't call and I stay awake anyway and there is a pile of cigarette butts by my trailer now as the sun rises and it does not inspire me and it's a cool dawn and I have a slight chill and I watch soldiers in flip-flops and shorts and gray army T-shirts with towels slung over their shoulders stumble to the latrines to shower and shave and shit and so I go to the latrines, too, long white trailers provided by KBR and they smell like strong disinfectant and feces and mouthwash and aftershave, but it is warmer inside because the heating units are on full blast and I throw water on my face and wipe it off with paper towels but some drops remain in my thin beard. Then I go find the public affairs officer who takes me to a helicopter pad at Camp Liberty and my stomach hurts because I've smoked too much and my embed is over, and reports like those that Captain Greg Stone, twenty-eight, from Potsdam, New York, compiled from the field and I, Michael Hastings, twenty-six, from Malone, New York, witnessed him compile, reports with digital pictures of mosques from different angles, are sent up the chain of command to give the U.S. military command the confidence to say, as Major General Rick Lynch does during a press conference in the days following the bombing and repeats after I've left Camp Liberty and after the two soldiers have been shipped home and their parents notified along with the fifty-three other soldiers killed that month: "We're not seeing civil war."

And the closer you look it's you and it's not you and you think everything becomes clearer but a force beyond human control like gravity but much more personal pulls you deeper and deeper and you no longer know what it is you're looking at.

We don't see the abyss. We're Americans.

There is a state of emergency in Iraq. Beginning February 22 permanent curfews are enforced. The death toll climbs, Shiite militias attack Sunni mosques, Sunni insurgents attack more Shiite mosques. There are open gun battles in the streets. The media reports on the spiraling situation (though still with a question mark—are we in a civil war?). The abyss spreads and horrifies and excites everyone it touches.

My two months are up. It is the first week of March. I want only to get on my flight to Amman then get on my flight to Vienna and then to meet Andi. I have to get to Andi. I have promised her, and that's all that matters. I am supposed to leave on Wednesday, March 1, but there's a curfew. I am supposed to leave on Thursday, March 2, but there's a curfew. I am supposed to leave on Friday, but the curfew holds. I try to sound cool about it when I talk to her. A fluid situation, baby. Just get on the plane. I'll be there.

The curfew lifts on Saturday. I go to the airport.

Andi catches her plane from New York, and is picked up at the airport with a sign that says MRS ANDREA HASTINGS, she tells me, and I think that's funny. The car takes her to the Hotel Imperial, a five-star European hotel, where they knew I was going to run late because I sent an email to the front desk saying: "Dear Sir, due to the fluid nature of the situation in Baghdad, the civil war and such, my fiancée Andrea will be checking in first under the room reserved in my name . . . Please let me know if this will be an issue. Sincerely . . ."

I arrive in Vienna on Sunday morning, March 5. Andi greets me at the door wearing a white top from Banana Republic and she just glows goodness and she is the most beautiful thing I have ever seen.

We order room service. We sit on the bed. We stare at each other. We order more desserts, including an elaborate cheese plate.

CHAPTER 12

March-July 2006

VIENNA, PRAGUE, NEW YORK

Two days in Vienna then we catch a train to Prague. (Budapest or Prague—Andi wants Prague. She makes the right choice.) We check in at the hotel near the river. The room is large; Andi puts on the slippers and the oversized white bathrobe. We take a walking tour of the city. Kafka and Kundera, the Brothers Grimm. Castles and Gothic structures, small, dark mysterious streets. We have a picture taken of us on top of a famous clock house; a picture near the castle overlooking the city; a picture on the Charles Bridge. Dana, a sweet woman who once gave Jackie O. a tour, shows us around. "You look like a Czech model," she tells Andi. "Except for the sneakers." Andi likes this and she likes the Czechs—a people who elected a poet for president, who've managed to overcome their troubled past and are now safe and happy and fond of freedom. We eat dinner at Allegro, overlooking the river and the Charles Bridge. We walk across it before midnight, holding hands.

There are issues, there always are—those things that for the last two months have gone unsaid, all the fears, paranoias, small aggravations that you can't really get at over the phone. On the train to Prague, we discuss them at length, sitting in a passenger compartment we have to ourselves. Andi takes out a pen and piece of white paper. She wants to write them down; she wants a document listing our anxieties and demands and grievances. She starts to write, dating the top of the page "The March 6 Agreement."

1) MH will not "seek attention" from other females . . .

2) MH will not flirt . . .

3) MH will not "emotionally cheat" . . .

4) MH will not "be nasty" and "attack" ASP if in bad mood . . .

I object to the conditions as stated and I tell Andi to add an amendment clarifying that "MH is denying that he has engaged" in the activities stipulated by ASP, and I add my own clauses to the agreement.

5) ASP will not break up with MH every time she is upset with MH . . .

6) ASP will not "threaten our love" by telling MH to "let ASP go" . . .

7) ASP will not break up with MH over the phone while he is in Baghdad . . .

8) ASP will not threaten to leave MH for remainder of vacation (as ASP did on second night in Vienna, when, after a fight, she said she was "going to the airport now") . . .

The list fills up both sides of the page—she furiously scribbles, each new clause bringing a smile to her face. "It's our Treaty of Versailles," she says. We both are required to sign on the bottom of the page. "We hereby agree to love each other . . ."

Andi senses, too, that I'm still tweaked from Iraq. On the days when we travel, I wake up early in the hotel and pack my bags and place them near the door. She wakes up and looks at them: "Is the convoy coming yet?" I am wound up, jumpy. As we are crossing a trolley track in Vienna on a cold sunlit morning a teenager screams—I jerk back. Nothing, just the teenager yelling to a friend, but I'm startled. My temper is short. At the reception desk to the hotel, I ask the man to break a fifty-euro bill and he looks at me like I've requested him to scrape shit off my shoe. "Are you kidding me," I snap, "I'm paying fucking seven hundred dollars a night and you're giving me a hard time about making change?" Andi walks up behind me, pulls me away from the desk, slightly embarrassed by my outburst. She wants me to shave my beard: "You're not in Baghdad anymore," she says, "and it hurts my face."

After a week together, though, the tension starts to disappear. And Prague is a city where we can repeatedly say what we've been longing to say to each other, face-to-face. "Why do you love me?" she asks one morning, waiting for room service to deliver breakfast.

I list all the reasons. Because you are pure of heart, because you are beautiful, because you are honest, because you believe in things and I don't know if I do, because you don't compromise your principles and sometimes I think I am always compromising my own, because you are brilliant, because you are mine, because you love me and you are willing to put up with my bullshit; because we fit.

"We are stuck together," she says, "no matter how difficult you can be."

"Me difficult?"

"You are difficult, Newsie."

"So are you!"

A pause, a squeeze of her hand—two squeezes back means she loves me. She draws her knees up to her chest, the bed's comforter wrapped around her. There is a look of concern on her face. I know the look well by now. I can already imagine what's coming next—I know that even though the tension over our relationship can fade, it's always close to the surface. We are always a moment away from what she says next. "Is love enough, though?"

"Yes, yes of course it is," I assure her. "We've made the decision to be together. That's that. Now it will just take time."

But I know my response doesn't put her at ease. I'm still going to go back to Iraq, and no matter how many times I explain that I'm laying the groundwork for my career, that I'm trying to establish myself, that when I go I'm not leaving her, she still thinks that my commitment to work trumps my commitment to her. I try to say that I understand that she worries about me, that it's harder on her, that it's not fair, and that I know I am asking her to make the sacrifice, while I do what I want.

"I'm not your priority. Work is. The magazine is. I'm like number five on your list."

"There is no ranking! You are equal. I have to work all the time. It's what I love to do. But I am not doing it just for myself, I'm doing it for our future."

"Oh, lies. Spin. Spinner."

"I'm not lying. I just don't see it as ranking, you are not in a category, you are in your own separate place."

"But if something happened to me, you'd file first!"

"Oh, stop. Who says things like that!"

We dance in the room, music from iTunes on the laptop, a dance party, we call it—Frank Sinatra, the Beach Boys ("God Only Knows"), Johnny Cash.

As we dance, I tell her: "Look, baby, it's a trade-off. Look where we are. We are in Prague. With my job we'll be able to travel around the world when we want to; yes, it's a steep trade-off, but being the significant other of a foreign correspondent does have its perks."

"Why don't you get the Paris bureau job?" she jokes.

Back to Vienna to catch the plane to New York. Hot chocolate and coffee and Easter eggs at Demels; more cheese; a visit to Freud's house; a stop by Franz Josef and Empress Sisi's palace, where Andi buys *The Empress*, about the life of Empress Sisi.

She gets a migraine on the way to the airport. As we pass customs, she says, I'm going to get sick, I don't feel well. I had already anticipated this, already scoped the airport terminal for receptacles and bathrooms in case of an emergency, and I grab her head and guide her toward the wastebasket as the vomit comes up. I go to the gift shop to buy napkins and the only ones I can find have black roses on them, which I hand to her to wipe her mouth off.

I have a business–first class ticket courtesy of the magazine (overseas flights of eight hours or more are automatically business class) and she has coach. I ask about getting her ticket upgraded and they keep saying, At the gate, you can upgrade at the gate, but when we finally get to the gate, we have to part—her back to economy and me to first class. "Don't worry, don't worry," I say. "I'll get you up here or you can take my seat." There is one seat available, the flight attendant tells me as the plane starts taxiing out. I walk back, the seat belt sign solid red, and there she is, sleeping, and I wake her up and grab her bag from the overhead compartment. It feels as if everyone in the plane is going to start clapping as she follows me up the aisle to join me in first class. We watch *The Constant Gardener* on the flight.

Back to New York, back to the office, back to reality—or something.

Andi has been working on a big event; the Bring Them Home concert at the Hammerstein Ballroom on 34th Street. She's arranged for Air America to be one of the primary sponsors. The guests for the March 22 concert included Susan Sarandon, Cindy Sheehan, Rufus Wainwright, Moby, Michael Stipe, Bright Eyes, and a veteran to speak to the crowd about his experiences in Iraq. I am there in the role of significant other, in the VIP lounge, and am so proud of her. She looks so capable and so stunning and the event raises Air America's profile and gets new subscribers to their Internet service and at the end of the night everyone is pleased.

I am getting back into the pace of office life. It chafes. It seems pointless and dull and I don't feel like I'm going forward. I'm doing the same things I'd done for the previous three years. It's hard to take the daily workplace drama seriously. There are times when I want to yell—in the office, at dinner parties, in conversation—"I just got back from fucking Baghdad, motherfucker! What you are saying means nothing!" It is an irrational urge, unfair, self-important—because I can answer the scream myself: "So? Who gives a shit? Good for you, asshole. Pass the salad." But I can't really connect to what I'm doing and I don't know when I'm going back to Iraq again; I could be stuck in New York for four months or more. The magazine wants me here, where I can report and help with editing from a cubicle on West 57th Street. I get to work on Iraq stories, but I'm also writing extensively about luxury goods for a section of the international edition called "The Good Life."

In May, two military investigations confirm *Time's* story on the Haditha massacre. A platoon of marines are accused of executing twenty-four Iraqi civilians after a marine lance corporal named Miguel Terrazas was killed in an IED attack. The incident occurred in November 2005, and the marines tried to cover it up. I call marines who were in Haditha that day to get their opinion. The consensus: If you weren't there, you can't judge. Soon after that, I write a story about a designer shoe company in SoHo, whose shoes, some of which are made from alligator skin, go for up to $3,200 a pair.

In June, another war crime is reported in the Iraqi town of Yusafiya. An American soldier named Steven Green is accused of raping a fourteen-year-old Iraqi girl then killing her family. The rest of his squad allegedly watched it happen; before the attack, the soldiers had a barbecue and drank beer. I drive to Chambersburg, Pennsylvania, to interview the mother of one of the accused soldiers. I wear a jacket and tie. I talk to her for two hours at her kitchen table. She is still in shock. She doesn't believe her son could have been involved in something so horrible. She has pictures of him around her house, dressed in his army best. He looks like a hero; in her eyes, he still is.

I write a story about expensive flat-screen televisions that work outdoors. I profile a New Yorker who makes custom suits. He made the suit Michael Douglas wore in the movie *Wall Street*.

I want to get back to Iraq as soon as I can. I feel like I'm missing out on the story. I used to enjoy writing about anything—shoes, suits, yachts, whatever—but all I want to do now is cover what's happening in Baghdad.

Andi senses this. She interprets it as me not wanting to be with her. I try, again, to dissuade her of this notion, but it is this feeling that causes our one serious rough patch, the only time we actually break up, which lasts for a period of about twelve hours.

It's a Sunday. I don't even remember what we are fighting about. She threatens to leave my apartment. She is crying. I am very upset. "I'm leaving," she says.

"Then leave—I'm not coming after you this time!"

"No one will ever love you like I do," she says.

I remember this. I thought it might be true though it sounded like a threat.

She leaves and I don't go after her. I sit on the futon and flip to a NASCAR race. I lock the door. She is not coming back, I realize. I turn on HBO. It's *Big Love,* and the song on the soundtrack is our song—Sunday nights are our nights, the nights we watched our shows together, and it's the Beach Boys that get me—

God only knows what I'd be without you.

I pick up the phone and make call after call and finally get an answer very late at night. I shouldn't have let you leave, I tell her. She agrees.

Two weeks later, *Newsweek*'s publicity department asks me to go on a Fox News show to talk about a story I had worked on about IEDs. Radio and television interviews were a regular weekly duty for the magazine's Iraq reporters. Shows in the U.S. were always looking to get the on-the-ground perspective from Baghdad, to talk about the news of the day, and stories we had written; it was also a good way to promote the *Newsweek* brand.

Andi decides to come with me to the Fox studio on 50th Street and Sixth Avenue—the heart of the enemy, she says, the belly of the beast. Before the show, a producer does a preinterview with me. The producer asks what I will say. I tell her that IEDs are the number one killer of American troops in Iraq, responsible for two thirds of the casualties, and that the bombs are very easy to make and hard to detect. Apparently this isn't good enough news for Fox. "Is there anything positive you can say?" the producer asks. "Uh, sure, I guess it's good that the DoD is putting like two billion dollars into something called the Joint IED Defeat Task Force (JIEDD, better than Joint Defeat IED, which would be J-DIED, hah). So that's progress, right?"

The TV spot goes smoothly. I sit in a room staring at a camera, answering questions from the anchorman who is on the floor above. As I talk, the show runs b-roll of American Humvees getting blown up.

We leave the Fox News studio. It's a Sunday afternoon.

"You have to promise me never to do Fox again," she says.

"Why? It's basically all the same shit."

"They're evil," she says. "Seriously."

"If I'm asked, I can't say no. It's good to be out there."

"Not on Fox," she says.

I don't remember who came up with the next idea, but we stop talking about Fox News and agree that the thing we need to do is go look at engagement rings at Tiffany. It sounds almost like a dare.

We browse the rings on the second floor for thirty minutes. We don't actually talk much, we just look. When we walk back outside, we both seem to be thinking, this is a serious thing, this looking at rings. Are we really ready to do this?

We stroll back toward her apartment in silence.

A homeless man walks by us.

"What a beautiful couple," he says.

She stops at the next block, Columbus Circle. "That was a sign," she says. "Okay, this can work. But when you do get me a ring, make sure you get the right one. I don't trust you going by yourself."

We talk about moving in together and start looking at new apartments. The magazine still hasn't told me how often I will be going to Iraq in the future, so it looks like my home base will still be in New York. A few months in Iraq, a few months back at the office. The plan is that we'll move in together once my lease finishes at the end of July.

And then in June, *Newsweek* offers me the job of permanent Baghdad correspondent. This means I'll go for another year in Iraq, and I'll be based overseas in Cairo. The rotation works out to be ten weeks in Baghdad, four weeks in Cairo.

I tell Andi. As soon as she takes in the news, I tell her, too, that I want us to stay together.

"But how can we stay together if you're gone a year?"

"We'll see each other. We'll meet in Europe or Asia." I try to explain to her how important this is to me, what a great opportunity it is, and how she knows and I know I have to take it. But it's hard—I am happy and excited about it, and she's not, she can't be.

"You want to take it."

"Of course I do. But it will work out. It will be a rough year, but we can make it, I'm sure."

"You're lucky," she says. "Not everyone is as lucky as you. You know exactly what you want to do. You know what your dreams are, and for whatever reason, your dreams do come true. You get what you want. I don't. I don't know what my path is. I need to find my path, too."

"But you do know what your path is. You're successful and brilliant and young. You know you want to get into politics, eventually, and that's going to happen."

"Well, I have always wanted to go overseas," she says. "And maybe now is the time . . ."

Andi was outgrowing her job at Air America. She was used to change, used to jumping around. She'd held four big jobs in the past seven years—including writing speeches for a Massachusetts governor and working for Harvey Weinstein's publicity department at Miramax—before signing on with Air America where she thought she could help spread the progressive Democratic message. But lately she'd been thinking of joining a presidential campaign if she could find a candidate she believed in. In July, she met with people who worked on Democratic campaigns, and during one of those meetings, the subject of Baghdad came up. Would she be interested in going over there? Yes, she said, going overseas had always interested her. We're not hiring for the campaign right now, but time in Baghdad would give you great foreign policy experience. And when you got back, you could work for the campaign.

We discussed this—what do you think about Iraq?

"I think you'd thrive once you started working there. I think it will be difficult and challenging and how they treat women will be quite a shock, but I think you'd like it."

"I'm going to apply for jobs at IRI and NDI."

The International Republican Institute and the National Democratic Institute were two nongovernmental organizations that had over 140 offices in countries across the world. Their most important operations were currently in Iraq. Both worked in countries that were trying to develop democratic institutions and practices, funded by grants from the U.S. State Department and private donations. The chairman of IRI was Senator John McCain, while NDI was chaired by Madeleine Albright. (IRI was founded by Ronald Reagan; NDI's first chairman was

President Jimmy Carter.) They were in the Ukraine, in Sierra Leone, in Afghanistan; in 2003 they established programs in Baghdad.

"Okay," I said, "let me know if I can help."

"Are you uncomfortable with me going to Iraq? You think it's weird, right?"

We talk about it at length, every day. I support her desire to go. If I have one worry, it's that she might get to Baghdad and not like her new job and be unhappy. I'm actually not worried about the danger. Or if I do worry, it's in an abstract way, and pushed very far back in my mind. Aid workers and State Department officials had been killed there occasionally, but so had journalists. Iraq was demystified for me. It was still a big deal to go, but it also wasn't. It was part of my life; it didn't seem unnatural. I'd been going there, my brother was on his way there, and so Andi would be in Baghdad, as well. My friends and colleagues worked in Iraq, and to work effectively, you couldn't spend much time worrying. Bad things happened, but the odds were that the bad things usually happened to someone else. I don't even know if I went that far in my thinking—bad things were a possibility I couldn't entertain.

For Memorial Day weekend, we flew to Puerto Rico (she wanted to go to Savannah to stay in a bed-and-breakfast with a *Gone With the Wind*–themed room, her favorite book; I wanted to go to Puerto Rico so I could gamble and get sunburned). I gambled for a few hours; she watched over my shoulder. When are you going to lose all your chips so we can go to the beach? she asked. The point is to get more chips, not lose them, I told her.

For her birthday in June, I surprised her with a suite at the Four Seasons and a dinner in Tudor City. We took pictures of each other that night. She wore white summer clothes. I have this memory of filming her on the digital camera I got her for Christmas, but I don't know where that video is now, and I don't remember what she said, sitting on the windowsill, looking out over the city.

CHAPTER 13

August 2006

BAGHDAD

Baghdad life is no longer new to me, it is just the routine. Wake up in the morning, feel your bed shake slightly, hear the windows rattle, a boom in the distance. Did I dream it? Close your eyes, back to sleep. The house shakes again. No, that's a car bomb. It's 8:15 A.M., I don't need to get up for another half hour.

Munib brings an omelet and toast with a glass of unidentified juice and Happy Cow cheese wrapped in colorful tinfoil.

"Boom cars this morning," he says. "Boom car" is his translation for car bomb.

Scott, whose room is on the second floor, comes downstairs.

"Did you hear the explosion this morning?" I ask, sipping coffee.

"Yeah, it was a big one."

"Woke me up, that's for sure. Beats any alarm clock."

We hear machine-gun fire, probably from one of the ranges set up nearby to train the Iraqi security forces.

I take a shower. There is a bare lightbulb and a red-tiled floor, damp though it's over 115 degrees outside. The mirror is cracked. The toothpaste is some local brand—Sino—and it feels like it burns away the enamel; the tap water is dirty so you swig and spit from the two-liter plastic bottle and the bottle top tastes like stale toothpaste, left over from last night when you brushed your teeth before going to bed. The shower water is either hot or burning hot; steam fills the room; the shower curtain won't close properly and the water splashes out on the floor; a cockroach runs out of the drain and I step on it with my flip-flops—exterminate the brutes. There is surprisingly decent water pressure, all other things considered. It's not an exaggeration to say that even after your hair dries and your Gillette Arctic Fresh deodorant is on you still don't feel clean.

I put on what I wear around the house: baggy brown cargo shorts and a white T-shirt, keeping my flip-flops on.

It's 9:30 A.M. I talk to Scott about reporting, or we talk about sleep.

"Did you sleep well last night?"

"Mosquitoes again. They ate me alive. I had to sleep in my hoodie with the hood up and at 4 A.M. I decided to fuck it and turn the light on and hunt the bastard down."

Mosquitoes always find their way inside the house, like we're living in a swamp and not the desert. The only explanation I can figure is that we are in walking distance of the Tigris River. Various other insects live in the house and faded green lizards sneak in through gaps and crawl up the walls to hide in plain view on the ceiling. At night, bats whip through the darkness.

Mosquitoes, lizards, bats. Extreme heat in the summer, air on your face like a blow-dryer switched to high. Noisy ceiling fans, dust everywhere, nasal-clogging sandstorms. Bad food washed down with unidentifiable juice. Boom cars. More people blowing themselves up in Iraq than at any other point in modern history. Baghdad is the deadliest city on earth.

What is it that Ranya, our fixer in Amman, said? She said she can't stand Iraqis. She said her grandmother blamed the Tigris. When they are children they drink from the Tigris and it makes them savages. Look what they did in 1990 to Kuwait, how brutal they were when they invaded, and look what they are doing to themselves now.

Our British security manager stands in the kitchen discussing his great annoyance with Iraqi soccer. Every time the Iraqi national team wins, there is celebratory gunfire all around us. The Iraqi national team is on a roll; they finished second in the Asian Games in 2006. It is a bright spot for the country, a source of pride. Our security manager hates it. After each match the city comes alive with AK-47s aimed to the sky, and he has to tell us to stay inside while he paces in the kitchen and keeps saying under his breath, these fucking savages, these bloody savages.

What's wrong with this place? What's wrong with these people?

Is it Islam? Is it the climate? The culture?

Is it us?

I start asking these questions and then I think back to Graham Greene's 1955 novel *The Quiet American* when old Fowler chastises the naive Pyle about his views on the Vietnamese people Pyle claims to have come to help: "Is that what you've learned in a few months? You'll be calling them childlike next."

Robert Byron arrives in a muddy Baghdad in 1933 and writes of the city: "For only one thing is it now justly famous: a kind of boil which takes nine months to heal and leaves a scar."

In Tim O'Brien's 1969 memoir *If I Die in a Combat Zone: Box Me Up and Ship Me Home,* an American captain criticizes a local Vietnamese soldier for skipping a mission. "Now damn it," the captain said. "This is your goddamn war. I'm here to fight it with you and to help you, and I'll do it. But you have to sacrifice too. Tell me how this war's gonna be won when you and others like you are running off when things get tight? How? . . . If I come over here and bust my balls, well, shouldn't you take the shit with everyone else?" The Vietnamese soldier responds, "You are here for one year. I've been in war for many billion years. Many billion years to go."

Even as Scott and I speak, sitting at our computers and finishing up our omelets, dozens of people are being killed or are about to be killed in this city. Could be a day when it's over a hundred. The violence is unbelievable, unimaginable, incomprehensible.

Those words are inadequate. It should be easy for us to believe, imagine, and comprehend because it happens all the time. Maybe "unfeelable" is a better word, though it's not even a real one. You can't let yourself feel it.

Time to start reporting. I sit down behind my desk in the dining room, converted into our office, my back facing a picture window that is covered by a blast blanket. I begin to send emails, arrange interviews, plan trips. I send orders to the Iraqi staff over Skype: Can you please call this Iraqi guy now? It is frustrating to try to get them to do anything. What do they do all day but sit on their asses and whine and watch porn on the satellite TV? They haven't worked in over a week, I complain to Scott.

The cell phone network is down; it always goes down. Iraqna, the country's largest service provider, was given an operating license after the U.S. invasion in 2003. Its cell phone towers are targeted by insurgents; its engineers are kidnapped from time to time. Perhaps the signal is getting interrupted by jamming frequencies sent out from U.S. military convoys to stop IEDs from detonating. Or perhaps it's the weather, or the network is overloaded with calls—a record number of Iraqis, more than five million, are new mobile phone subscribers. Iraqna, a subsidiary of the Egyptian-based Orascom Telecommunications, is posting annual revenues of over $250 million. (The most reliable phone network in Iraq is not available to civilians; it's a network set up by MCI for American and Iraqi officials—the phones come with the Westchester County 914 area code.)

The Internet goes down. The Iraqi man whom we get our service from runs his server from a power generator, and he tells our office manager that his generator has run out of gas. He can't get more gas right now because he hasn't been able to leave his house since the most recent curfew.

The cell phone network is back up. Rarely does a call go through on the first try. Call five times. Six times. The seventh time there is a response, but it's a bad connection.

"Allo?"

"Hello, yes, can I please speak to Mr. al-Dabagh?" Or Mr. Mashandani or Maliki or Abdul or whatever.

"Allo?"

"Hello?"

"Allo?"

"Hi, yes, hello. This is Michael."

"Allo?"

The connection gets better.

"Yes, Mr. al-Dabagh? This is Michael Hastings from *Newsweek*."

The connection gets worse.

"Yes, Mr. al-Dabagh—this is . . . from . . . magazine . . ."

"Yes, yes. What can I do for you?"

Now I am practically shouting into the phone. My colleague in the office looks at me severely. I grab a notebook and take the call outside, where I can pace and speak at high volume.

The connection goes dead.

I call back.

"Allo?"

"Hello?"

"Yes, I just called . . ."

By now at least twenty minutes have passed for one phone call. Maybe an interview is set up. Maybe there's a quote. Maybe the person I'm trying to reach is out of the country, or in a meeting, or doesn't want to talk to me, or will talk to me only in person because he thinks the phone lines are tapped. There is usually some kind of resolution and sometimes it is satisfying just to have someone pick up. And then the call is over.

"Thank you, *shukrun*. Goodbye, allo, allo."

Allo, allo, what you say in Iraq at the beginning and end of a conversation. I think it was Rod, the former bureau chief, who said Iraq is where hello means goodbye.

The news cycle catches up with me. There is a new "security crackdown." Operation Together Forward Phase II, which begins on August 8, 2006. Things are happening. They're calling it the Battle of Baghdad in press statements. This could be a story.

I start getting excited. Something different is happening. Something other than car bombs and death squads. The attention of the world media is turning back toward Iraq.

My interpreter calls. He has finally reached the important Iraqi guy I've been wanting to interview for a week. The guy agrees to meet with me in person tomorrow at his compound.

Progress, a rush knowing there is an exciting trip to take the next day.

A mortar falls nearby, a whistling shriek while I am outside smoking. Munib comes running inside—did he shut the gate to the driveway? I take cover in the living room.

CNN is always on. I stop and take another phone call or five of them and I send more emails and plan more trips and the sun has gone down and I eat dinner and call New York and call Washington, and Washington has heard such and such and what do I think about that—does it jibe with what I'm hearing on the ground—crash, and the blast blanket hanging on the window actually sways. Scott just found a piece of olive-green shrapnel in the driveway from a rocket that hit three doors down—it blew out the kitchen window, knocked our security manager down, he spilled his tea. Scott shows the chunk of shrapnel to me—he'll keep it in his top desk drawer—then I drink some tea or some instant coffee and I start talking to my colleagues about stories and big ideas and what's going on. The images on CNN and the BBC are the images that I see right outside my own window. The next day the FedEx shipment arrives via the U.S. embassy with copies of the magazine with my stories from two weeks ago, and there's my name, and there are the pictures to prove I was there, but I don't have time to read because it's Thursday or Friday and I am on deadline again and I'm awake for twenty-four hours or forty-eight hours or it feels like that or it's Tuesday and I'm writing a story for the website and then it's the next week.

There's a great joke going around.

Sarah, another magazine correspondent, tells it to me. She heard it from her interpreter. It's about a death squad. An Iraqi man who runs a hardware store in Baghdad is targeted at his workplace. (Let's say he was a Sunni, death squad was Shiite, though it could be the other way around.) It's time to torture and kill him and the death squad leader looks around. "We forgot our tools! You idiot, you didn't bring the drill! How can we do our job without our tools?" The lightbulb in the death squad leader's head flickers on (it's running on generator power, hah). Oh, right, they are in a hardware store. There is a drill and a saw right there. They pin the Sunni man down and use brand-new tools off the shelf to drill his kneecaps. Then they kill him. They leave the body in the store and steal the tools.

Sarah first heard this with other reporters, and they all started laughing before the story was finished. They were laughing because of course an Iraqi death squad would forget the tools. It's hard to stop laughing at something like that.

Time here does not move like it does in the rest of the world. It has its own laws. You wake up and start to work and hear the bombs and it's 5 P.M. so quickly and nothing has really been accomplished. The days blur together. You leave and come back a few months later and nothing has changed, except that you know it is somehow worse this time. You can see it in the eyes of the Iraqis who work for you. You have been gone a few months, back to "real life," and they have been stuck here. It is real life for them, and it shows in the way they talk and in their faces that are not even frightened but resigned, numb, as if they know their name is on a list somewhere marking them for dead. Are they the same men I knew a few months ago? How long have I really been gone? Am I remembering them correctly? Have they aged in years, not months?

I call home. "I've only been back here a week, baby, can you believe it?"

It is August 2006. The situation has drastically deteriorated since June when the new Iraqi government took over under Shiite Prime Minister Nouri al-Maliki. It is the fourth new Iraqi government in four years. The government is barely functioning; on most days it is nonexistent. Parliamentary sessions are regularly canceled because less than half the 275 members show up for work. The U.S. military is scrambling to contain the rising sectarian violence and is promising to restore law and order to Baghdad. No one I talk to who knows what's going on—Iraqis, reporters, diplomats, soldiers—believes that it's possible to do that. The next five months will cap off the deadliest year for Iraqi civilians since the war began. In October, a record 3,709 Iraqis will be killed. Record high levels of American soldiers are going to start dying again soon. The situation, according to an official 2006 State Department report, includes a "pervasive climate of violence" and "arbitrary deprivation of life" and "misappropriation of official authority." The insurgency and the militias continue to gain strength. Average daily attacks across the country will rise from a hundred per day in June when the government took over to 185 per day in December.

During the first week of August, Mohammed and I go to interview Abdel Aziz al-Hakim. Al-Hakim is an influential Iraqi leader, and head of a large Shiite political party called SCIRI. SCIRI stands for "The Supreme Council for Islamic Revolution in Iraq." Al-Hakim is considered an American ally; U.S. diplomats call him "a moderate." This is despite, as the name of his party suggests, he advocates an Islamic fundamentalist government similar to Iran's. In fact, al-Hakim spent much of the past twenty years in Iran, where SCIRI was formed with Iranian backing. His party also controls a militia called the Badr Brigade, which is accused of organizing the first Shiite death squads within the Ministry of Interior. American officials are counting on al-Hakim and his political allies to help stop the sectarian violence.

The interview with al-Hakim is at the SCIRI compound, a three-minute drive outside the Green Zone. It used to be the home of a high-ranking Baathist official. After making us wait a half hour, al-Hakim sweeps into his marble chamber, wearing brown robes and a black turban, and takes a seat on a red and gold chair. His teeth are yellowing; he's known for chain-smoking Marlboro Reds. Mohammed interprets. Al-Hakim says he doesn't think there is sectarian violence, but if there is, it is probably justified. The interview lasts fifteen minutes.

After the interview, Mohammed and I head back to the Green Zone. I'm in the backseat of the Mercedes. At the first traffic circle a small gunfight breaks out. I don't see who's shooting, or what they are shooting at. I just hear the shots. We keep driving.

At the bureau, we get tea and sit outside on the lawn at a white plastic picnic table. It is the first time I've seen Mohammed since getting back to Baghdad this week. He looks much older and more tired now. I've noticed he sighs more. He could say the same thing about me: When I get my Green Zone badge this time I need to get a new picture taken. The other military press ID I wear around my neck has the photo that was taken on my first day in Iraq, a year ago. I cringe at the side-by-side comparison. In the old photo I'm grinning; my hair is short, my face is flush. I look young. In the new photo, I'm tired, bloated, and pale. I'm not smiling. We compare notes on the al-Hakim interview.

"Asshole?" I ask.

"Asshole," Mohammed agrees.

"He didn't fucking say anything," I complain.

We talk for a half hour.

"Mike, I don't trust anyone anymore," he tells me.

There is desperation in his voice. He goes through a list of grievances that is familiar to all Iraqis living in Baghdad. He only gets one to four hours of electricity every day; there is no clean drinking water flowing from the taps; it takes at least fifteen hours of waiting in line at a gas station to fill up.

He tells me he is doing everything he can to try to leave. He's applied for the Fulbright, he's taken GREs for grad school, he's practicing his English. He tells me the risks of working for the magazine are becoming greater. A few months earlier, he was visiting a mosque for a story, and was detained by a militia and accused of being a spy. He feels very lucky that he was finally released.

Mohammed's predicament is not unusual. Tens of thousands more, like him, are trying to get out of the country. The refugee crisis will continue to grow throughout the rest of the year. Camps for internally displaced people start popping up in and around Baghdad; neighborhoods in the city are increasingly divided along ethnic lines. In total, an estimated two million Iraqis will have left the country by the end of 2006, and two million more will be displaced within its fractured borders.

To quote the State Department report: The country's "social fabric remains under intense strain."

To quote Mohammed, the situation is "fucking shit."

CHAPTER 14

August-September 2006

BAGHDAD

I step outside to take her phone call.

"Hi, baby."

"Hi, Cub."

"I have news."

"Tell me."

"I got the job."

What I feel first is pride. To give up a prestigious public relations job in New York to come to Iraq to help fix this mistake, to help this country function, to work for democratic ideals and women's rights and to work for half the pay. I am immensely impressed with Andi, and proud. This is what I tell her in that first conversation, and I believe it. I am excited that she is coming. She will be working at the International Republican Institute's Baghdad office. Her job description is media development, working with Iraqi leaders and their parliament to set up a public affairs office, with the larger goal of getting Iraq to establish a free and independent press. I love her bravery and her guts. We discuss the logistics: when she's going to get here, what kind of training she has to do, when she will go to D.C. to meet with IRI for orientation. We agree this is a great opportunity. There are a lot of great opportunities if you're young and willing to risk your life, I tell her, quoting a friend who told me the same thing. You'll get to experience something most people won't experience. You'll get to work in what is the most challenging and difficult environment you can imagine. If you can work in Baghdad, you can work anywhere. If you like it, you can go other places overseas, places much nicer than here. Or you can move from this job to work on one of the campaigns, and you'll probably have more foreign policy experience than the candidate you work for. You'll enjoy it, being in the center of things, where history is being made. ("Center of things falling apart," she jokes.)

"It doesn't make you uncomfortable that I'm coming?"

"No, honestly, I'm excited for you. But this a very bad and dangerous place. It's a real shithole. And I'll worry . . ."

"You don't worry."

"I'll worry. You're not going to like a lot of things about this place—and like I've said before, being a woman here will be hard. Women aren't treated well here by anyone, and you'll get more unwanted attention than you ever have gotten before. But I'm honestly excited for you. I'll support you, whatever you want to do."

Was I totally okay with it? No. I don't think it's possible to be completely comfortable with the notion that someone you care about is in a war zone. It's just something you learn to accept. I knew from the moment she told me she was coming that it would be tough, a real shock for us. So I tried to focus on the positives. She really wanted to do this, and I wanted her to have confidence that she was making the right choice. She was going into an unknown. I knew it would be extremely stressful for her—I'd been through it myself—and it would be extremely stressful for me. What if she didn't like it? What if she was miserable? Just being in Iraq is stressful in ways you don't even realize. And going to Baghdad at the start of one of the most violent periods of the war, in the fall of 2006, couldn't be a truly good idea for anyone, but that never stopped those of us who wanted to go from going.

Andi began to prepare for Iraq. She packed up her apartment in New York; her mom picked her up and drove her back to Ohio to put her boxes in storage. Her family was very worried about her going, but they knew, too, that once Andi decided to do something, she was going to do it. She headed to D.C. for orientation with IRI, got all of her necessary ID cards, and found out she'd be staying in the Green Zone, near the Blue Star restaurant, just five minutes away from my house.

While Andi was closing up her life in New York, I was getting more deeply involved in the "Battle of Baghdad." American military officials came up with the name—a pitch to get the media interested, and to let those back in Washington know they were serious about stopping "sectarian violence." It was the first major American operation explicitly aimed at stopping the civil war. (Though, according to the military, it still wasn't a civil war; just a number of different factions in the same country fighting against the government.) Sunni insurgents would be targeted, as would Shiite militias (or as the military now preferred to call all of them, "illegally armed groups").

The plan, dubbed Operation Together Forward Phase II, called for sending an additional 6,000 Iraqi soldiers and police to Baghdad, along with 5,500 more American troops. The strategy was "to clear, hold, and build." To "clear" meant going into neighborhoods in Baghdad to find the insurgents; the Americans would act as backup to the Iraqi forces. Once the neighborhoods were cleared, the Americans and the Iraqis would try to establish a more permanent presence, to "hold" the area. The final step, "build," involved $650 million worth of initiatives like new job programs and fixing electricity and sewage.

The "clear, hold, build" strategy had failed when it was tried in 2005, and at other times during the war. The Americans cleared the neighborhoods fine (often because the insurgents, knowing of the operation, had already "melted away," as military intelligence officials would say, to other parts of the country), but there were never enough soldiers to hold on to the neighborhoods for the months—or probably years—required to truly pacify them. And after the Americans exited the neighborhoods, leaving them in the hands of the Iraqi security forces, the violence would start up again, which prevented the U.S. from ever really getting around to the "build" part.

This time around, the U.S. wanted to make sure there were enough troops. But where were they going to get them? The army was already feeling the strain from the "high operational tempo" of fighting the war for five years in Iraq and Afghanistan. Operation Together Forward Phase II was a last-minute plan drawn up in July, a desperate attempt to slow down the violence that had been let loose by the Samarra mosque bombing in February. There just weren't any more troops ready to go. So what to do?

The answer: Don't let the 172nd Stryker Brigade go home.

I'd spent time with 172nd Stryker Brigade in Mosul in October 2005, embedding with them on the second month of their deployment in Iraq. Ten months later, in August, they were scheduled to complete their one-year tour and go back to Fort Lewis and Fort Richardson in Alaska, where they were stationed. But when the army looked around for more troops to send to Baghdad for the security crackdown, the Stryker Brigade was picked—and the 172nd got extended for three more months. I put in a request for an embed.

On August 10, 2006, I took a helicopter out to Camp Striker, one of the five or so bases surrounding the Baghdad Airport. I was going to hook up with the same battalion I'd covered in Mosul, the 4-23 Tomahawks, whose motto was "Unleash Hell." It was late in the evening when I stumbled into 4-23's makeshift tactical operations center—lots of bare plywood, without even a coffeepot set up yet. They had just arrived in Baghdad from Mosul a few days earlier.

Lieutenant Colonel John Norris, the battalion commander, greeted me warmly. It was good to see him. I'd followed the forty-one-year-old commander around Mosul when I was embedded with the 4-23 and had written a profile of him for the *Newsweek* website. He was a blunt, five-foot-eight, no-bullshit, crew-cut leader who went out on the ground with the troops almost every day. His officers had a nickname for him— RPG Magnet, a title he received after a firefight the previous September. He had started his military career in the early eighties as a marine, then he switched over to the army, became an officer, and rose through the ranks. He assumed command of the Stryker battalion in 2003. He embodied the American military ethos at its best—he liked to kick ass, but in an intelligent way. He considered his time in Mosul a success. The Iraqi police force and army were functioning at a higher level than when he arrived, and violence had been kept relatively low. I had a great deal of respect for him.

Norris told me there was a mission going out first thing in the morning, around 4 A.M. I said I was going to get some sleep.

"Where's the XO?" I asked him, referring to his executive officer, whom I'd met last year.

Norris grinned. "Major Hammond went home to Alaska two weeks ago, but he's on his way back here now."

The extension was such a last-minute decision that a third of the 3,500-strong Stryker Brigade had already returned to Alaska, and another third was waiting in Kuwait to go home. The soldiers who'd returned to Alaska were greeted with WELCOME HOME banners and had settled in with their families for a few days when they heard the news—that they would have to return to Baghdad. They'd already sent back equipment, given away spare parts to the unit that relieved them in Mosul, and shipped out their personal belongings, including extra uniforms. Most of the men in 4-23 had only one uniform left with them.

I went to the tent where I'd be sleeping. I saw Captain John Grauer, the 4-23's chaplain. I knew him from Mosul, too. He had an athletic, mountain climber's build and was an optimist by nature. When I first met him, he was newly arrived and hopeful. He told me in October 2005 about how he would go out on raids with the troops and try to make life just a little bit better for the Iraqi children that the soldiers had to roust from bed in the middle of the night. He'd give them candy, he said, and try in whatever small way possible to ease their pain. The intervening year had changed him. His nickname now was the "combat chaplain." Seven different Humvees he'd been riding in had been hit by IEDs.

I asked him how the men were taking the extension.

"Traumatized," he said. "I think we're all still in shock."

Many of the soldiers first learned about the extension from their families back in Alaska, who'd seen the news on CNN and frantically begun emailing and instant-messaging their loved ones still in Iraq. *Is it true? Are you really not coming home?*

Grauer told me he'd already worked on at least ten Red Cross letters, requests from soldiers who needed to get back to the States to deal with family emergencies. "There was a rush of soldiers trying to get on the phone to call home. Some literally threw up when they heard the news. Some were extremely angry. Some went to sleep for a couple of days, hoping maybe it was all just a bad dream." Even Grauer, the eternal optimist, now questioned the mission's purpose—what were they doing here?

And something else was weighing on Grauer's mind, a worry shared by others in the 4-23. Miraculously, after a year in Iraq, no one in the seven-hundred-man battalion had been killed. There'd been plenty of close calls—Captain Benjamin Nagy, nicknamed Ox, got IED'd fifteen times—but not a single soldier had been killed in action. When they started to ship out to Alaska, there was a collective sigh of relief and disbelief that they'd beaten the odds. Now they had three more months in Baghdad.

It wasn't even the three months that bothered them. Professional soldiers are used to putting up with a lot of crap; it comes with the job. The soldiers knew it was much worse for their families in Alaska who'd been waiting, for those wives, kids, and girlfriends who'd been counting the days. It wasn't the delayed vacation plans—the battalion surgeon had already lined up a hard-to-obtain moose-hunting permit, and now he'd have to miss the season; Specialist Mott's wedding invitations had already been sent out, and now had to be recalled. What they struggled to deal with was their sense of betrayal. They had done their tour; they had served their time. And now, because of poor planning and a lack of foresight on the part of the Bush administration and Donald Rumsfeld's Pentagon and the top military commanders (it's not like Baghdad just suddenly got worse; the U.S. leadership simply preferred not to recognize it until now), they were being yanked back at the last minute to the war they'd survived. "If we lose anyone, the blood will be on the hands of Bush and Rumsfeld," the battalion surgeon told me.

For the next three weeks, I stayed embedded with the 4-23. My editors were interested in the story of the 4-23's extension. It showed how strained the army was to meet the demands of this war, it underscored the emotional burden on military families, and it illustrated how the Battle for Baghdad, an operation that General Casey called yet another "critical point," never had a chance of success.

*   *   *

Day One. At 3:30 A.M., the alarm on my cell phone goes off. I grab my cleanup kit and walk in a daze down an avenue of blast walls and endless tents to a trailer of showers. I shower, but don't have time to drink or eat anything, and I forget there is no coffee in the TOC.

This is the first day of the operation. The plan is to clear a neighborhood in Baghdad. It is very hot out, even before the sun comes up. By 7 A.M., I am sweating and smoking; by noon I am sweating more than I ever have before and I'm chugging two-liter bottles of water to no effect; by 4 P.M., as we head back to base, I am sitting inside the Stryker trying not to pass out or puke. Finally, we are there, we make it back. I made it. Oops, not quite. We took a wrong turn. We are at Camp Liberty, not Camp Striker. I'm dizzy. "Shit," I say to anyone who's listening. "Can you pass me a bag or something?"

I throw up in a canvas bag. I am dehydrated. They try to give me an IV at the TOC, but it doesn't stick; the needle won't stay in my arm, so eventually we give up and I drink more water and vow that tomorrow I'm going to take rehydration tablets.

Five soldiers ask me that night: "So you're the reporter who threw up in the vehicle commander's bag?"

Week One. The neighborhood the 4-23 is clearing is called Ghazaliya. During Saddam's time, it was a wealthy, Sunni area, a prestigious place to live in the western part of the city. Over the past six months, the neighborhood has turned into a battleground.

I'm in Lieutenant Colonel Norris's vehicle. We arrive at the starting point for the operation, a road running parallel to a train track on the edge of the neighborhood. More than fifteen Stryker vehicles rumble to a stop, dust rising in the pink sun. The Strykers are massive, multiton green machines that remind me of the kind of vehicle I'd want to be riding in during an alien invasion. It is the first time in the war the Strykers, a relatively new vehicle, are being used in Baghdad. The Stryker armor is better than Humvee armor. Eight men can sit inside the troop compartment; the driver is in the nose; there are four portholes in the roof; two "air guards" in the back, where soldiers stand guard, their bodies half exposed; the other two portholes are for the vehicle commander and the machine gunner; the machine gun can also be operated by joystick from inside the vehicle.

A fleet of Iraqi police cars and Iraqi Army trucks pulls up, twenty minutes late. The Americans and Iraqis huddle to discuss the plan for the day, deciding which unit gets which block to search.

Norris surveys the scene. The road is next to two football-sized fields full of trash. A lone woman in a black hijab is picking through the garbage.

"Hundreds of bodies have been dumped here," Norris says. "This is the dead zone. This is the kill zone."

Ghazaliya is on a "sectarian fault line," Norris explains. The neighborhood to the north, Shula, is mostly Shiite and Shiite militias and death squads have been making frequent attacks on Ghazaliya: lobbing mortars and firing rockets, kidnappings and executions at illegal checkpoints. Insurgents in Ghazaliya do the same to the residents of Shula.

Norris tells me a story he heard from a high-ranking Iraqi officer. The insurgents took a baby, cut off the head, sewed a dog's head on the baby, "cooked the baby in an oven and left it on someone's front doorstep."

I doubt if the story is true, but it's the kind of story that's going around.

Around noon, I walk onto a small residential street with a platoon from the 4-23. Two widows greet us, holding photos of their lost husbands and brothers. Can you help me, they cry, can you help me?

The widows explain that fifty men from their neighborhood were kidnapped by men in security forces uniforms in September 2005. They don't know where they are. I take the names down, though there is an understanding that it is futile; the women know they are gone.

An American officer I'm with asks one of the widows: "Did you contact the police about it?"

The widow looks at him, incredulous: "It was the police who kidnapped them!"

Week Two. The clearing operation in Ghazaliya continues. The heat is intense, 115 degrees, sometimes 120 degrees and climbing.

I walk with the soldiers. There is no action, no bang-bang, so I try to describe what the soldiers are going through, the monotony and the boredom and the heat. I focus on the sweat.

You start to sweat before you even start to move. You sweat more than humanly possible. Your eyebrows and mustache leak with sweat. Your pants are soaked with sweat and leave a damp mark where you sit. You drink liter after liter of water and Gatorade, which makes you sweat more, and the sweat becomes even saltier and collects in the Wiley X eye protection you wear and stings your eyes. Cramped in the Stryker, the heat reaches 140 degrees. You feel the sweat coming through the soldier's clothes next to you, mixed with the sweat soaked in your uniform. The uniforms are heavy and love sweat. You must have your sleeves rolled down for safety, a regulation in place to protect your skin from possible exposure to fire damage in case of attack. You must be wearing thirty-one pounds of body armor, along with a three-pound helmet which actually feels like it's baking the brain, seven clips of 5.56mm ammunition, carrying a seven-pound M-4 rifle, a radio, or a shovel, or a pair of bolt cutters. You start climbing over walls to get into locked houses, breaking down doors, looking for a bomb that could explode or sniper ready to shoot you in the face.

This is Baghdad in the summer, this is the mission assigned to the 4-23 Tomahawks, which they are doing instead of going home. The soldiers have a word for it: the Suck. "Baghdad is a real suckfest," says twenty-one-year-old Phillip Jereza, as he sits in the back of a Stryker. "At least you're not the only one in the suckfest. We have each other." One soldier has his company's unofficial motto scrawled on a white undershirt: WE SUCK THE LEAST.

There is a certain bitterness among the men, a well-earned cynicism, openly expressed. Sergeant Brian Patton believes there is a political motive behind the extension and the Battle for Baghdad. Midterm elections are coming up in November; the Republicans want to show that Baghdad is stable. "We're fighting for the House of Representatives," says Patton. "You could call this the November 2 extension." As we walk, a young private grabs a lemon from a lemon tree: "This country sucks," he says, inhaling the lemon. "This lemon smells good." He throws the lemon at a house. A veteran sergeant who asks me not use his name because he doesn't want to get in trouble blames Donald Rumsfeld personally. "I wish I could meet Don," he says. "I call him Don. I'd like to punch him in the face, then I'd like to punch him in the gut. It's like he doesn't realize he's destroying families."

Streets in Ghazaliya stink like raw sewage. A sickening, acrid smell of shit and chemicals. The sewage floods the pavement and stretches along the street like a liquid sidewalk, bluish-gray pools warming in the sun.

These streets used to be nice; the houses were owned by upper-class families. Now every third house we enter is abandoned, the Iraqi families who once lived here having left the country or the city. It is an exodus of the educated—doctors, lawyers, professors, businessmen. Those with the resources and skills to play a role in rebuilding the country are gone.

I go into an abandoned three-floor home with a few soldiers. The soldiers kick down the expensive wooden door. Dust on everything. Toilet still works. It feels like an invasion of privacy. On the bookshelf are engineering texts in German. This Iraqi must be a professor or something. The photo albums have been left behind. I look at the family, at their wedding photos, the snapshots of sons and daughters and relatives.

I stop and look at the photo albums in half a dozen other empty homes.

After ten days, the 172nd Brigade has searched over twenty thousand homes. And what are the soldiers looking for? Weapons, explosives, bad guys. The problem is that the Iraqi Army and police are infiltrated with spies, and the spies tip off the bad guys to move their weapons to other places before the soldiers arrive.

Iraqi law: Each household is allowed one AK-47 with two magazines. Mosques are allowed five AK-47s. At one house, the soldiers take away a pistol from an old man who lives with four women. "How can I defend my family," he says. "Sir, it's our orders," replies the soldier. The old man, hunched over, frail, white hair on the rim of his balding head, continues to plead his case but loses his pistol.

And where are the bad guys? Where are the terrorists, the insurgents, the death squads? They are lying low; they have melted away; they are probably not going to launch a large attack when the Americans are on the streets in these numbers. Maybe a bomb or a sniper, but nothing big. They prefer to wait and hide and attack the soldiers when they travel in small convoys, with IEDs, by ambush. It's the classic strategy of guerrilla warfare when facing a foe that is superiorly armed. I hear soldiers complain: "If they'd just come out and fight, they wouldn't stand a chance." And that's exactly why they don't; they don't need to; they aren't facing midterm elections; the insurgents have all the time in the world. It's their country, after all.

I remember reading somewhere that once you start complaining that the enemy isn't playing by the rules, you're in trouble.

A group of Iraqi teenagers watches us move from home to home. I start to interview them—one of them, a twenty-two-year-old named Saif, speaks English. I ask him if he is a Sunni or a Shiite. He hates that question, though he admits he's a Shiite. We are standing next to an ankle-deep puddle of waste. "Look, look at least if I am going to die, I accept that, but at least give me a clean street to die in!" He likes journalism but is in dental school; we exchange email addresses and keep in touch. Over the next eight months, Saif and his family move to three different neighborhoods. He continues to go to dental school. He sends me a text one day that reads "breaking news school under attack." I call him. He tells me that his school is being attacked by a gunman. "The girls are screaming," he says, "can you hear them?" He says he will write something for me about it. The next day, the bridge he takes on the way to school is destroyed in a bombing.

Still Week Two, still in Ghazaliya. Half the Iraqi Army soldiers and police don't show up for the searches, and the half that do show up want to quit at noon. We search three mosques. They are minifortresses, with sandbags and fighting positions. Weapons are discovered in all of them. At one mosque, where the largest stash was found, mortar rounds are hidden in the minarets; magazines of AK-47 ammunition are stuffed in a plastic bag behind an air conditioner. A beheading knife is buried in the grounds; a soldier finds it with a metal detector. Behind the mosque, the metal detector goes off again; the Americans start to dig up the grass yard, and they find an entire arsenal, including rocket-launching tubes.

An American general comes out to check on the action. He tours the mosque, and gives the soldiers coins: pocket-sized medallions with the 4th Infantry Division crest. I ask the general what gives him confidence in the plan to secure Baghdad if we are working with the Iraqi police force, which is known to be infiltrated by militias and death squads. "We're trying to make these neighborhoods into little Mayberries," he says instead. He is not joking.

A week later, the 4-23 gets chastised for searching the mosques so thoroughly, and they are told by the division command that they aren't allowed to go into mosques anymore. Political sensitivities; we are in a Muslim country and it understandably angers Iraq's Muslim politicians and their constituents when the American military enters their places of worship, even if they are being used as staging grounds for attacks on both Americans and Iraqis. The 4-23 gets a new rule: Iraqi soldiers can search the mosques first, and if they find anything, then the Americans can enter. But the Iraqi soldiers never seem to find anything.

We search the Ghazaliya branch office of the Iraqi Islamic Party and find materials to make IEDs and a stash of grenades and heavy machine gun ammo. The Americans believe the IED materials are being used to attack Coalition forces. Captain Brad Velotta questions the head of the office, an Iraqi politician who is a member of the local government, for two hours, but the politician is not detained.

Week Three. A young captain is giving his men a lecture on the base at Striker. "Water conservation is in effect," he says. "They're serious this time. So if you're going to rub one out, do it in the Port-a-John." The Port-a-Johns are spaced in groups of twos and fours and sixes on the hot gravel, behind blast walls, and are cleaned daily by Filipinos who spray water and disinfectant on them from a large truck. The Port-a-Johns are like plastic saunas with graffiti. "I lost ten pounds taking a five-pound shit," says one bit of scrawl. Another line of graffiti is about Operation Iraqi Freedom—every year or so, the military updates the OIF mission name with a number to mark the passing of time. "OIF 1, OIF 2, OIF 3, how much fucking freedom do these Iraqis need?"

I spend the day on base, writing up my reporting. I put my laptop on the metal cot and type. After I'm finished, I bring the laptop outside, with my BGAN satellite modem. I set the modem up, resting the gray box on a concrete duck-and-cover bunker, and send my file by email to New York.

Newsweek also sends a reporter to Alaska, to interview the families of the soldiers I've interviewed, including those of Captain Velotta and Captain Grauer.

Rumsfeld goes to Alaska, too, and meets with soldiers' wives at Fort Lewis. One wife asks the secretary of defense: "Why is the 172nd doing all the house searches? Isn't that the Iraqis' job?" "Over 90 percent of the house clearings are being handled by the Iraqis," Rumsfeld responds. The women in the audience start shouting, "No!" and, "That's not true!" Rumsfeld shoots back, "No? What do you mean? Don't say 'no,' that's what I've been told. It's the task of the Iraqis to go through the buildings."

A midnight raid is planned for a "high value" target. The target is a middle-aged Iraqi man who runs an insurgent cell. There's good intel from the S-2 shop. (S-2 is the code name for military intelligence.) At 1:30 A.M., I climb into the Stryker vehicle, sitting in the troop compartment on a bench next to six soldiers. Two of them just got back to Iraq after going home to Alaska. I ask them how they feel, and one closes his eyes and shakes his head. The other says, "I thought this shit was over for me." There isn't much conversation; everyone is tired, after having spent the day searching houses on the street. Heads nod, as the soldiers catch twenty minutes of sleep on the drive into Baghdad.

When we get close to the objective, the vehicle commander says: "Drop ramp," and the back of the Stryker opens up slowly. I follow the soldiers out onto the street. It's dark and the city at night is like an empty movie set called "Downtown Baghdad." A four-block area is cordoned off. We stick close to the buildings, jogging, heading toward the apartment complex where the target is suspected to live. But the homes next to the target's apartment building must be secured as well. I follow three soldiers through a metal gate to a front door. One of them pushes the buzzer. No answer. He knocks on the door. Knocks again. Nothing. One soldier steps back to cover the other, who takes a running kick at the door. The door busts open. The three soldiers run inside, rifles ready, illuminating the inside of the house with flashlights attached to the scopes of their M-4s. A woman starts to scream. The flashlights and rifle barrels point to a bed. A husband and wife are lying on a queen-sized bed, an infant cradled between them. The woman is hyperventilating; she does not stop screaming, she is in a white and pink nightgown and she keeps screaming and hyperventilating and her husband tries to calm her as she holds the infant. The soldiers look mildly embarrassed and don't point their weapons at her anymore. When we walk out, I ask one of the soldiers if that happens often, finding a man and woman in bed. "Yes," the soldier says. "Once we came in a house and the husband was doing his old lady on the couch."

"Was she naked?" I asked. "Was she hot?"

"Hell, yes, she was fine," says the soldier. "But her old man was pissed."

A few days before my embed is over, my younger brother Jeff arrives in Iraq with the 10th Mountain Division. He happens to be assigned to Camp Striker. We see each other and hang out. I hadn't seen him since the spring, when he went out to dinner with Andi and me in New York. Very odd, very strange—totally surreal. To see him brings the feeling of home—that feeling doesn't fit with this environment. We call our parents in Vermont on my Iraqna—it is 7 A.M. their time. "Hi, Mom and Dad, we're calling from Baghdad . . ."

My embed is over. Captain Velotta brings me back to the Green Zone in a convoy of three Strykers. The soldiers I'm sitting next to bullshit throughout the half-hour drive: "If the bitch finds out I got promoted, she's gonna want more alimony." Another: "I don't want to go home, fucking lawyer is after me. I hope they keep extending me." It's an easy run, a fluff mission, a relaxed drive from the base down Airport Road to the Green Zone on a Saturday. No searches, no patrols; they're even planning to stop at the Crossed Swords.

And then, about fifteen minutes into the drive, an IED goes off on the other side of the street. Velotta orders the convoy to stop, the ramp drops, and we rush out. An eight-year-old boy is sitting cross-legged on the sidewalk, bleeding from the neck. He looks up at us as we stand over him. The medic gives him first aid, a simple white bandage on his neck, and he is saved. Velotta has his men do a quick search of the area to see if they can find the triggerman, but there is no one around except the eight-year-old boy and his father, who just happened to be in the wrong place at the wrong time. We pile back into the vehicles, and continue into the Green Zone. We do have time to stop at the Crossed Swords, and we pose for a group photograph.

My story on the embed gets edited and closes in the magazine the next day. I end the story on the note that, remarkably, still no soldiers have been killed in the 4-23. On Sunday, the magazine comes out. The same day, Lucian Read, the photographer working for *Newsweek* who had been with me during the embed, decides to go out with the 4-23 on one more patrol. I don't go, I have my story; but Lucian is freelance so he takes the chance to get more pictures. That evening, he calls me. He is waiting at the hospital in the Green Zone, the CASH, and he tells me while they were out, Corporal Alexander Jordan, twenty-four, was killed by a sniper. They didn't catch the sniper. They drove as fast as they could to get Jordan to the hospital for medical attention, but he died en route. I drive to the hospital to pick up Lucian; the Strykers are parked in a line outside; Norris is standing in the vehicle commander's porthole, his face taut and unresponsive.

Later at the bureau, Lucian has a few beers. He has taken some of the best-known pictures of the war, including photos from the battle of Fallujah and of the Haditha massacre. "Of all the pictures I've taken," he says, "the only ones that matter are dead people. The rest are bullshit."

I know that Norris is not going to like the story when he reads it. Much of my material on the soldiers, detailing the day-to-day missions, was cut, leaving the focus on how difficult the extension has been for the 4-23 and their families. It also contains criticism, from his men, of the

Bush administration and Donald Rumsfeld. I feel uneasy, because I have respect for Norris, and I want him to like it. I know he won't like it, though. But I know most of the soldiers will.

The story runs. Norris is not happy with it. He sends me an email and says I betrayed his trust and asks if my magazine is pushing a liberal media agenda. I say my story is based on interviews with dozens of soldiers over a month and it is accurate. It's just not very good news.

CHAPTER 15

September 2006

BAGHDAD

"Is it weird seeing me here?"

"No. Yes."

"This is awkward."

"It's always awkward, isn't it?"

"It is. It is."

"Did you think it wasn't going to be awkward?"

"No, I knew it was going to be awkward."

"Well, it's great to see you."

We'd last seen each other in New York six weeks earlier, hours before I got on a plane, wondering when we would see each other next. When would I get her a ring? Was our love strong enough to make it through a year apart? Now we were together again, in totally weird circumstances, trying to process our emotions over a dinner at the best restaurant in the Green Zone—which wasn't saying much. We were sitting at a white plastic table on the patio of the Blue Star, the restaurant that replaced the

Green Zone Café after it was destroyed by two suicide bombers in October 2004. It was one of two restaurants in the IZ—the other was called the Baghdad Country Club. The food was decent—chicken tikka, soggy French fries, hummus, grilled tomatoes—and guests could order hookahs with apple-scented tobacco and other flavors. It had a simple layout, a patio area with a dozen tables out front, and inside a very plain, overly lit dining room. Military personnel and embassy staffers were not allowed to eat there—it was considered unsanitary by U.S. government health regulations—but most I knew broke the rule and ate there anyway. We'd chosen a table in the back of the patio where it was private and the light was dim. Under the table, we held hands. We didn't want to draw attention to ourselves.

It was a cool night. Helicopters flew in pairs overhead. The restaurant sat directly beneath the flight path to LZ Washington, and the gusts of air from Black Hawks passing over forced patrons to clamp down on their napkins and pita bread in red plastic baskets.

There was a flash of green; a flare dropped, illuminating our table for a moment and making me jump and look up. Andi wasn't fazed.

"This is what I hear every night," she said. "It shakes the roof of my trailer."

Andi had arrived in Baghdad three days earlier on September 16. I wasn't in the city that day; I didn't get back until the nineteenth. After my embed with the 172nd, I'd taken an Iraqi Airways flight to Kurdistan to do a story on Kurdish rebel groups that were regularly attacking Turkey and Iran from the mountains on Iraq's northern border. While I was in Kurdistan, Andi was in Amman, spending the first two weeks of September at a conference for Iraqi politicians hosted by the International Republican Institute. We communicated by phone, me calling via satellite to her hotel room. She told me she was enjoying her time in Jordan, her first experience with the Middle East. As a blond, she was something of a novelty, and the politicians asked to pose with her for a digital picture. She received more than one impulsive marriage proposal. ("No, thank you," she told the three Arab men who asked her to marry them. "I'm already engaged." *When are you going to get me the ring,* she'd IM me.) She helped organize the event—and she had that instant observation all Americans have when they start working in the Middle East: *Does anything happen on time? It's like herding cats to get these guys to do anything.* She learned about eating goat and hummus from communal plates with her hands. ("I mean, I had a plate of hummus, and this fat man in a dishdasha started eating off it!") She took it all in stride, enjoying the culture clash, the new experience. She found it particularly amusing that one of the Iraqi leaders who spoke at the conference began his remarks by denouncing the Americans and the American occupation, even though it was an American organization that had footed the bill for this gentleman's airfare and accommodations, and, more important, given him an excuse not to be in Baghdad.

Her arrival in Baghdad was uneventful, the airport run smooth, except that she was too small and so there was no body armor that fit her. IRI had to special-order one for her size. She learned her meals would be mostly in the military dining facility (the DFAC; I sympathized) or at the Blue Star, where she kept to a strict diet of French fries and hummus, or she'd eat Zone bars and cereal and oatmeal in her trailer.

As predicted, she got a lot of attention around the Green Zone, more than she expected. "Welcome to Baghdad," I said. The population of the Green Zone was overwhelmingly male—something like 70 percent. The lack of women and the high level of testosterone in the air—combined with some jobs that required little work—made some men tend toward the barbaric, gaping at and trying to pick up any woman that crossed their path. (Fraternizing with local Iraqi women was very much frowned upon. Iraqi men didn't appreciate it, for reasons of pride and culture, and it could get the man or the woman killed.) So it wasn't a shock that Andi received that much attention. It annoyed me, even stressed me out, for sure, more than I was willing to admit. (As one of my friends remarked, when he learned she was coming, "Andi's pretty even in New York," a comment that left me ill at ease.) I would tell her, "You're the most beautiful girl in Baghdad," and she would respond, "Oh, stop it!" I wasn't proud of how jealous and possessive I sometimes felt, but I trusted her, and in my heart I knew I had nothing to worry about except her safety.

After we ate dinner, Andi showed me her new home. It was a trailer, or CHU—pronounced "chew"—for containable housing unit. She had already made her modifications. The sink, which was just part of the living room, now had a curtain (a "sink shield," she called it, because she couldn't stand looking at a bare sink in a living room), and she had rigged her air conditioner with sheets of fabric softener that blew a fresh, lemon-scented breeze and overpowered the vague smell of sewage in her unit. She had a single bed with brand-new sheets, a TV with a satellite hookup, and a desk where she worked on her laptop, using the wireless Internet access when it wasn't down.

"Nice accommodations," I said. "It's not that bad."

"You live in a house. With a cook."

"Yes, I have it pretty good here," I admitted, just to annoy her.

"I just want to kick you."

And she walked over and kicked me with the instep of her small sneakered foot.

We spent time together in her room. There wasn't much privacy, and I couldn't spend the night. I wanted to, but it wouldn't have been good for me to be away from the bureau for too long in case anything happened, and like a high school student borrowing his parents' car, I couldn't keep the Mercedes out all night. As a woman, Andi knew she needed to be taken seriously, and she felt it wouldn't have made a good impression on her supervisors if I was already sleeping over. For security reasons, she wasn't allowed to spend the night in the *Newsweek* bureau—IRI's policy required her to have two Blackwater security guards with her wherever she went outside her compound. It was another challenge of having a relationship in Baghdad; we were both there to work, and having a job in Baghdad is a twenty-four-hour occupation.

I left after our first date, passing through the checkpoints manned by Iraqis, and then Georgians, getting into the Mercedes I'd parked in the gravel lot behind her compound. I drove home and texted her when I arrived—even though it was only a few minutes away—to tell her I got there safely.

For the next month, while she lived in the IRI compound, I went to see her three or four times a week. She'd also visit the bureau when she had a chance in the evening. Her security guards would drop her off for a few hours, then pick her up and bring her back to her trailer for IRI's midnight curfew.

Andi fell into her routine. She worked at the Iraqi parliament—the Convention Center—during the day trying to build a media center for the Iraqi press. Her predecessor had started the project a year earlier but it still wasn't even close to being complete. She encountered the common frustration in Iraq—it took forever to get even the smallest things done. The media center was held up because one of the Iraqi spokespeople did not want to give up his large corner office, an office that the other parliamentarians agreed would make a perfect media center. Then, when they finally settled on a floor space for the center, on the second floor, and mapped out where computers and dividers would be put up, the Speaker of the House decided to temporarily ban all press from the parliament. Still, Andi got to know Iraqi leaders and helped them send out press releases, set up press conferences, and trained them how to deal with the media. She worked out in the mornings, even finding a yoga class to attend called Baghdad Yoga. She described her days to me as if she were Alice in a disturbed Wonderland, where every conversation took on the air of the Mad Hatter's tea party. I'd laugh and say what I'd come to say a lot to her: "Welcome to Iraq."

On the evening of October 10, I was sitting at my desk in the bureau's office when I heard what sounded like a mortar land nearby. I ignored it and kept typing up a story I was working on. Less than a minute passed, and there was another explosion; the windows shook. In the next five minutes, there were a series of seven or eight more blasts. It sounded like someone was shelling the hell out of the Green Zone.

I was the only correspondent at the bureau that night. The other person in the house was a Scottish private security manager who was filling in for a few days for a friend of his. He walked into the office and he suggested we move into the living room, the designated safe area. I brought my computer with me, and then my phone rang—it was our Iraqi office manager. He told me he thought there was heavy fighting in his neighborhood; in fact, he said, he hadn't heard these kinds of explosions since the bombing of Baghdad in 2003.

I sent a text message to Andi, asking if she was okay.

Then I went up to the third-floor roof of the bureau with the security manager. In the distance, off in the city, we could see the red glow of a large fire, lighting up the dark skyline in a rhythm of pink blasts. I called New York and filed an audio report on the scene for the website: "Mysterious explosions, like a fireworks show, there goes another one, sounds like heavy fighting, nobody knows what it is . . ."

Andi hadn't texted me back, and I started to get concerned.

After fifteen minutes of watching the explosions, I went back inside. The TV news was covering it, and the military had just issued a press release: There had been an insurgent mortar attack on one of the U.S. bases in Baghdad, FOB Falcon, and the mortar had landed on an ammo depot, starting a fire and setting off the explosions that were being felt across the city. I called New York again to tell them that it wasn't heavy fighting after all. I felt a bit silly, thinking I had jumped the gun a little.

I called Andi and she picked up.

"Are you okay?" I asked.

"Yes," she said.

"Why didn't you respond to me? You can't do that—you have to text me back you're okay."

Andi ignored what I said and explained she'd been at the Blue Star with colleagues. They'd all laughed off the explosions at first and continued with their dinner, but after about five minutes, her boss started to get worried. He'd been in Iraq for two years, and these were the worst explosions he'd heard. So they all moved to shelter in one of IRI's houses.

"You could see the glow of the explosions on my face," she told me.

I let go of my annoyance, and told her about going up on the roof. We were both still excited over what had happened, though Andi sensed some disappointment in my voice.

"Oh, my Newsie, you were hoping the Green Zone was under attack, so you'd have a big story!"

Five days later, I was scheduled to leave Iraq—yet another unique stress that came with having a relationship in Baghdad. American civilians working in Iraq—journalists, State Department officials, U.N. workers, contractors, aid workers—were all on a rotating schedule. For mental health reasons, most organizations didn't want their staff staying in Iraq for long periods at a time. A few months in, a few weeks out. *Newsweek* didn't like it when correspondents stayed more than two months, and by the middle of October, I was approaching ten weeks. Another reporter had already been slated to relieve me, but my schedule wasn't yet aligned with Andi's. She wouldn't be due for an out until the end of November.

I went over to see her on my last night. Our dinner at the Blue Star was strained. Together in her trailer, we had a repeat of the same conversation we'd had many times over the last year, only in reverse. I was heading to Dubai, where I promised her I was going to look at diamond rings.

"Dubai," she said.

"Yes," I said, "I know a guy there who just a got a diamond ring for his fiancée, and he told me he'd hook me up."

"I don't know if I trust you getting a diamond ring in Dubai, Newsie," she said.

"Don't worry, I can trust this guy. I'll see what he has to offer."

We kept the lights off in her trailer.

"How are you going to handle it now that I'm in Baghdad and you're not?"

"I'll worry. I see what you mean. It's not so fun when the shoe is on the other foot."

"You don't worry."

"I do, I do. Just promise me you'll be careful."

I left for the airport at 6:30 the next morning, then got stuck there all day and night. I hung out with a friend I met there named Ahmed, who was nineteen and worked at the airport. He lived there with his father in an office on the second floor that they'd converted to a bedroom because it was too dangerous for him to go back and forth from his neighborhood every day. His cousin had been killed, he told me, and his mother and sister had fled the country to Syria. So he stayed at the airport, sleeping and eating there, picking up odd jobs, while his father ran airport security for the Ministry of Defense. We listened to his iPod on my laptop—he had many more songs than I did—and chilled out watching *Scrubs* on satellite TV. At night we wandered the airport corridors. For me it was a strange sense of freedom, being able to walk anywhere in the airport, through customs and back, into the departure gate, down to where lost luggage was kept, with no one stopping us. I felt like a child running in the halls of his parent's office on a Saturday. There were over a hundred stranded passengers sleeping on the floor and on the sticky gray couches at the departure gate—mostly Arab businessmen, but also women on the way to Saudi Arabia for the hajj who had been stuck there five days. Sitting back in his room, which had a view of the airport parking lot, Ahmed quizzed me on how hard it was to get into the U.S. from Mexico. I said it probably wasn't too hard. He shook his head. Neither of us said it, but I could see the despair of his position—wanting to leave every day, wanting to escape, and being in the one place in Iraq where each day everyone around him was leaving, going, getting the hell out.

I spoke to Andi from the airport, telling her I was stuck but okay.

"I miss you," she said.

"I miss you already."

The next morning, Ahmed and his father told the security I was a VIP. (I was wearing a blue blazer with flannels, after all, having realized before that if I wore that outfit I wouldn't get searched as much.) Ahmed escorted me to the front of the line. I got on the plane. There was not much of an adrenaline rush, no thrill like I'd felt a year ago. I was just leaving—and for the first time, Andi would be in Baghdad without me.

CHAPTER 16

November 2006–January 1, 2007

DUBAI, SAIGON, JERUSALEM, AMMAN

After leaving Baghdad, I spent a few days of downtime in Dubai. I checked in with my friend about his diamond connection—he showed me the ring he'd bought his fiancée. It looked nice, but I wanted to wait before I made the purchase. I knew Andi had very specific tastes, and I wanted to take my time and get it right.

The week before I left Iraq, I'd planned a trip to Vietnam to write a piece comparing the two wars. After a week in Vietnam, I was supposed to head to Cairo to set up an apartment, where I thought I'd be staying when not in Baghdad. But before I left for Vietnam, I got a phone call from Scott, who was in Mexico at the time. He was planning the upcoming rotation schedule for reporters, he said, and he wanted *Newsweek's* Jerusalem bureau chief, Kevin Peraino, to go to Baghdad in November. Would I be interested in covering Israel for the month Kevin was in Iraq? I said yes, and discussed it with Andi, who started making plans to visit me in Israel on her break.

I arrived in Vietnam at the end of October. I spent a few days in Ho Chi Minh City, staying at the Continental Hotel, made famous in *The Quiet American*. It was where Fowler first met the idealistic Pyle, on Rue Catinat (changed to Freedom Street when the Americans took over the city, renamed Dong Khoi by the Vietnamese after the U.S. left). The hotel, which had once been a haven for spies, diplomats, and journalists, still maintained its French colonial design. I visited old battlefields in the jungle, crawled through the tunnels of Cu Chi that the Vietcong had dug. I looked at exhibits of the booby traps and equipment the guerrillas had used: punji sticks, punji pits, grenades set to invisible trip wires, rubber-soled sandals, black pajamas. I took a sampan down to the Mekong Delta. I ate dinner atop the Rex Hotel, looking out over a peaceful city where thirty-five years earlier American military officials and journalists watched the war get closer and closer to Saigon, closer and closer to the end. I stopped next in Hanoi, where I reported a story about Vietnam's economic recovery, pegged to President George W. Bush's scheduled November visit to the city for a regional economic summit, which would make him the second American president to have set foot in Vietnam since 1975.

The country was booming. It had the second-fastest-growing economy in Asia after China. The students and businessmen I spoke to seemed optimistic, and not resentful of Americans at all. In fact, they idolized the U.S.—in an opinion poll taken of teenagers in Vietnam in 2000, Bill Gates and Bill Clinton ranked as popular as Ho Chi Minh.

Could Iraq possibly turn out this way? Would I be able to visit Baghdad in thirty years with a copy of the Lonely Planet tourist guide? "Stay in the Paul Wolfowitz suite at the Al Rasheed Hotel, the room that was hit by a rocket in October 2003 during the deputy defense secretary's visit . . . Take a bus to Fallujah for an overpriced soda and a look at an exhibit of IEDs, the honorable resistance camouflaged in the trash . . . Here's the infrared sensor, garage-door opener, and 60mm mortar shell; on the left is the EFP, or explosive formed projectile, supplied by Iran, that could pierce even the toughest American armor; up above is the famous DBIED, or donkey-borne improvised explosive device."

It was hard for me to imagine Iraq turning out like Vietnam; we'd be lucky if it did.

I arrived in Jerusalem in November. I spent my first days going to the Palestinian territories. I talked to a one-armed Hamas commander in Gaza, black flies buzzing around his head, who told me he wished all his seven children to be martyrs.

Andi took trips to IRI's office in the Red Zone. "Our private security guards almost shot someone," she told me over the phone. She watched an Iraqi man, working in the Green Zone, get taunted by an American soldier. "These poor people, these poor people," she said.

I interviewed a Palestinian rocket maker in Khan Younis, a town in the Gaza Strip where three journalists had been kidnapped in the previous six months. The kidnapping threat was still high. The interview went well. A masked Palestinian gunman stood guard in an abandoned concrete building as a twenty-year-old showed me how to pour explosive powder into a rocket tube.

Andi worked in the Iraqi parliament and experienced another close call. She was in the Convention Center when two car bombs were found just outside, part of an assassination attempt against the man whose staff she was training. The Green Zone was locked down, and it was getting dark—she led a group of people on foot back to her compound, a few mortars falling along the way. "Well, baby," I said, "now you have a war story." The story about the assassination attempt appeared on the front page of the *New York Times* the next day.

Was any of this real? The stress, the drama, the concern—it all felt too much sometimes, too much to actually be our lives. Andi worrying about me in Gaza, me worrying about her in Baghdad. The two of us arguing and threatening to break up, then threatening to get married, then deciding on the names of our kids (Hayden Gray, girl, Emerson, boy). When are you coming to Jerusalem and when are you getting back to Baghdad, everything so intense and desperate and insecure and then absolutely sure, all of it expressed over bad phone lines and emails and Skypes. We try to stay close, we try to stay connected, we look to the future. "I have a five-year plan," I tell her. "That's so long," she says. "This is the long run we are in for, right?" "When will we have a normal life?" "We don't want a normal life now. We'll have time for a normal life later."

A month passes, a precious month, a useless month—November ends. Then there's a change of plan. Andi's contract with IRI ends much sooner than she expected, so she switches jobs to the National Democratic Institute. She leaves Baghdad. What relief I feel now that she's out safely. It dawns on me for the first time how deeply worried I was, and it surprises me to realize how capable I was of putting it so far back in my mind. She comes to visit me in Jerusalem for one week, Sunday to Sunday. On Monday, we walk in Jerusalem's Old City, getting lost in the crowds and tunnels of the Arab quarter, seeing the most important Muslim shrine—the Dome of the Rock—and the most important Jewish shrine—the Wailing Wall—and the spot where Christ was crucified. On Tuesday, despite State Department warnings for Americans to avoid it, we go to the West Bank. In the town of Nablus, in a valley between the Mountain of Blessings and the Mountain of Curses, we visit with Samaritan mystics, and get our fortunes told. As we leave, we pass Israeli Army vehicles that have closed off a road because of a stone-throwing incident. On Wednesday morning, we go to Ramallah and interview Fatah activists. Andi spends the afternoon with our Palestinian fixer, Nuha, looking at jewelry and running errands for her children. (She picks up Nuha's son, Abdul Nasser, from school. His teacher wants him to sing "O Come All Ye Faithful"; he is a Muslim!) I interview the mayor of Jerusalem and write a story for the international edition about Iraq's economy. On Thursday, we plan a trip to Bethlehem, and I get a haircut. ("He cut your hair way too short," she tells me.) Friday night we relax at the American Colony Hotel, eating room service and watching movies on my laptop. The week is almost over.

On Saturday, we drive to Amman. We drive around the Dead Sea, across the King Hussein border crossing. We hire another car, and drive as the sun is setting over the ancient hills. So much history, so much bloodshed. The Romans were here putting down revolts in Jerusalem two millennia ago, leaving ruins in Jordanian towns, crumbling forums and aqueducts. The Israelis and Palestinians fought along these winding roads three decades ago. There was a shooting in the West Bank just last week. The hills and valleys are burned orange, baked, worn down, beautiful. I pass Andi a bottle of water and I drink a Pepsi, and we fall asleep on the ride to Amman, back to the Four Seasons.

It's our last night together. I'm scheduled to take a flight from Amman to Baghdad on Sunday. Should I stay another day? Yes, I should, but I need to get back to work, back to Baghdad, that's the schedule, that's the plan, so I go.

Another goodbye. Fuck, this doesn't get easier.

Andi spends a few more days in Amman and then flies to D.C. via Paris to go to NDI's head office on K Street. We want to spend Christmas together—we're going to try.

Andi flies back to Baghdad on Christmas Eve; she is no longer in the Green Zone, though. NDI's compound is at the Ramal Hotel, in the Red Zone, which poses some serious difficulties. There is a security gulf between the two of us now. You can't just drive over whenever you want. I want her to come to the *Newsweek* bureau; we are having a Christmas party. Munib has decorated the house with pink and yellow balloons and purchased a three-foot-high plastic tree that you can plug in and it rotates. "Scott and I made eggnog," I tell her. "My laptop is playing Frank Sinatra Christmas carols, Baby, it's cold outside. Your friends from the U.S. embassy are going to be here." But for her to get to me, she has to get a security detail to bring her, and it's too short notice to arrange it. She just got to Baghdad that day, and again she's starting a new job, and taking a security detail for personal reasons is frowned upon. I have the same problem—whenever a *Newsweek* reporter leaves the Green Zone, we follow strict security procedures, whether we're going to the airport or to an interview, or in this case, to visit a girlfriend. For me to get to her, I need to have three cars of Iraqi guards, who have to know at least a day in advance that a trip is planned. The guards and driver have the day off, our security manager would also need to go with us, and we're still busy working on a cover story. So close to spending Christmas together! She's a ten-minute drive away, but there's no getting to her. It's too much of a risk to be together on Christmas this year, and so we text: Merry Christmas, Mog. Merry Christmas, Cub.

New Year's Eve is the same story. Andi has to stay in her compound; I have to stick around the bureau. Happy New Year, Cub. Happy New Year, Love.

Celebratory fire goes off around the city. The tracers light up the sky.

Andi sends me another text message, at 12:04 A.M.: baby I almost just got shot!

I call her, and she explains she heard a bullet whiz by her head.

She takes a picture of herself smiling and sends it to me.

I go out that night for a few hours. I tell her I tried to get into the CIA bar in the Green Zone—it's called Babble On or Babylon—but I don't get in, I'm not on the list. She asks if I am going to the BCC—the Baghdad Country Club, a white house with a lawn that's been converted to a bar and restaurant and is frequented by mercenaries and contractors. I tell her no, and instead I find myself in the back of a Pajaro sport utility vehicle with a drunk American official behind the wheel yelling, "Happy New Year. Let's go over the bridge and see some Iraqis!"

Pop, pop, pop, more gunfire in the air.

The year 2006 has come to an end. Thirty-six thousand dead Iraqis, 822 dead Americans, $50 billion gone. Bodies and dollars, bodies and dollars.

I go back to the bureau and we talk on the phone until 5 A.M. "I'll come to see you as soon as I can," I tell her.

CHAPTER 17

January 7-9, 2007

BAGHDAD

I plan a trip to visit Andi at the National Democratic Institute's compound in Karrada. To get there, I have to follow *Newsweek*'s security procedures. The planning started with X, our new security manager.

X, or the X-Man, as he likes to be called, used to be in the Special Forces. He's in his early forties now, with a goatee and silver and black hair. He did a tour in Iraq at the beginning of the war, and then went home and worked as a bouncer in a Nevada casino. That job ended, he tells me, because he beat up a man who was harassing a female customer at the casino. The beating was justified, he wants me to know that. But it was also caught on tape by the security cameras. The video was shown at his hearing; he was not allowed to continue his work as a security guard in Nevada after the incident. Earlier in his life, X had started a business as a bail bondsman, but it didn't last very long. X is divorced. He likes his job now. He likes being in Iraq. He has a white business card that says "X-Man"; he writes his Iraqna number on the back of the card.

X is the fifth Western security manager we've had in a year. It's been getting harder to find well-trained security professionals (or, as one of my colleagues referred to them, "well-trained psychopaths") to come to Iraq. My friends who work in the security business say quality control has slipped. At the beginning of the war, most of the guys were legitimate ex–Special Forces or veterans of other conflicts. But the demand for PSDs—private security details—remains high and the supply of qualified pros is low. Now companies are hiring guys who look the part of the mercenary—bouncers or retired cops or ex-soldiers from developing countries—but who don't have the training.

In October, *Newsweek* switched security companies to a firm called CTU (the name taken from the organization Jack Bauer works for in *24*). Our old security provider, the company Jack Tapes worked for, was too small to handle the magazine's growing needs. CTU was better established. They had a number of contracts with the military, including one to add extra armor to Iraqi Humvees, and they could provide *Newsweek* with the setup we preferred: a Western security guard to live with us at the house, whose responsibilities included planning trips and making the bureau safe by installing security cameras, sandbags, sniper screens, bunkers for the guards.

We plan the route to NDI the day before I'm supposed to go. X loads on his computer a Google satellite map of Baghdad, zooming in on the neighborhood, marking the path we'd take to get to Karrada. He looks at the attacks in the area over the past week; nothing significant nearby. During heavy traffic hours, the main road we'll be on has been hit by car bombs, but not recently. An okay neighborhood, relatively safe, and traffic shouldn't be that bad if we leave in the afternoon. When we get close to arriving, X will call NDI's security chief to let him know.

Thirty minutes before we are scheduled to leave, X-Man gives us the briefing. We go through standard operating procedures in the living room. If A happens, what do you do? If B happens, how do you react? What about C? When do you return fire? When do you keep going? What are the SOPs? The Iraqi guards, sitting on the couches in the living room, listen and answer the questions. Checkpoints—these are tricky. Do you stop at a checkpoint? If you get to a checkpoint and you think it might be illegal, you turn around if you can because there have been attacks and kidnappings at illegal checkpoints. But then it's also a risk to disobey legit Iraqi police. Best to try to avoid checkpoints, try to avoid the Iraqi Army and Iraqi police, and if worst comes to worst you drive through it, keep driving, don't stop. I sit there, trying to stay awake as he talks. X likes it when we sit in on the briefing; he prefers his client to know what's going on.

I'm bringing along two large black trunks full of Andi's stuff that she had left with IRI. Clothes and new supplies—a few crates of Ocean Spray cranberry juice, Pringles, microwave popcorn, peanut butter, jam, a new mug for tea. X, who picked up the supplies for me, even got a bottle of perfume. ("You should give this to her," he says, "give her this perfume." And then he tells me that his girlfriend, whom he told about the mission, thinks it is terribly romantic—to go through all of this because of love.)

It is the first free weekend for Andi and me since she came back to Baghdad. Andi was settling into her new job, and I was swamped with reporting. The two weeks after Christmas were extremely busy for news in Iraq; Saddam Hussein was executed on December 30.

Hussein was captured by the Americans in December 2003, and they had held him in custody at a U.S. base called Camp Cropper near the airport. In October 2005, he went on trial in a renovated courthouse in the Green Zone for "crimes against humanity," at a cost to the U.S. taxpayer of over $100 million. The first case against Saddam and eight other codefendants dragged out over ten months. Three of Saddam's defense attorneys were killed, another was seriously wounded and had to leave the country. The chief judge resigned in the middle of the trial, saying there was too much "political interference." Throughout, Saddam and his codefendants made a mockery of the trial, shouting insults at the judge ("daughter of a whore") and the Americans, sometimes refusing to show up in court, and other times getting thrown out by the judge. It made for good TV.

Print reporters covered the trial using a pool system, with news organizations sharing the responsibility of going to the courthouse and filing daily dispatches that everyone had access to. As the trial dragged on, it became a tedious duty—it was hard for the pool's organizer, the veteran journalist Larry Kaplow, to find reporters willing to go. Especially after Saddam was found guilty in the first of the cases against him (massacring 146 residents from the Shiite town of Dujaili), and the second case started (a genocidal campaign against Kurds in 1988 in the northern town of Anfal). It was a foregone conclusion that Saddam was going to get the death penalty, so the daily mechanics of the courtroom were only newsworthy when Saddam would go off on a tirade. And even that soon got old. The trial seemed like another bad joke. Amnesty International called it "deeply flawed" and "unfair."

I went to the courthouse once in October 2006. I was excited to be there. After seeing pictures of Saddam on television since I was ten years old, after writing about his country on a weekly basis, I would finally get to see the man in person—assuming he decided to show up. The morning of the trial, I joined the State Department official who was in charge of taking the media to the courthouse and a small group of other reporters at a bus near the Convention Center. The bus shuttled us to the courthouse, a new and heavily defended building, renovated just for the trial. Security was extra tight—no tape recorders, no metal at all, no notebooks or pens. Writing materials would be provided for us once we were inside. I walked up three floors to the media viewing chamber, which was like a darkened home theater, a few rows of seats in front of a large and thick bulletproof glass window looking into the courtroom. The red curtains on the window were drawn and they would be opened once the trial started. (They were often closed when events got out of hand in the courtroom.) I put on a headset to hear the translation.

The curtains opened.

Saddam walked in. There he was, in a dark suit and tie with a red handkerchief in the pocket, a thick gray beard. The tyrant, the man America had fought two wars against, the man who was once the most feared dictator in the Middle East, a man who'd ordered the executions of thousands. He took a seat fifteen feet away from me. He had the look of a depressed businessman, a former CEO in a corporate fraud case, resigned, circles under the eyes hinting at long nights in his cell, awake in disbelief: Could this really be happening to me? Could I have fallen this far?

I filed a pool report on the testimony of the day: Kurdish women describing how the town of Anfal was gassed with poison, how they barely escaped and their families were killed, disappeared. "Anfalized"— the new word used to describe it.

A month later, the court announced Saddam's penalty: death by hanging.

The only remaining question was when?

On December 26, the court denied Saddam's appeal and confirmed the sentence. On December 28, I got a phone call from a U.S. military source. "Keep your phone on Saturday morning," the source told me. On December 29, the "Saddam death watch" was in full effect—the cable news shows were giving it wall-to-wall coverage—but where he would be killed and at what time was still a secret. The best guess was Saturday morning, December 30, at first light.

Scott and I were up at 5:30 A.M. on Saturday, after only a few hours of sleep. We figured if the execution was going to happen, VIPs in the prime minister's office would be involved, and they lived in the Green Zone. There were also rumors that the execution might take place somewhere inside the zone. Scott suggested I drive around to see if anything was going on. X volunteered to drive, I rode shotgun.

We drove down to the Convention Center. Nothing. We drove past the parade ground at the Crossed Swords monument. It was deserted. We swung by the courthouse but didn't see a thing.

Since we were out, I suggested we might as well get some coffee at the Green Bean in the U.S. embassy. As we approached the embassy, I saw a long line of SUVs parked on the street outside of LZ Washington. At least thirty Iraqi guards stood by the cars, smoking. This was something.

X parked in the lot across from the LZ Washington. He went to the embassy to pick up coffee. I walked across the street to see what I could find out.

I offered a guard a cigarette. He took one.

"Saddam," I said, and pointed to the line of cars.

He smiled, and nodded. I chatted with a few more guards.

I returned to the car and got my coffee, then I called Scott and told him that we'd found the security detail to the prime minister's advisors and other court officials waiting at the helicopter pad. The guards were waiting for their bosses, those who'd gone to the execution, to return. Scott told me to stay put.

X and I waited in the car, warming up with caffeine. I heard helicopters, and then the guards started to move around, firing up the engines on the SUVs. As I walked back across the street, two helicopters landed inside LZ Washington.

The gates to the helicopter pad opened and about ten Iraqi men in suits came through. The guards rushed to meet them, and they all started shouting and jumping with excitement. One man was holding a camera phone up in the air, and the men flocked around him. Saddam was dead, Saddam was dead, Saddam was gone. They were hearing the news for the first time. Another man was holding a Sony HDTV camcorder. He was being congratulated by his friends. An Iraqi man pointed to the guy holding the camcorder: "He was the one who filmed the execution."

His name was Ali al-Massedy; he was the official videographer for Prime Minister Nouri al-Maliki. He had shot the official film of the dictator's death. I tried to get as many details as I could—what did he look like, what were Saddam's last words, what happened when he died? I scribbled notes. I was the only journalist there. I talked to him for five minutes before he got in an SUV and rushed off.

My adrenaline was high as I rushed back to the bureau.

I wrote the story in thirty minutes—I had just enough detail—and it went up on the website at around midnight New York time.

The story headline: "I SAW FEAR, HE WAS AFRAID."

It was an exclusive interview, and one of the first published accounts of Saddam's death. The story got a link on the Drudge Report. I was asked to do phone interviews with MSNBC, calling in on the satellite phone throughout the day.

But the scoop was fleeting. By noon, a small portion of the video Ali had shot was released to the press. It showed Saddam walking to the gallows, then the video froze right before he dropped to his death. There was no sound on the video. Iraqi officials who'd witnessed the execution said it was a dignified event. Mowfak Rubaie, Prime Minister al-Maliki's security advisor, told the BBC he was "very proud" of the hanging, that Saddam was given "respect" and it met "international standards."

By that afternoon, though, another video version of the event leaked out through an Arab TV channel. It was taken from a camera phone. (I suspected it was probably from the other guy the guards swarmed at the landing pad, but I didn't know who he was.)

The camera phone version was much more disturbing. It did not look like a respectable execution. There was sound, and you could hear the people assembled taunting Saddam. You got a good look at his execution-ers: two men in leather jackets wearing black ski masks. They looked like thugs. They looked like a death squad. After Saddam fell through the gal-lows, the unknown man holding the camera phone rushed in to get a closer look, while others in the chamber started to dance around the dictator's body.

The video didn't play well with the international media. The U.S. mil-itary tried to distance itself from the event, embarrassed by the lynch-moblike display. The U.S. had captured Saddam, paid for and orchestrated his trial, kept him safe in jail, and now their triumph had ended in humiliation. The military did not respond to questions about the execution that day. Finally, at a press conference a few days later, the U.S. military spokesperson said the Americans played "no role" in the exe-cution. That was a lie. The U.S. had brought Saddam to Camp Justice (a joint U.S.-Iraqi base in Baghdad where the gallows were located), handed him over to Iraqi custody, and flown twenty Iraqi officials to wit-ness the execution. When the execution was completed, the U.S. flew the top officials back to the Green Zone, along with Saddam's body. Techni-cally, the Americans turned custody of Saddam over at 5:30 A.M.; the exe-cution took place at 6:05. And what had happened in those thirty-five minutes? What happened after Saddam was turned over completely to the new Iraqi government? It was time for insults and old-fashioned revenge. One executioner taunted Saddam: "Moqtada, Moqtada, Moqtada." Another told him to go to hell. At least two witnesses filmed it with their camera phones. I saw it as a window into the new Shiite government—given the responsibility of executing Saddam, a longtime enemy, they fucked it up. They made a spectacle of themselves. They somehow made Saddam appear dignified, while they looked like a bunch of crim-inals in black ski masks and leather jackets. This was the new face of Iraq.

This was "an important milestone on Iraq's course to becoming a democracy," as Bush would say in a statement on the day of the execution. The democratic course of the new Iraqi government: executioners in hoods and officials with camera phones and bloodlust. It reinforced the worst fears of many Iraqis, especially in the Sunni community, that while one evil found his fate another was eclipsing the future.

The reporting pace didn't slow up. The next week Scott and I worked on a story called "How the U.S. Is Losing the PR War." We pegged the story to an exclusive draft memo we'd obtained, written by the director of strategic communications for the U.S. mission in Iraq, that outlined a media strategy for the military and the embassy: "Without popular support from US population, there is the risk that troops will be pulled back . . . Thus there is a vital need to save popular support via message." "Insurgents, sectarian elements, and others are taking control of the message at the public level."

The heart of the military's public relations campaign was located in a parking garage behind the Iraqi parliament. At the end of 2005, the parking garage had been converted into the headquarters for the Combined Press Information Center, or CPIC, pronounced "See-Pic." The building was called, rather misleadingly, Ocean Cliffs. Inside Ocean Cliffs, CPIC held weekly press conferences, or "operational updates," in a carpeted room with TV monitors and a large screen for slide shows. The format for the press conferences had just changed. For four years, the U.S. military spokesman had stood behind an official-looking wooden podium. Now, as part of the military's new strategy to influence the press, the spokesman, Major General William Caldwell, would sit at the head of a "media roundtable." More friendly, more approachable.

I'd go to the press conferences each week if I was free. It was always good to get the military's official line. The spokesman would dutifully explain how the U.S. was making progress and how the Iraqis were taking the lead. We'd get new slogans—2006 was "The Year of the Police"; 2007 was "The Year of Transition and Adaptation." We'd hear talking points like: "the majority of Iraq's violence is in only four provinces," meaning Iraq's other fourteen provinces were not so violent. Sounds impressive, until one considers that the majority of Iraq's population lives in those four provinces.

There were times when only a handful of journalists would show up, outnumbered in the briefing room by public affairs officers and the civilian media advisors. At one press conference in the spring of 2006, as the country descended into civil war, only two journalists attended.

A constant stream of press releases was also meant to spread the message. I'd get at least ten a day from CPIC, sometimes as many as twenty. Only a fraction were informative—mainly those that listed attacks against Americans. The subject line on the email would read something like "MND-B Soldier targeted during combat operations," and the body of the email would contain about three paragraphs. The first would explain the kind of attack and give the general location (west of Baghdad, north of Baghdad, etc.); the second paragraph would inform you of the point of the mission, and justify it ("Units operating in this area of Iraq continue to conduct targeted raid and clearing operations . . . Destroying these cells reduces overall sectarian violence and helps set the conditions for the improvement of essential services, economic growth and aids in the transition of Iraqi-led security operations"); then the third paragraph would read: "The Soldier's name is being withheld pending notification of next of kin and release by the Department of Defense." Almost every day I would receive emails from the Department of Defense, reading "DoD Identifies Army Casualties" (or marine casualties); and there would be a few lines with the soldier's name, his rank, his unit, where he was based, and a phone number at the bottom listing a number to call for more information.

The press releases were written with a stilted, half-literate mix of military lingo and public relations spin. "Foreign fighter facilitators nabbed." "Two AQI with SVESTS Killed." "Soldiers keep route clearance vehicle going." Operation Geronimo Strike III. Operation Bastogne. Operation Arrowhead Ripper. Hundreds of the releases focused on weapons caches: "Desert Rogues find two weapons caches." The caches were a way for the military to keep score, along with the body count—look how many mortars and AK-47s we found today!—but in a country teeming with firearms and explosives, the notion that the finds could possibly make a dent in the overall level of violence seemed absurd.

The public affairs officers would spend hours writing the press releases, hours reviewing them, hours finding pictures to go along with them. As the months went on and the situation did not improve, the press releases seemed to become more cheerful, more detached from reality, dispatches from a la-la land of their own.

My favorite: "Polar Bears storm Quarghuli Village by air, land and water." This release described a unit nicknamed the Polar Bears whose mission was to clear insurgents from the town of Quarghuli, using boats. The press release included the following line and quote from a soldier involved in the operation: "The Polar Bears chose to launch Operation Polar Valor on Dec. 7, the anniversary of Pearl Harbor. 'We try to pick days that the enemy knows are holidays to the Americans,' Griggs said. 'It is during those times that the enemy is less likely to think we are going to do anything.'"

I read it and thought: Pearl Harbor is not a holiday, and I seriously doubt that any insurgent in Iraq would have it marked on their calendar.

Strange doublespeak would creep in. When the U.S. military announced a new strategy of building walls around neighborhoods in Baghdad—to keep the bad guys in, or the bad guys out—the release I received read: "Paratroopers create gated community in Adhamiya." It began: CAMP TAJI, Iraq—"According to an old proverb, good fences make good neighbors. Paratroopers from the 82nd Airborne are putting that idea to the test in Baghdad's Adhamiya district by building a three mile protective wall on the dividing line between a Sunni enclave and the surrounding Shiite neighborhood." "Gated community"—a term that originated to describe wealthy suburban residential complexes in the United States.

"Why can't we get our message out there?" a U.S. government media consultant once asked me. "How can we compete with car bombs? It's not fair."

The answer: Stop the car bombs.

"Why won't you report the good news?" U.S. military officers and right-wing critics would constantly ask us.

The answer: Actually, we don't even come close to reporting all the bad news. There's too much of it.

Our enemies, on the other hand, had the PR war down; the insurgents weren't having a problem getting their message out there. There was a popular new satellite TV station, Iraqi run, called Al-Zawra. It was a snuff channel. Snuff films, 24/7.

Those being snuffed out were Americans. The Humvee drives along—boom—an IED hits. The crosshairs focus on a soldier—bang. Two Humvees pass over the bomb, the third doesn't. A body flies in the air.

All day long, seven days a week, Americans getting blown up. The channel was run by a former member of the Iraqi government, a politician named Mishaan al-Jabouri, who had come in with the American invasion in 2003. His channel now "fomented sectarian violence," as the military would say. (On Al-Zawra the Shiites were called dogs, and worse, Persians, and it went without saying that all Shiites were part of a plot hatched in Iran to take over the country.) The channel had a soundtrack of patriotic Iraqi songs from Saddam's era.

It was hypnotic and eerie and popular among Iraqis. Our staff liked the channel. Our Iraqi stringer in Najaf said even Shiites in the south thought the channel was great—despite its being anti-Shiite—because everyone loved to watch Americans get blown up.

Al-Zawra was allegedly being broadcast from a mobile TV van somewhere inside Iraq, and was being hosted by an Egyptian satellite TV company called Nile Sat.

The Americans weren't doing much about it—free speech and all, a U.S. military spokesperson told me. Free speech?

The U.S. and Iraqi governments talked of negotiations, talked of progress, talked of ending the violence—but the talk was not real. Just turn on the TV. Have a look at Al-Zawra. This was progress. Satellite dishes were banned during Saddam's time, but as soon as he fell, they sprouted up across the capital and the country, as popular as cell phones and air conditioners. Al-Zawra was a hit in cafés, in homes, on the street.

You can actually see the body. You can see his legs fly up, damn, must be ten feet high.

I watched Al-Zawra with my interpreter. We kept the channel on in the bureau office for a few days, until we couldn't watch it anymore. There was a video of a man being tortured, interrogated, bloodied—an Iraqi man, a Shiite, confessing to some kind of conspiracy to blow up other Shiites. Insurgents filmed their attacks, and sent them to the network. Death by IED. Death by VBIED. Death by SBVIED. By ambush. By pressure-activated mines. By remote-control-activated mines. By trip wires. By EFPs. The videos could also be found on the Internet; they could be purchased on DVDs at the local market; this was on TV. And no one seemed to give a shit. It wasn't that big of a deal.

On Saturday, January 6, we close the public relations story. I'm now free to go see Andi at the NDI compound. Scott is leaving Iraq the following week. After twenty-two months, he's handing over his responsibilities to the new bureau chief, Babak Dehghanpisheh. With both Babak and Scott at the bureau for now, it's not a problem for me to take the weekend off.

The Iraqi guards wait out in the bureau parking lot at the side of the house. They each have an AK-47 and two clips of ammunition. Two have pistols. The engines are humming on the three cars we are going to take. The tail car and the lead car are both nondescript Chevrolet sedans. I'll be riding in the client vehicle, the Mercedes armored car.

X wants me to practice the drills before we leave. It's only my third trip out into the Red Zone with him and he wants us to run through a mock incident.

Okay, Mike, if the car is disabled, here's what you're going to do.

I act it out, with my body armor on. The other car pulls up at an angle, creating a V-shape. I open the armored door, using it as cover. I keep my head down. Uday puts his hand on my shoulder and pushes me into the car that isn't broken. Ammad gives covering fire over the hood. Head down, pretending the bullets are flying, I transfer safely into the follow car, the whole time thinking, Jesus, if this was real, we're totally fucked.

Going to see Andi was a risk that had to be weighed carefully. It wasn't just my life I was risking—that would be fine—it was X's life (but

X loved this kind of shit) and it was the lives of the guards, too, who'd be killed if anything happened. Three drivers and four guards in total: seven lives for me to visit her. Babak and Scott signed off on it, though. It was a relatively safe area, they figured—relative to the fact that nowhere was really safe—and you had to stay sane here, and staying sane meant seeing your significant other if you had one. I wanted to see her badly, but I knew if anything did happen there would be questions. Still, I wanted to see her, and she wanted to see me, and it would probably be fine. Most of the time it's fine, right?

Until it's not.

The lead car leaves the driveway. A minute later my car follows, then the third car. I sit in the backseat. We reach the checkpoint to leave the Green Zone and I take off the ID that I carry around my neck and put it in my pocket. No more need for these IDs, not once you leave the Green Zone, not once you leave the pocket of rules and regulations and law and order.

X has his sunglasses on. The car is silent. I button my jacket, exhale, and slouch down in the backseat, my face partially protected from view by a flimsy dark sunscreen pulled down over the window.

I look at the sniper screens on the side of the two-lane road, sheet metal built up along the guard rails to prevent potshots from insurgents. A convoy of Iraqi police flies by, firing in the air. I remember what Ahmer told me, that despite the resentment toward Americans, most Iraqis would rather see an American convoy than an Iraqi convoy. After Abu Ghraib and everything else, an Iraqi would much prefer to be detained by the Americans than by the Iraqi security forces. The Americans most likely wouldn't execute you; the Americans didn't really torture, or at least they probably wouldn't torture you like an Iraqi would; the Americans would probably let you go, eventually; the Iraqi security forces on the other hand—shit, you were likely to be done for, disappeared.

I don't see any other Americans around. This is only the third time in the last month I've left the zone without a military escort, and I have the odd sensation of being the only unarmed Westerner driving through Baghdad.

X phones NDI. "We're coming in," he says.

We make our way down Karrada Street. NDI has decided to keep its main office in the Red Zone because, as a nonprofit organization with humanitarian aims, it doesn't want to be seen as part of the occupation. It also makes it easier for the Iraqis they're working with to visit the compound; no special privileges or badges are needed.

"Mike, I don't want you getting out of the car until we know it's clear; I don't want you standing around, even in the compound; once we make sure it's clear, once the hotel is okay, then you can."

I nod, though I think he's being a little paranoid.

The NDI guards open one gate, check our car, then open another gate. We drive into a small street—a hotel on each side—that seems like a quiet cul-de-sac, its own separate world. Andi pops out from behind a blast wall protecting her hotel, the Ramal. Our car backs into a parking spot.

I wait a few seconds then get out, take my body armor off, and go over to see Andi. We stand there being watched by my security contingent and hers, and we can't shake the somewhat self-conscious feeling that this is something of an event, me coming to see her.

My guards carry her two trunks and prop them up against the blast wall.

"We need to have those trunks checked," an NDI security man says, seemingly annoyed. "Why didn't anyone tell us about those trunks?"

X actually had told them we would have substantial luggage, but somewhere there was miscommunication.

I tell X goodbye and wave to my guards, who are standing around the Chevy. I'll call them in the morning.

"This is quite the spectacle, hunh? Always a production."

"Let's get inside," Andi says. I can tell she's embarrassed by all the fuss we've caused. Three cars. Eight guards standing around. Two black trunks, now being sniffed by guard dogs.

We walk up to her room on the fourth floor, and finally, once we're behind the closed door, we embrace. She's been five miles away from me, but I haven't seen her in person since Amman, almost a month earlier.

One of NDI's security managers, dragging the trunks behind him, plods down the hallway to Andi's room.

"Oh, no, this is so bad," she says.

"What?"

"They brought up the trunks! We should have done that! They're going to think I'm high maintenance!"

"Well, you are!"

"What! Take that back!"

"I'm kidding."

She opens the trunks and I hand her another bag of supplies.

"No cookies?"

Fuck, I forgot the cookies. She didn't ask for cookies, but I knew she would want them and I forgot to pick them up at the PX.

"I got you chips and jam and peanut butter and Ocean Spray!" I say. "It's huckleberry jam!"

"Why did you get huckleberry jam?" She thinks for a second. "Wait, didn't you get this for Christmas? Didn't your parents send you huckleberry jam and pancake mix?"

"Well, I'm giving it to you!"

"You're regifting!"

We wait for things to calm down outside, for X and my security convoy to leave the compound. I plug in my cell phone chargers and settle in.

"This is a pretty nice room. You finally got your wish, you're living in a hotel."

"I had them take out one of the beds, for my yoga mat."

"Hah."

I hand her a stack of DVDs.

"Here you go, these are for you."

She looks through them: *Black Dahlia, Borat, Casino Royale,* and other new releases.

"Did you get *Babel*?"

Babel. We'd tried to watch it together in Jerusalem, but the bootleg copy was so bad we stopped.

"No, I couldn't find it at the Rashid."

"Did you actually look for it?"

Hmm. A trick question. I actually hadn't looked for it. I'd picked up the DVDs from the bureau's collection.

"Of course I looked for it!"

"You're lying, I can tell."

I sighed and lay down on the bed.

"You're right—I didn't look for *Babel*. I don't want to see that movie! What we did see of it was kind of depressing."

"Selfish!"

We make love. We order room service. French fries, chicken tikka, hummus, coffee, tea. We decide to watch a movie on the laptop. We start with *Little Miss Sunshine*—"I knew you'd like this one," I say—but she's already seen it. Then we try *Blood Diamond*, but the copy is in horrible condition; you can't really make out what DiCaprio is saying, and the frame has an odd distorted shape to it. We lie down on the single bed. I twirl her hair.

"You're going to have to send me another pregnancy test," she says.

"Baby, you always think you're pregnant. I've gotten you like five of those tests."

"Well, it's your fault."

"Okay, okay, I'll get the test for you."

She pauses. I can feel a trick question coming.

"If I was pregnant and giving birth to our child would you leave work to come see me?"

"Yes, I would leave work to come see you."

"You wouldn't file first?"

"No, I would not file first."

"Okay. Just checking."

We talk more—about Iraq, about the projects she's been working on, about the friends she's making at NDI, about how she's adjusting to being back in Baghdad, about my story on Saddam, about *Newsweek*'s Palestinian fixer, Nuha, whom we had spent time with in Jerusalem. Andi tells me she likes the idea of working in Jerusalem. We discuss our next vacation—I've made reservations in Paris for Valentine's Day. We were aiming for that date, hoping we could both get out at the same time. We drift off to sleep.

At around 7 A.M. a loud explosion wakes me.

Andi opens her eyes.

"Did you hear that?" I ask.

"Yes, every morning."

"You can hear the booms pretty good from here."

We order coffee. I pack up my gear. X calls. They're on their way. We embrace for a long time, for minutes, it seems, and then we walk downstairs and wait. She says hello to the hotel workers.

X pulls up with the same cars and guards, and I leave Andi at the compound.

At 11 A.M., I'm on a quick helicopter flight with a handful of other journalists out to Camp Victory near the airport, to witness a TOA, pronounced "Toe-Ah," a transfer of authority ceremony. Lieutenant General Ray Ordierno is taking over daily operations in Iraq from Lieutenant General Peter Chiarelli. It marks the completion of Chiarelli's second Iraq tour. There are a lot of flags and a band, lots of saluting. The military loves their uniforms and flags and salutes. Chiarelli, along with his superior, General George Casey, has presided over a year in Iraq in which the violence has spiraled completely out of control. The attempt to restore security to Baghdad during the summer and fall has failed.

In his farewell address, Chiarelli quotes Teddy Roosevelt: "It is not the critic who counts; not the man who points out how the strong man stumbles or whether the doer of deeds could have done them better. The credit belongs to the man in the arena, whose face is marred by dust . . . who errs and comes short again and again . . . who at the best knows in the end the triumph of high achievement and who at the worst, if he fails, at least he fails while daring greatly . . ."

As he speaks, you can hear gunfire and helicopters in the distance.

Chiarelli said he and General Casey had often discussed that quote. I try to figure out if any of the two hundred or so soldiers in the crowd, or any of the other journalists at the ceremony, notice this remark.

This was our military's attitude behind our Iraq policy? It's better to have tried and failed daringly than not to have tried at all? Maybe if you're playing football, but in war?

I fly back to the Green Zone and look up the Roosevelt quote on the Internet. It was a speech he'd given at the Sorbonne, in 1910, called "Citizen of the Republic." He delivered it two years after he'd left the White House. It was a complex, nuanced treatise on his views on citizenship. The passage Chiarelli quoted didn't quite apply to TR's views on war.

I speak to Andi that night. "Baby, you should have heard what he said—better to have tried and failed?"

Andi sends me an email Sunday night. "Just wanted to thank you for coming to visit me and risking your life to do it! I want there to be a time when we welcome each other home after work and kiss each other goodbye before work. Do you think we'll ever have that?"

CHAPTER 18

January 11-16, 2007

BAGHDAD

Andi came over to the bureau Thursday at noon. She had had a meeting with an Iraqi politician at the parliament in the morning, then her security guards dropped her off at the house. We wouldn't have much time together. I was scheduled to go on embed that afternoon to cover a battle that had broken out on Haifa Street, a main avenue in walking distance of the Green Zone.

I'd first heard about the fighting over the weekend, and by Tuesday Apache attack helicopters were flying overhead, F-15 fighter jets thundering above. If you went on a drive to the edge of Green Zone, you could hear the steady shots from rifles and heavy machine guns. The battle picked up, and so did the body count. No Americans killed yet, but eleven soldiers from the Iraqi Army and a reported fifty insurgents were dead. I requested an embed with a unit that was involved in the fighting. I wanted to get to Haifa Street, what was being called "an insurgent stronghold." It took two days to process the request.

Andi and I were sitting at my desk in the bureau. Everything was going well until I was about to leave her alone in the office to get her tea. I got worried she would check my email on the screen of my computer.

"I have to close my email account . . ."

"Why, what are you hiding?"

"Nothing. But I know if you see the name of any girl you'll get upset."

She didn't like this. I started in on a series of apologies that lasted for about fifteen minutes before we went to my bedroom.

This time she forgave me quickly. She seemed to have gotten upset only because that was what was expected, the role we were so used to having her play. I say something stupid, or do something stupid, she gets angry at me, I beg and apologize, tell her she is the love of my life, and we make up.

We lay down for about an hour or so. We didn't have sex. It was the middle of the day, and she didn't want the other correspondent in the house or any of the security guards to get the wrong idea. There wasn't much privacy anyway. My bedroom window looked out to a lot on the side of the house where we parked our cars and the guards roamed. So we held each other on the bed and talked. I was sick, too, running a fever and coughing. She put her head on my shoulder. I had a radio interview to do at two o'clock. Andi sat on the bed as I talked about the war over a satellite phone to a radio station in New York, the *Armstrong Williams Radio Show*. Heavy fighting, I told the host, open fighting in the streets.

She had to go back to her compound before it got too late. I walked her to the house gate, where her private security guard, a Fijian, was waiting for her in an SUV. I hugged her before we opened the gate, and kissed her lightly. Once we were in public, I knew a display of affection would make her uncomfortable. It was one of her quirks, she liked her privacy. She got in the car and I watched it disappear down the street.

I went back inside to pack for my thirteenth embed. Body armor, blue, with O POSITIVE blood type written on silver masking tape, weight about ten pounds. Two plates front and back. Can stop a 7.62 round, with the material along the sides able to repulse a 9mm bullet. Helmet, black and scratched, big enough for my head, the one I always used. The helmet had been to Najaf, Fallujah, and Mosul. Wiley X Ballistic eye protection. Two mobile phones: my Iraqna and my international cell phone, a T-Mobile, with a 212 New York area code, running a three-dollar-a-minute roaming charge for an average monthly bill of about $5,000. A Thuraya satellite phone, a long string of numbers starting with +863 to be used in case the Iraqi network went down. I packed my Sony Vaio laptop that I never cleaned, which still had dust on it from Najaf, and a BGAN satellite modem. There was a subscription fee and charges based on data transferred. The record in one month for the bureau was $30,000 for thirty days of uninterrupted use. A blue Ethernet cord for the BGAN. A Sony digital camera, seven megapixels with video function. Power chargers and cords for everything—laptop, mobile phones, sat phone, BGAN, camera. A cheap power bar imported from China. A silver and red sleeping bag, a towel, cleanup kit. Tylenol, high-powered decongestion bought earlier from an Iraqi drugstore, the antibiotic Cipro given to me by Andi, and a rubber tourniquet my security manager had handed to me to stop massive blood loss in case of injury. A pair of Old Navy khakis with lots of pockets, a pair of jeans, a sweater. A Motorola radio to communicate with the *Newsweek* bureau. Lightweight hiking boots, which I had bought eighteen months earlier in New York, while shopping with Andi, on the recommendation of a salesman who had been in Iraq for the invasion with the 82nd Airborne Division. You want these for the desert, he said. Two packs of cigarettes, Marlboro Lights. Lighter. Two packs of Wrigley's Extra Professional chewing gum, the brand sold in the Amman, Jordan, airport duty-free shop. Sony digital tape recorder with USB connector, twelve hours of recording time, two fresh notebooks and three notebooks filled up with information from other stories I might have to respond to while away from the bureau. Five pens, stuffed in pockets. Wallet, about two hundred U.S. dollars. Flashlight. Identification, two pieces, one military press ID issued CPIC. One gigabyte thumb drive. All packed into my black Victornox laptop bag and a silver Welty hiking pack, a gift from Andi a year earlier. Together, the bags weighed about thirty-five pounds. I set the bags next to each other in the living room, resting the body armor and helmet up against them, and told my security manager I was ready to be dropped off near the Iraqi parliament building for a pickup by the public affairs officer for the 2nd Brigade, 1st Cavalry.

It is January 2007, three and half years into the war. At this moment, there are over 120,000 soldiers stationed in Iraq, close to 14,000 in Baghdad. Over 3,000 American military personnel have been killed since the invasion; the previous months had been among the most deadly—112 killed in December, 70 in November, and 106 in October. Estimates vary on the number of Iraqi civilians killed, ranging from 50,000 to over

100,000. According to the U.S. Department of Labor, 771 foreign civilian contractors have been killed in Iraq. Ninety-five journalists and thirty-seven members of their staffs have been killed. At least 80 aid workers—working for international relief organizations, the United Nations, and NGOs—have been killed. Another 20,000 U.S. troops are on the way as part of the latest security offensive to secure the capital city of Baghdad, home to 8 million Iraqis. It is being dubbed the start of "the surge," of which Haifa Street is a part, a "last-ditch" attempt to "win," another "turning point" in a war that I'd seen go in only one direction, down.

I am on the embed.

We drive to Forward Operating Base Prosperity, inside the Green Zone. I am introduced to an American advisory team, the unit that was in the first fight on Haifa Street a week earlier. Their headquarters is in a guest residence in one of Saddam's palace complexes. I meet Lieutenant Colonel Steven Duke, a forty-two-year-old from Tennessee with a bald head and blue eyes. He asks what I want to talk about. Haifa Street, I say. He laughs along with his men, a kind of absurd laugh. Like of course, what else would I want to know about except the fight.

He sips a coffee standing in front of a map of Baghdad and indicates his "AO," or area of operations, which until recently, he tells me, included Haifa Street. No longer, he says.

I am somewhat disappointed but don't say anything. I wanted to get to the unit that was fighting now, getting shot at now, patrolling that street now, but as often happens with the military, you never get exactly what you request. But then he starts talking. He says his unit commander, a patriotic Sunni general, was removed by people in the prime minister's office and replaced by a Shiite commander only twenty-four hours after the fighting started.

This is news.

I know instantly that this is the story. The Haifa Street operation was being called a model for how the war was now going to be fought, and the new model had come with promises that there wouldn't be sectarian and political interference from the Shiite government—that the prime minister wouldn't care if a policeman, a soldier, or a citizen was a Sunni or Shiite, only that he or she was an Iraqi.

Already it appeared the Iraqi government was going back on its promise.

Lieutenant Colonel Duke tells me about the fight. It started over twenty-seven dead bodies. The twenty-seven were found executed, all members of the family of a local Iraqi police chief. The men, women, children, and teenage boys had been dumped in an empty lot. Duke's unit tried to remove them from the lot. Everyone else—the Iraqi police, the locals, the Iraqi Army—was too afraid to touch them.

The fighting starts, a "big shitfight," Duke calls it. I see the digital pictures tacked up on the wall—the insurgents with sandbagged positions in the alleyways, the vacant lot with the dead bodies, a new kind of armor-piercing round they discovered that can penetrate the armor on the Humvees.

He starts saying things that I have never heard said so bluntly—what observers and critics and analysts have worried about, what those in the military have been privately thinking, what I assumed was happening, but that he, an active duty lieutenant colonel in Baghdad, is saying on the record. (Sometimes reporting is finding out what you don't know, sometimes it's hearing something said that everyone knows, but that no one has had the guts to say, because they aren't supposed to say it.)

"I get it," he says, talking about the battle and the crack of bullets and having soldiers killed. "I get it, okay? I've been here three months now, and I get it, I understand, that's enough for me, no need to stay for the other nine." He laughs.

Duke says he thinks the Shiite Iraqi government wants the Americans to move out of the cities so they can "pull back the red curtain, do their business, and say, you guys don't need to see this." That business is killing Sunnis. Eliminating them. Ethnic cleansing, or as an Iraqi politician called it a few days earlier, "sectarian cleansing." Every war gets new words to describe it, new and improved terminology, though in practical terms not very much changes. One group killing the other. Block by block, street by street, bedroom by bedroom. Name by name. At midnight or in broad daylight, it doesn't matter. Us versus them, so we better get them before they get us.

Duke says he thinks we're doing the Shiite militias' work for them, that they are "sitting on the fifty-yard line, eating popcorn," while we go after the Sunnis. If I was a Sunni, he says, I would feel fairly besieged. He points to the map of the Green Zone and notes that it is now surrounded by Ministry of Interior forces and Iraqi police, who all likely have militia affiliations. The less sectarian-minded Iraqi Army unit, the nearest to the Green Zone at least, is undermanned and underequipped.

What the fuck is this shit? I've seen it and heard it all before. Death squads. Shots to the head. Drill to the kneecaps. Mass graves and body dumps and bullshit. I've spent a year and half writing about it, quoting numbers from official reports—one hundred dead Iraqis per day says the U.N.; 2.2 American soldiers killed a day, according to the DoD. The statistics keep saying the same thing but nothing gets better.

"If you looked at a map of South Vietnam and Saigon in late 1967," Duke says, "you would have seen that the city was surrounded by Vietcong." Nobody saw it, he says, only in hindsight did the pattern become clear. Why did no one see that coming? "Look at this map. The Green Zone is surrounded and no one sees it. The Green Zone could be overrun. It's just my conspiracy theory," he says.

"Our enemies are attacking us with impunity," he points out. "We got rocketed the other day—knocked me on my ass. We know where the rockets are coming from, our antiartillery technology tells us, but we don't do anything about it. We didn't respond. Not allowed to."

Duke also tells me about the mission I was supposed to go on tomorrow. A raid with American and Iraqi forces. It has been canceled. Why is that? The raid appeared to have sectarian motivations. Duke's soldiers suspect the new Shiite commander is targeting the office of a Sunni political party without evidence. Well, there is some evidence the Shiite commander has pointed to, but it's fairly inconclusive—an Iraqi patrol was fired on by men who fled in the general direction of that office. The new Iraqi commander has intentionally kept the Americans out of the loop. They are planning the mission on their own, "taking the lead," as the military likes to say. Duke suspects the lead they are taking involves illegal detentions and executions, perhaps some torture. One soldier jokes about it bluntly: "If it's raining tomorrow, they'll probably cancel it themselves. Who likes to commit a war crime in the rain?"

I know that the canceled mission does not matter at all. One mission cannot make a difference. So how many more missions and patrols would it take to make a difference? Is there a number? Does anyone know it? How many missions have been done already? Tens of thousands? And what a difference they have fucking made! Why go out at all? You can make as much of a difference by doing nothing, right?

I have a cot to sleep on under the map at Duke's headquarters. The map is a satellite printout of Baghdad, all grids and multicolored lines showing the main routes, each part of the city divided by unit. I am still feverish and sick. I make a phone call to the bureau chief, Babak. I smoke cigarettes with the soldiers. I talk to an officer who also has a girlfriend stationed in Baghdad, a nurse at a medical unit whom he sees about once a month for a few hours. We commiserate on the difficulties of relationships in Baghdad.

It's all about logistics. We're all under stress. It's not easy. The officer says he tries to get missions where he has an excuse to take a helicopter to her base, but she has more opportunities to come to the Green Zone. Same here, I say, it's easier for her to come see me than the other way around.

I call Andi. The conversation is pleasant. She is happy.

After two weeks readjusting to Baghdad and her new job, she is making friends. She tells me about a girl named Anne; another blond from the Midwest, also dating a reporter, who shares Andi's interests in spirituality. Magic stones and whatnot. I smile when I hear this. She is excited because she ran into a reporter from *The New Yorker*, George Packer, in the lobby of her hotel compound. She says she wished I could have been there, because she knows how much I like his work. Packer had supported the war in the beginning, but his reporting had shown what a mistake it had been.

"Who runs into George Packer in Baghdad?" she asks.

"I suppose that is the place to run into him," I say.

I have to go. She says she's going to talk to Anne and her new friends. I smoke more cigarettes. I call back a half hour later and we talk again.

She is happy. I am happy she is happy.

The next morning I go out on a patrol with Lieutenant Xeon Simpson, a soft-spoken black kid from the Bronx. He's twenty-four years old; graduated from Fordham. I hook up with him at the Muthanna Airfield, in the vicinity of Haifa Street, where his team works with an Iraqi Army company.

It is raining and muddy. All the buildings are cold, the same Iraqi industrial-style buildings with small offices, all with beds and ashtrays for officers, spotty electricity, and the occasional overflowing toilet. The white squat kind, a black hole in between two muddy grooves for your feet.

There are gray pillars looming in the fog on the base, hundreds of them with metal poles sticking upright, the leftovers of a mosque that Saddam Hussein wanted to construct. The ruins appear not to have been touched since the first bombs started to fall on the city almost four years earlier.

I am pushing to get to Haifa Street, and I am promised that Simpson's platoon will take me there. We drive in a three-Humvee convoy through the neighborhoods around Haifa Street. We stop outside the Karkh Children's Teaching Hospital. We are warned about a sniper who killed a man there earlier in the week. He was sitting across the street on the top floor of a school.

The platoon leader demands that the hospital guards take down a poster supporting Moqtada al-Sadr, the popular Shiite militia and religious leader whose father was killed by Saddam. I take pictures. How to describe all this, I think to myself, and all I come up with is:

It looks like Baghdad.

The ink on my notebook runs in the rain. Al-Sadr propaganda is everywhere. He always gets described as an anti-American cleric, though that doesn't do him justice; his Mehdi Army has killed Americans; his Medhi Army fires rockets into the Green Zone with impunity; his Mehdi Army is now part of the new Iraqi government, a cornerstone.

The hospital guard refuses at first, saying he is being watched and he will be killed if he takes the poster down.

"Being watched by who?" the young lieutenant asks. "I thought you didn't know who hung up the poster?"

The guard shrugs and finally takes the poster down.

The patrol continues.

It's Friday, the Muslim day of prayer, so there is a curfew and the streets are clear. The curfew is to keep young men from causing trouble after they go to the mosques; "Fighting Friday's," the soldiers call them. An hour passes, and we start heading back to the Muthanna base. We haven't gone to Haifa Street. I don't say anything, though I am nervous I won't get the story I wanted. Simpson, sitting in front of me in the Humvee, reads my mind.

"I'm not comfortable with bringing my men to Haifa Street right now," he says.

It's not in his AO and he doesn't know the area.

"Maybe the major can bring you when he takes you back to the Green Zone?"

Five minutes later, we return to the base. As if on cue, machine-gun fire starts. Loud. Nearby. Just over the blast walls of the compound. All coming from Haifa Street. It doesn't stop. We move behind the Humvees. Insurgents regularly fire over the walls at the base, aiming at anything, including the power generators ten feet away.

We all laugh, me and the soldiers, thinking that had we gone to Haifa Street those machine guns would have been trained on us.

That night, I file a story for the website about the patrol, using a computer in Duke's headquarters. I answer emails from my editors in New York about the cover story we are working on, called "The Next Jihadists," about Iraq's lost and disfigured youth growing up on revenge, death, and hatred. I get a call from *Newsweek*'s foreign affairs columnist and international editor, Fareed Zakaria, who has seen my email advisory about what Duke told me. He says he'd like to use some of the material in his column. I say no problem, and send a file with Duke's quotes to him. I tell Fareed I tried to get down to Haifa Street, but could only get so close. He reminds me to stay safe: "Hastings, you got ninety percent of the story, don't get killed trying to get the other ten percent."

I text Andi. I can't talk because I am on deadline.

I am up until 3 or 4 A.M. answering emails. I am nervous because I want to stay another day, and the story will be up on the website. If the unit doesn't like what they read, they'll get angry and stop talking. I'm anxious about this all the next day, when I go out on patrol again. It is uneventful. Rainy still. One neighborhood after the other with another young lieutenant, who happens to know my younger brother, Jeff. He went to officer candidate school with him.

We check on things like winter clothing for the Iraqi soldiers, if a space heater is working right, do they have enough bullets, have they received orders for the upcoming operation. You need to find a good patrol base. You need to figure out how to get food there. Bathrooms. Blast walls. The nuts and bolts of war, the unglamorous day-to-day work.

We go out on patrol to talk to the residents of Baghdad. To get "atmospherics," what the people are feeling, the intangibles.

The residents we talk to in each neighborhood all say basically the same thing. It is dangerous, yes.

This is the same response I've heard on nearly every patrol I have been on with Americans in Iraq when they "engage the local population."

Where does the danger come from?

The danger comes from over there, the other neighborhood, other people, other countries.

We are not involved in anything, it is someone else.

There are no militia members here. There are no insurgents here.

There are conspiracies.

There are outsiders, strangers, foreigners, spies, takfiris, sawafis, agents, Iranians, Saudis, Syrians, Algerians, Egyptians, Israelis, Kurds, Kuwaitis, Sunnis or Shiites. Jaish Omar. Jaish Mehdi. Zarqawi. Al Qaeda. Ali babas. Criminals.

The response to the Americans is always the same. We don't know who is doing this. We just know it is not us.

We know the danger is over there.

After forty-eight hours, my embed is over. An SUV driven by Army Public Affairs brings me back to the bureau.

It is Saturday night. I am still feverish and tired. I eat dinner, email, then put on episode eleven, season two of *The Wire*. I've been told *The Wire* is probably the best show on TV—a cop drama set in Baltimore—but it has taken me a few tries to get into the narrative. I watched the first four episodes on my last tour a few months earlier, and picked up where I'd left off when I got back in December. The season finale is one episode away. I stretch out on the couch in the living room. The DVD player, a generic model with the brand name Super General, is acting up, so I have to get up and eject the DVD and put it back in. I finally get comfortable on the couch.

My cell phone starts beeping and vibrating, a text message.

"I'm scared."

The message is from Andi. I know she's at her hotel in the NDI compound. I press pause on the DVD player remote control.

I pick up my cheap black and gray Nokia phone resting on the small table next to the couch and push the button to reply.

I text back:

"Why?"

The phone works, saying the message has been sent to Andi.

I feel like watching TV, not talking.

The Wire finishes twenty minutes later. I take my Iraqna from the table and step outside on the driveway where the reception is better. It is still cold and damp. I light a cigarette and call her.

"Oh, hi."

"Hi. What's wrong?"

"Nothing is wrong."

"You texted me 'I'm scared.' What's happening?"

"It's fine now."

"Tell me what happened."

"No, you're in a bad mood."

"Tell me what happened."

203

"I'm not going to tell you. You have an attitude."

"I am tired and sick and I just got back from an embed."

"Did I interrupt something?"

"No."

"You want to go watch TV? Are you watching *Lost*?"

"Just tell me what happened. Why are you scared? You've never sent me a message like that before—it's not like you. So why are you sending me a message saying you are scared? Then you won't tell me? Was it bombs? Was it shooting? If you texted and said, 'There's shooting outside,' I would call. If you said, 'Car bomb just went off,' I would call. But you say 'I'm scared,' what kind of bullshit is that? It's like you're trying to manipulate me into calling you. Crying fucking wolf."

"Oh my god oh my god. I can't talk to you right now. You are accusing me of being a horrible person. I'm hanging up."

"Don't fucking hang up. I want to know. I am concerned, I do worry. I got shot at today, too, you know."

"Are you done lecturing me?"

"I'm not lecturing you, but you can't say you're scared and not tell me what happened. Was there shooting or explosions or what?"

"I don't want to talk about it. Stop lecturing me."

"Jesus Christ."

She hangs up. She never hangs up, or very rarely. I call back and apologize. I'm sorry to have snapped. I am stressed and tired. I am not feeling well.

And I think to myself, yes, you're scared, I'm scared, we're scared. We should be.

I go to sleep. I wake up at 8 A.M. from a nightmare. In the dream it is all black, but I see Andi, a blond color, a Lego version of a person, and there is green, a vague impression. She is in a car; something happens. I reach over to my Iraqna and send her a text message. I have never sent a text message like this before. The text message reads: hi cubbi had dream you were kidnapped are you okay call me.

She doesn't call. She's still somewhat upset with me. I send more text messages and apologetic emails throughout the day. The usual pattern.

The evening of Sunday, January 14, she finally picks up the phone when I call again. We talk.

She is happy, I am happy.

Monday night. We talk. We plan for the future. I think I could get a job working with the Palestinians in Jerusalem if you were assigned to Israel, she says. Or maybe the presidential campaign—she has been looking into making the jump. She likes Barack Obama. She doesn't know, though, she is enjoying the work overseas. We discuss Paris again—I say I have confirmed the reservations. She sends me an email with specifications for a diamond ring from DeBeers. Ring size six, princess cut, platinum band. She says I better propose to her in a romantic location. I say, how about on a train? She tells me to come up with a better idea. We say good night.

Tuesday, January 16, we are busy. We don't talk. We text.

Love you.

Hug.

CHAPTER 19

January 17, 2007

BAGHDAD

I wake from a nap. My laptop is next to me on my bed, along with my two mobile phones. I've been sleeping for about twenty minutes, resting up before starting to write a story about Prime Minister Nouri al-Maliki. That afternoon, the Shiite leader held a rare press conference for the Western press that I attended. I'm wearing gray sweatpants and a sweater. It's a damp and dark Baghdad winter night. It's 7:40 P.M. and the sun is gone.

My phone beeps, my international number, the T-Mobile. There are three new voice mails and three missed calls. I don't know when I missed those calls or when the voice mails arrived. It's a little odd; most of my phone calls are on the Iraqna, unless it is New York calling, a radio or television interview, or occasionally my family.

I check email from my bed. I see there are two emails, both unusual. One is from a man whose name is unfamiliar, Tom Ramsay. Subject line: Please call. It says: "Dear Michael, could you call me at one of the

numbers below? Thanks, Tom." His signer says he is the country director for NDI's Iraq Program. Another is from a woman in the publicity
department at *Newsweek,* subject heading: National Democratic Institute.
The email says that someone at NDI called the magazine and wants to
speak with me. "The matter is urgent," the email says.

I carry the laptop into the office. I hit reply.

"Thanks, did they say what it was about?"

A response comes four minutes later.

"No, they didn't say."

I call Andi on my Iraqna.

It rings, rings again, and then goes to the familiar message, in Arabic
then English—"The subscriber you are trying to reach is either switched
off or out of the coverage area."

Her phone is off.

I try calling the number Tom Ramsay gave me, but my call doesn't go
through.

I try again.

I respond to Tom Ramsay's email. I write that I tried to call but my call
isn't going through. I give him all my contact numbers—the bureau's
satellite phone number, my T-Mobile, and my Iraqna.

I go to my room and change into jeans and put my shoes on. I am
preparing to act; perhaps she is hurt or sick or has had to be hospitalized,
I think.

I try calling from the bureau's satellite phone. It is a +88 number working off the Thuraya satellite network. It is sometimes more reliable. I dial
Tom Ramsay again. It rings.

He answers.

"Tom Ramsay."

"Hi, Tom, this is Michael Hastings from *Newsweek.*"

"Michael."

He recognizes the name. There is no pause, but I will pause here.
There is this moment before I know, before I have this piece of information. A moment before when life was normal, when life was good, when

I was in Baghdad with Andi and my career was skyrocketing and I was writing stories about the war, when we were planning trips to Paris, to Budapest, to Istanbul, when I looked at a diamond ring in Dubai, when I got an American Express Platinum Card because it gave me a free complimentary business or first class ticket so we could travel together. The life before I have this piece of information, before the three missed calls and the three new voice mails and the two cryptic emails, this life, my life, our life. There is the moment when the information has not been delivered. The moment before 7:58 P.M., Baghdad time. This moment before I know, but not before I understand because there is no understanding moments like this, the moment before the future no longer matters, before the future is nothing but a wish for the past.

"Michael, I have terrible news. We lost Andi today."

"What? You have to be fucking kidding me."

"No, Michael, we lost Andi today."

"You're kidding me, right?"

"No Michael, no Michael. I'm sorry. Her convoy was attacked. She was ambushed, we think her car was hit by rocket-propelled grenades. Three security guards were killed with her. We think it was a setup, we think she was set up."

"Oh my god, oh my god, oh my god, oh my god."

I am repeating oh my god oh my god oh my god you have to be fucking kidding me. We lost Andi today. She has been killed. A setup. RPGs. Ambush.

"Have you called her family?" I ask.

"Yes," he says.

"Do you want to call me back?" he says.

"Yes," I say, trying to understand exactly what he has just told me. Three-car convoy. Machine guns. Setup. RPGs. Armor-piercing rounds.

My brain feels like it has been smashed.

I act. I need to respond, right now. X, the security manager, is not at the house; he is over at the embassy. I call him but the phones are not working. I send a text message: X need you back now.

The message doesn't go through.

I walk outside to the guardhouse. They have radios to contact him.

"Guys, tell X to get back here now. Call X now and tell him to get back here."

I go back inside.

Fuck fuck fuck fuck fuck.

Call home.

I dial my parents' number in Vermont from the satellite phone.

My grandmother answers.

"Ruthgram, this is Michael."

"Hi Michael."

"Ruthgram, is my mom or dad around?"

"No, Brent is out and Molly is at work."

"Okay, you need to get in touch with them. I have terrible news. Andi was killed."

"Oh, no," she says.

I don't feel like she understands.

"Ruthgram, take this number down." I rattle off the bureau number. "Have them call me when they get in."

Her family has been contacted already.

I send an email to Jaime Horn, her best friend and former coworker at Air America Radio.

"Subject line: urgent.

"Jaime, when you get this give me a call at the number below or if there is a number I can reach you at, please send it to me."

She responds with a number.

She doesn't expect the news.

"Hi," she says, and I can tell she doesn't expect it.

"Jaime, I have terrible news. They killed Andi."

"What, what, what?"

I explain I am serious. I explain she is dead. I explain what they think happened.

"I'm sorry, Jaime, I'm so sorry, I know you told me to protect her, I'm so sorry. Jaime, I'm so fucking sorry."

"What?"

"I'm sorry."

"But she sent me an email this morning."

"I know, I'm sorry, Jaime, I'm so sorry. You told me to protect her and I couldn't. She loved you, Jaime, she loved you."

"She sent me an email this morning . . ."

"Jaime, you need time to think about this, you can call me back, you have my numbers."

An email to Babak, the new bureau chief, who is up on an embed near Tikrit. "Urgent. Hi Babak, give the bureau a call if you have a second."

I go outside to smoke a cigarette.

X comes around the corner.

"They killed her, man, they killed Andi."

X grabs my shoulder.

"They fucking killed her."

The bureau phone rings.

It is my mother.

"Oh Michael oh Michael oh Michael."

I can't believe it is my mother because I have never heard my mother's voice like this. She is strong, she does not cry, yet she is crying now. I don't remember what I said though I break down, I break down and say, fuck how could this happen, and I explain what I have been told.

Tom Ramsay calls again.

I know I was called first because I was listed as her emergency contact.

I am pacing in the bureau, back and forth, I kick something, a file cabinet, a wall. I stare at the ceiling, I keep saying, fuck fuck fuck fuck fuck they killed her, they killed my baby, how could this fucking happen, how the fuck could they have killed my baby?

I call her family. It is Marci, she is crying. I'm so sorry, is all I can say, I'm so sorry I'm so sorry, I'm so sorry, I can't even stop crying now, I am so sorry.

Her mom is on the phone. Vicki I am so sorry I am so sorry.

"Why are you saying you're sorry?" she says.

Babak calls. He can't believe it, either. He says he'll contact the editors in New York.

I am smoking in the bureau, sitting at the desk. CNN is on the television set. The news crawl reads, every five minutes or so:

AMERICAN AID WORKER AND THREE SECURITY GUARDS
KILLED IN BAGHDAD AMBUSH.

It's terrible news.

CHAPTER 20

January 18-19, 2007

BAGHDAD

There are more phone calls, more ringing phones, more discussions on what to do next. I feel the need to get to Ohio to see her family. My younger brother, Jeff, the infantry platoon leader, happens to be home in Vermont on a two-week leave. I talk to him. "I can't believe it, man, I can't fucking believe it. This is so fucked up."

"I know, dude, I know," he says.

My mother calls again. She is calm now, her voice steady, her priority now is getting me home safely.

"This phone call," she says. "It could have been Andi on the phone calling about you, it could have been you calling about Jeff, it could have been Jeff calling about you."

But it wasn't. It was Andi. It was me calling about her.

I tell whoever I am talking to that this should not have happened. I say it should have been me. I would trade anything for it to have been me. I'm the one who is supposed to take those kinds of risks; I'm the one who is supposed to pay for them with my life. At 5 A.M., I lie down on my bed. She gave me a stuffed panda bear that I keep at my bedside, or in my bag when traveling. I hold the panda. A brain-dead sleep comes for two hours.

I wake up at 7 A.M., put on sweatpants, a navy blue hoodie that she hated, a red Washington Nationals baseball cap that she gave me, and sunglasses. It is Thursday.

I'm told by NDI that they don't actually know where Andi's body is right now. After the attack, a U.S. patrol secured the scene. They recovered the car her body was in. NDI tells me the military has apparently misplaced it. This is not too surprising to me.

I talk to X.

"Find out where she is, man, find out where she is."

X goes to the CASH, the Combat Army Support Hospital in the Green Zone. No word of her there, though he is given the name of the person who will eventually receive her body, if her body shows up. He gets the DSN number for him. DSN, defense switched network, the phone system only the military has access to.

NDI is trying to get an answer from the military, with no luck.

I want to go home with her, on her plane. The idea is floated. What needs to be done to make that happen? NDI is working on it. I have little faith in them, so I work it, too.

I call the U.S. embassy spokesperson, Lou Fintor. Lou is very good at his job and he is a friend. He arrived in Baghdad six months ago after serving two years in Afghanistan. "Is there any way to make that happen?" Lou says he will bring it to the attention of the ambassador. He'll make it happen.

I also start working an alternative plan of escape. If the military flight falls through, *Newsweek*'s contact in Amman, Ranya Khadri, has gotten me a seat on any Royal Jordanian flight I want. She spoke directly to the president of RJ.

"The Iraqis," she says to me over the phone. "Iraq."

The question is whether I wait to go home with her body or, if that seems like it will take too long, leave on an RJ flight.

It is still unclear where her body is, when we will fly home. Later that night, Lou Fintor tells me it could be as early as tomorrow, Friday, which in militaryspeak probably means Sunday. A seventy-two-hour window of hurry up and wait.

Another embassy official tells me that I may or may not be able to get on the plane with her. "We don't reserve seats like that," he says. "You can fly Space A"—space available. He tells me he is very busy, and under a lot of pressure. I say I understand, but I am angry. I don't want space fucking available, I want a seat on the flight. I call Lou back. Lou says Ambassador Khalilzad has personally said to make this top priority, to get me on the flight. The embassy also issues a statement written by Lou. He tells me it is one of the most strongly worded statements on a civilian attack: "We vow to honor the memory of those killed by finding and bringing to justice all those who committed and assisted in these senseless and cowardly acts of murder. We will work with the Government of Iraq to relentlessly pursue those responsible."

Her killers also put out a press release. It is from the Islamic State of Iraq, the name of a jihadist umbrella group, affiliated with Al Qaeda in Iraq. They are claiming responsibility. "Oh Allah land of three rivers we have killed the Zionist occupiers," they say of Andi and the three guards, in a statement distributed online and translated by the SITE institute. I receive that in my in-box.

Andi's body is still missing, as Thursday night comes to a close. Her name has been released to the press. Her photograph is released, too. I want to talk to the press about it. I don't want Andi to be a one-day story. I don't want her to be just a headline on the wires. I call a friend at the *Los Angeles Times*. I tell her why I loved Andi; I try to explain who Andi was, what she believed in. It is the first of ten interviews I do on her death. The headline in the *L.A. Times* on Friday reads: "American Woman Follows Heart, Ideals, to Baghdad." The *New York Times* also calls; it is their guy from Cleveland.

So this happened today, right? he asks.

No, yesterday.

There is so much to say, so much anger that I am keeping in check. I want to kill someone and I want to scream at someone and I want to die and I want revenge.

A man from NDI calls; we talk about the media strategy. He requests that I speak only about Andi, that I keep the stories focused on her, on what great things she was doing, not on NDI, not on what NDI was doing. Security reasons, of course.

215

I hold my tongue. It is difficult not to say what is obvious to anyone who looks at this situation: NDI and its security company, Unity Resources Group, failed to protect their staff member. A catastrophic failure. The first thing out of the mouth of anyone I talk to—Iraqis, my journalist friends, my military contacts, the security personnel—is how could this trip to such a dangerous place have been approved? It seems like a clear fuckup. No American civilian should have been approved to go to the Iraqi Islamic Party headquarters in Yarmouk. Yarmouk is considered one of the most dangerous neighborhoods in Baghdad. There was no need to meet members of the Iraqi Islamic Party, a party known to have ties with insurgent groups, at their headquarters. Bad things happened at their headquarters. Two Iraqi journalists were killed while leaving a press conference there—kidnapped and executed—six months ago. Eight months earlier, Jill Carroll's kidnappers released her to the Iraqi Islamic Party. The IIP asked her to make a videotaped statement, saying they had had nothing to do with it. They assured her it would not be broadcast, then showed the interview on their own TV station. The last Western journalist I knew who had visited the compound had gone there in May 2006, against the advice of his translator, and he didn't tell the IIP the time he was coming, he just showed up.

I start looking into Unity Resources Group. They're based out of Dubai and Australia. Why had the URG failed to accurately assess the threat level in the area, or in Baghdad itself, approving the trip without hesitation? The situation in Baghdad was extremely volatile. There was open fighting on Haifa Street only the week before. There had been three reported attacks in and around Yarmouk in the previous five days. On the day she was killed, there were sixty attacks in Baghdad alone. It was likely a setup. Her attackers probably knew well in advance the day and time she was coming. Enough time to get together a team of insurgents, to identify the target, to plot an attack. Everyone working in Baghdad knows you never give a set time for arrival when going to such a high-risk spot.

Yeah, don't worry, I'll keep it focused on Andi. The anger and blame is everywhere—myself, the insurgents, NDI, IIP, myself again. Yes, it's a war, yes, these things happen, yes, hindsight is twenty-twenty, but shouldn't security be the number one priority? What happened to security that day?

Will I ever get these answers? No, I probably won't get the answers, and I won't be satisfied if I do, and none of it is going to change a fucking thing.

Another phone call from NDI on Thursday night. I get the most detailed account of events so far. She is at the IIP compound for an hour and a half. She leaves the compound around noon. She is traveling in a convoy of three sedans. She is in a BMW. The first car leaves the compound; in it are an Iraqi driver and a security guard from Ireland. The first car is allowed to pass down the street. She is in the second car. Her car pulls out of the compound. About 150 to 300 meters from the entrance, the car is "disabled"—perhaps by heavy machine-gun fire with armor-piercing rounds. The third car is behind it. There is an explosion. The second car disappears in smoke. The third car takes heavy fire, from thirty to fifty men. They are shooting from all directions, it seems. The private security detail team leader in the third car is killed, the driver wounded, the other security guard shot. The first car radios for help and turns around. A gun battle ensues; they get a few of the insurgents. A second team of NDI security guards arrives fifteen minutes later. They are engaged in a gunfight. Forty-five minutes later the U.S. Army arrives on scene, the quick reaction force, or QRF. The insurgents are gone; two cars have been destroyed; everyone in the second car, which included a Hungarian PSD and an Iraqi driver and Andi, is dead.

It is unclear why the second car stopped; it is still unclear what happened. An FBI investigation is under way, I am told. The FBI investigates murders of American civilians overseas. The incident is being classified as a terrorism case. The survivors of the attack are being interviewed.

I need to get my own answers, launch my own investigation. This is what I do, I am a reporter. And NDI knows this, I think.

Calls from NBC, CBS. They want to talk to me about Andi.

The CBS crew comes to the *Newsweek* bureau in the Green Zone. We set a chair outside in front of sandbags blocking the office window. It is a sunny day.

I talk to the producer before the interview, offscreen.

"I'm still in shock, to be honest. I don't know how the fuck I'm supposed to be acting."

He nods, and chats, sympathetic.

The microphone is put on me, and I start talking. I sit down. The camera is on, the questions come.

I say things, most good, some angry. I talk about Andi.

"My brother's a soldier and he told me not to cry on camera," I say.

I say, "Ask whatever you need to ask, I know the deal, I've been on the other side of the questions, too." It's odd. As a journalist, I'd regularly talk to people after tragedies in their lives; after the worst moments, after deaths and killings, I would try to ask as politely as possible, How do you feel? I wondered sometimes how and why they would talk to me. I understand now. Getting people to pay attention makes you feel less helpless.

NBC, same thing. We go inside, I show them pictures of Andi and me on my laptop. That morning, I made a folder of pictures of us.

The Associated Press, Knight Ridder . . . I repeat myself. I want her story to be front-page news everywhere. I want people to know what kind of woman has been killed in this war. My editor asks me to send my thoughts about Andi for the "Editor's Note," the page at the front of the magazine. I write them down in between interviews. I say that if there was such a thing as love at first sight, this was it. I say that she hated the suffering she saw in Iraq, that she wanted to fix the mistake her country had made. I say she was the best and brightest of her generation. I say she was the best face America could offer to the world.

I go on for five hundred words. I don't know what they are going to do with this, but I hit send, and it's off to New York.

That night, ABC calls and asks if I can do an interview via satellite from the U.S. embassy. It is past ten o'clock. Lou sets it up for me. The studio is on the second floor of the embassy. An older man takes the lint and dandruff off my blue sweater with a piece of electrical tape. The lights in the studio are on me; the camera adjusted, the earpiece in. A voice from the ABC studio in New York tells me, "Don't look at the camera, look off to the side, like you're being interviewed in person."

We're rolling, questions coming into my earpiece.

I say that Andi is an angel; I speak of her as an angel, as a pure soul. I talk about plans for the engagement—she sent me specifications for the ring a week ago: DeBeers, princess cut, 1.5 karats, size six.

After the interview, another friend from the embassy pulls me aside. "I have some information," he tells me.

He has read a classified intelligence report on the attack. It was a setup, an attempted kidnapping. Andi was the likely target. Not a random target, not a target of opportunity. Andi, the girl from Ohio, blond hair and blue eyes, she was the target. The insurgents swarmed the car. They tried to open the doors, but couldn't. And then everything got worse. They rolled grenades under the car, boom boom boom, the fuel tank exploded and the whole car went up in smoke.

"The pictures are bad," my friend says. "The photographs are very, very bad. The driver of her car—he may have tried to run away."

The insurgent group responsible, my source tells me, is Islamic jihadist with ties to Al Qaeda. Al Qaeda wannabes. He says this group is known for kidnapping Iraqi women. They are known for torturing and raping Iraqi women—pulling their fingernails out, beheading them. They are bad men; they are not the kind of insurgents who negotiate.

"It is better she was killed than kidnapped by these men," he says.

I know this is true. I think I know.

It is becoming more apparent that the Iraqi Islamic Party, with their own contingent of armed guards a few hundred feet away, stood by and watched this happen. They did nothing to stop it.

I am sick of Iraq. I am sick at the thought that the people Andi was going to help had an active hand in setting her up. I am disturbed, too, that the Iraqi Islamic Party visited the Bush White House in December 2006. The IIP is considered a "moderate" Sunni political party. The head of the party, Tarek al-Hashemi, is one of Iraq's three vice presidents. According to what NDI told me, and what my source confirmed, a person or persons within the organization likely played a role in killing her by tipping off the men who did it. The White House is entertaining people who have links to Islamic extremists? This is our war on terror?

I know all this. I know the Iraqi Islamic Party is shady. I know they are hypocrites. I know most political parties in Iraq are complicit in the killing that is taking place in the country—SCIRI, the Supreme Council for Islamic Revolution, is America's most important Shiite ally. Does the Supreme Council for Islamic Revolution in Iraq, whose leaders lived for years in exile in Iran, sound like a moderate political party? Moqtada al-Sadr has thirty members in the Iraqi parliament; his Mehdi Army has death squads that attack Coalition forces regularly. The IIP is not much different. I know the IIP has ties to Sunni insurgent groups. I witnessed it myself in Baghdad in August 2006 with the 172nd Stryker Brigade. We searched an IIP branch office in the neighborhood of Ghazaliya and found an arsenal and IED-making materials. I even emailed Andi about the IIP in December, describing them as having known ties to "the honorable resistance." This is not hidden knowledge. Why did I not put all of it together when Andi told me she was going to visit with the IIP days earlier? She told me she was going to the IIP headquarters. All I said was, Be careful.

I did not look at the map. If I had looked at the map I would have been horrified at the distance of the trip. The headquarters is miles away from her compound, on the other side of the city. I would have been horrified that the neighborhood was Yarmouk. A neighborhood that *Newsweek* inquired about going to a week before this happened, and we were told within fifteen seconds by our security staff, "Are you crazy? There is no way you can go to Yarmouk, it is much too dangerous. Even Iraqis are afraid to go to Yarmouk."

So I know all of this.

I know, I know, I know.

I know that after the attack, the Iraqi Islamic Party blamed the Americans. They told the *New York Times* on the day Andi was killed that they had been asking the U.S. military for better security in the neighborhood. They did not publicly condemn the attack. It is not a popular position to be against the insurgents.

This is the Iraqi government. These are our allies, the moderates, the men we decided to work with, the men we have given billions of dollars to.

Fuck them all. Kill them all. Bomb this country and make one giant parking lot. Better yet, build a giant runway to go bomb every one of these other Arab countries off the face of the Earth.

Nuke everybody, put on protective antiradiation suits, take their goddamn oil.

Fuck all of them, these savages, this fucking criminal government. The birthplace of civilization, but there's a reason that civilized people left, migrated, got the fuck out this shithole.

I don't really mean that, I tell myself.

Do I?

I do at the moment, maybe, but there are good people here.

Are there?

And what are we doing here anyway?

We're not evil like this. We're not fucking savages.

Oh?

Stop, stop, stop. I wish a hundred more Hadithas on these fucks. Line them up—I will pull the trigger myself.

I have a change of heart on sectarian cleansing—let the Shiites wipe these Sunni fucks off the map. Let them kill them all, women and children. Let them pay.

I don't really believe that, right?

I don't think so.

Maybe sometimes.

Maybe not.

It is late Friday night. They have located her body. It has made it to the Army morgue at Camp Victory. The phone calls continue. Why didn't I say anything? Why didn't I stop her? You know Andi would have gone anyway; you know how she was; it was her job. She always told you not to go places and you didn't listen. You went anyway. You cannot blame yourself, I am told. Yes I can. I can blame myself and I can blame everybody. Blame is easy. Blame is easier than living with this terrible sadness and despair.

CHAPTER 21

January 20, 2007

BAGHDAD

It is Saturday. I learn the flight carrying Andi's body is scheduled for tomorrow. I will be helicoptered out from the Green Zone to the airport on a Black Hawk. There will be a small ceremony there. Ambassador Khalilzad will attend.

This afternoon, a few security guards from NDI dropped off Andi's belongings at the *Newsweek* bureau. Two large black trunks—the trunks I had brought to her two weeks earlier. Four suitcases. Two unopened cardboard care packages—they arrived on Thursday—FedEx boxes from her family and my family. Her laptop bag with her personal computer.

I move her things into my room and start to go through the trunks and bags. Her clothes, her perfume, her scent. I was planning to take the important things her family would want now, any of her writings and documents, with me on my flight.

In her laptop bag I find pictures of her and her two nieces. Folders from work. Letters that my father has written her. Gifts I have given her: a small gold Kurdistan pendant and a necklace I had bought for her from a woman in the West Bank, the digital camera I gave her for Christmas in Vermont. A few books: *Marie Antoinette,* Twain's *Joan of Arc,* the biography of Empress Sisi I bought her when we were in Vienna. I open up the care packages, and inside are finger paintings from Kayla and Abby, her nieces, with yellow hearts saying LOVE ANDI.

I find her personal writings and her diary. She wrote about what she hoped the universe would give her. She wrote about the readings she got from her psychic in Boston named Diana, whom she would call occasionally from Iraq. She liked to take notes on what Diana told her so she could compare it to what happened and prepare for what she should watch out for.

I find a note she wrote on stationery from the Amman Four Seasons in December. It says:

> Dear Angels dear God dear universe
> Please let me get this NDI job.
> The NDI job will work out fine.
> I am protected by light and love.

I open her diary, and my heart skips a beat as I read:

> Don't let MH find out about this, please forgive me,
> angels, please forgive me . . .

I read on. She had got access to my email account and sneaked a peek. I laugh for the first time in three days. I smile. I always wondered how she could guess who I was emailing—she always seemed to know! Part of it was her own intuition, of course, and knowing me so well, but it turns out she had had help, too. I don't know how she figured out my password.

I find a note that says: "career, death card." Another, dated January 12, says that she and I will "take the journey home together." She had written her favorite quote from Milan Kundera's *Immortality* on an index card: "Only obstacles, Paul thought, were capable of turning love into a love story." The note was dated August 25, 2006, a week before she left for Iraq.

I take out her clothes—the blue sweatshirt of mine she liked to wear, my favorite top of hers, the white one she wore when she met me in Vienna, her blue scarf and mittens. I take her perfume.

God, this is like out of a movie. So people do this.

I also take her underwear and put it in my bag. I know she would not want customs or anyone else seeing something so personal. But it feels weird all the same.

I find a plastic bag of extra large men's T-shirts, including one that says THE HUNGARIAN INTERNATIONAL SHOOTING CLUB. I assume it belongs to the dead Hungarian guard who was in Andi's car.

Later that afternoon, the security manager from NDI calls.

"You don't happen to have T-shirts, do you? Extra large? They belong to the bodyguard in the third car."

"Yes, I do."

"I'll come by and pick them up," he says. And then, "He's agreed to meet with you if you want. He's at the NDI compound in the IZ."

"I'd like to talk to him."

A few hours later, I drive with X to meet him. His name is Jacob. He was one of the two survivors in the third car. He's from a small town in Hungary. His English is okay. He was shot in the arm, but is doing fine.

NDI has three rows of trailers, next to three rows of IRI trailers, right next to the Blue Star restaurant. Not many people are at the restaurant. We walk down the row of trailers.

I've brought a notebook with me, though I don't know if I'll take notes.

Jacob opens the door to his trailer and we step in. He's finishing up a Skype chat with his wife, back in Hungary.

I want to thank him for trying to save Andi, but I don't really get a chance.

"I'm sorry we couldn't do more," he says, and then he starts talking, and I stare at him, listening.

He's a thick six feet two with a square head and soft brown hair. He's wearing sweatpants and a T-shirt. He has a cut on his chin and what look like stitches. He seems a bit shaky.

"She wasn't the only one who was killed, you know," he says.

I nod.

"My friend Yonni, he was in her car. He died, too, he was like a brother to me. He has a wife and a two-year-old baby back in Hungary."

I listen.

"They don't give a shit, you know, a PSD from Hungary gets killed, then it is no big deal, but she wasn't the only one who died.

"And you have to understand," he says, in broken English, "that I am usually in the client car. For the past six months I have been in the client car. I was not in the client car, my friend Yonni was instead. Brother to me."

So what happened?

He says he cannot answer all my questions—he would like to, but there is still an "ongoing investigation." He could even get in trouble speaking with me now. It appears no one high up at the organization has cleared this conversation. The NDI security manager who set it up was doing me a favor; he wanted to help me get answers. But Jacob wants to talk, too, wants to see me, to explain what he can.

They were at the IIP compound for about an hour and a half. He says he has been there seven times. That the last trip there was a month ago. I have talked to people with post-traumatic stress disorder before, watched as they recounted their experiences in combat, and he gets the same look as he goes through the events of that day.

He is about fifteen meters behind her car. For whatever reason—it is unclear to him, or he can't say—her car stops. Four or five men run at the car. At this point, there is a massive amount of shooting. Or maybe there is shooting before, too. The sequence of events, from his telling, is hard to pin down. There is an explosion. The car he is in crashes. Crashes into what? He can't say. The car is receiving fire from all directions—above, to the sides, everywhere, from what he guesses has to be at least thirty shooters. The PSD team leader, a Croatian, is sitting shotgun in the third car. The Croatian steps out of the car to move toward Andi's vehicle. It is unclear whether the explosion has happened yet, whether there still is a vehicle to move to. The team leader, says Jacob, is almost immediately killed. His boss, shot dead. Bullets are now pouring into his car. There is smoke everywhere. Jacob is in the backseat. The driver of his car, an Iraqi, has also been shot. Two hundred rounds hit our car, says Jacob, maybe more.

It is hazy, he says, foggy. He doesn't really know what happens next. It sounds like he stays in the car, in the backseat. It seems like he does not return fire or make any attempt to move to Andi's car. Maybe it is too late. Maybe he is in shock. Maybe the training does not kick in, and he is overwhelmed by what is going on. He hunkers down in the car and waits and at some point, he leaves the car to hide in a building with the wounded Iraqi driver of his car.

X has been listening carefully to the conversation. "There is tunnel vision," he points out. "When shit like this happens, it's hard to see everything."

I ask if the guards from the Iraqi Islamic Party compound responded.

He smirks and shakes his head, no.

He tells me the second team of NDI guards arrived maybe twenty minutes after the ambush started.

"Twenty minutes is an eternity," says X.

Jacob repeats his points.

"I am lucky to be alive," he says. "He was a brother. I am sorry we couldn't do more."

I nod, yes, lucky.

I take down his email address and I thank him for his time.

I go back to the bureau, and think about what he told me, and I come to the harsh conclusion that he failed, he froze, he did not return fire. He hid in the backseat. He told me instead that he was fortunate to have survived. I agree, he might not have been that fortunate had he been doing the job he is paid to do, which is to protect his client, even if it costs him his life. That is why he gets paid. I am sympathetic to his own shock, his own trauma, and I am probably being unfair, but I don't really give a shit that he lost a friend, another mercenary. I don't give a shit that he is usually in the client's car, and it was only the fate of switching with his friend that saved him. I care only that Andi is dead, murdered, and that she was not protected.

CHAPTER 22

January 20-21, 2007

BAGHDAD

On Saturday night, I print out an email containing my travel orders: authorization for "Fiance of Andrea Suzanne Parhamovich to Accompany her Remains . . . The State Department requests that the Department of Defense authorize Michael Mahon Hastings . . . to accompany the remains of Ms. Parhamovich aboard U.S. military aircraft . . ." The document, on DoD letterhead, notes she was "killed by terrorists in Baghdad."

The flight home will be Sunday morning. There will be a ceremony at the Baghdad Airport, which the ambassador, representatives from the State Department, NDI, URG, and I will attend. I will be accompanied on the flight by Karen, the head of the political parties program at NDI and Andi's direct supervisor in Iraq.

The first flight will take us from Baghdad to Kuwait. In Kuwait, we are scheduled to change planes then fly to a U.S. airbase in Germany. From Germany, we will make the last leg of the trip to Dover Air Force Base in Delaware. We are scheduled to arrive in Dover late Sunday night or early Monday morning. If there are no foul-ups, it is about eighteen hours of flying. It is important to me that there are no delays. The longer it takes to get to Dover, where the U.S. military may take as long as a week to release her body, the longer Andi's family has to wait to have a funeral for her.

The security guard who died in Andi's car, Yonni from Hungary, will also be coming with us back to Dover for processing. The air force base in Delaware has the military's largest morgue, and receives the bodies of almost all the American servicemen and women killed in Iraq, just over three thousand at this point.

That night, I pack my bags, just the essentials. My clothes, thrown into a Swiss Army duffel bag, are mixed with Andi's clothes. I put her laptop in a backpack I'm carrying. I have her mobile phone and diary, her folders from work, her perfume. I put a stick of lipstick in my pocket, where I'll keep it for the next few months. I'm also bringing body armor and a helmet for the helicopter ride to the airport and the C-130 flight out of the country. I fold up the printout of my DoD travel orders and slip it in my jacket.

Sunday morning is overcast and windy. "Show time" is 0700; the helicopter is supposed to take us to the airport for a flight around 0900. I get in the Mercedes, X drives. We leave the bureau, take a left from our house, pass the traffic circle, go underneath an arch from the Saddam era, then after a series of massive speed bumps we hang a left and are at the LZ Washington gate a few minutes before 7 A.M. I am the first to arrive. The Peruvian guards at the gate say we are not allowed to drive in and try to send us across the street.

"You don't have the right pass to drive in here," they say, in broken English and Spanish.

I get out of the car and unload my bags. They tell me to move.

"I am getting out here," I say, my voice rising. "If you have a problem, call the fucking ambassador."

The Peruvian guards start to circle around me, like they are going to physically restrain me. X moves near me, ready to intervene, ready to tackle the Peruvian who looks like he is ready to tackle me. I pick up my bags and walk inside. The guards watch. I put my bags down in the waiting area inside the LZ. I apologize to the guards for my outburst.

Reps from the embassy, including my friend Lou Fintor, turn up about fifteen minutes later.

"I've spent the last twelve hours trying to find a Hungarian flag," Lou says, when I ask what's in his hand. "The only one we could find was at the DFAC." The embassy dining hall has all the flags in the Coalition of the Willing—the thirty-two countries that originally supported the U.S. invasion of Iraq—hanging from the ceiling. Korea, Japan, Estonia, Fiji. Even though Hungary, as Lou points out, is no longer part of the Coalition (they dropped out in 2005), they still kept their flag hanging right above the salad bar, three meters from the Baskin Robbins ice cream counter.

"There is one problem," Lou says. "The flag smells like French fries and onion rings, all that grease from the chow hall." The loss of Yonni is front-page news in Hungary, Lou tells me. It's caused some controversy. Before Yonni was a hired gun, he served in the Hungarian military. Officially, the Hungarians aren't even supposed to be here, but they're part of the NATO mission. NATO has representatives stationed in Baghdad to watch the progress of the war. Lou, who speaks Hungarian from his time at the U.S. embassy in Budapest, has been in touch with the Hungarian NATO detachment to arrange their participation in the ceremony at the airport. They didn't know if they could get a flag in time, and Lou did not want to take any chances.

The wind picks up. I resign myself to the fact that we might be delayed.

No, I'm told, we're going.

The contingent from NDI arrives. I meet the man who gave me the news, Tom Ramsay. He tells me: "We are cooperating fully with the FBI investigation."

This statement perplexes me, and I get suspicious. Well, of course you're cooperating fully with the investigation. Why wouldn't you be? It is a sentence that reeks to me of legalese and evasiveness and guilt; cooperating fully with the investigation. No shit you are. Perhaps he says this because I'm a journalist. Perhaps he says it because it is stressful and he doesn't know what else to say. Perhaps he says it because he is not cooperating fully with an investigation that will show many mistakes were made, too many, and the responsibility for those mistakes might fall on his shoulders. Perhaps not. Perhaps I am just angry and tired and paranoid.

I meet Karen. She will be with me all the way to Dover. Karen was the last NDI staffer to see Andi. She is about five feet five, with tan skin and dark hair down to her shoulders. She looks tired and smokes Marb Lights. Do we have enough cigarettes? I ask. I have two packs—so does she. That should keep us until the afternoon, I say.

The two Black Hawks land, blowing wind and dirt against our faces as we follow the ground crew member out to the "birds." I dressed today in the blue blazer and gray flannels and a white button-down shirt that has light blue stripes in a crisscrossing pattern. I wanted to look respectable for the ceremony. I do the State Department chic thing, and put the body armor on under the navy blazer. I wear my Burberry coat, bought with Andi the year before, and button it to the top. I strap my helmet, pop on the eye protection, and stick in the yellow earplugs. I have the travel down to an art—two bags carried, one on my back. X and I hug before I get on the helicopter.

We lift off over Baghdad. There are heavy winds, winds that would cancel a normal flight. I am being buffeted around like never before. I feel so fucking strange. The city is waking up, three thousand feet below, maybe closer, it seems closer. We follow the river out, the other Black Hawk tailing behind us, whoomp whoomp whoomp, and I can't help but smile at the unbelievability of it all. I laugh to myself, an absurd, sad laugh. I think very briefly, I can't wait to tell Andi about this trip, she'll get a kick out of it—and it hits me again that I will never get the chance.

We land at Sather Airfield, or the Glass House, the military terminal at the Baghdad Airport where the C-130 is scheduled to meet us that morning. The Glass House was once the building where Saddam met VIPs arriving in Baghdad. There is not much glass anymore, most of it replaced by plywood to board up the windows. I can see the civilian air terminal across a large airfield, where the Royal Jordanian flights take off. We are informed that the C-130 is late and won't arrive until the afternoon, about eight or nine hours from now. They want to do the ceremony as the two coffins are loaded onto the plane, so we have to wait.

An army chaplain comes in, along with Lieutenant Colonel John Franks of Mortuary Affairs and the ambassador's speechwriter. They start to talk, going over the details of the ceremony—the honor guard, where the soldiers will stand, who will speak first. The ambassador's speechwriter shows her talking points to the chaplain so he can get a sense of what the ambassador is going to say. It is too much for me, and I go outside to smoke and look at the airplanes.

Lou joins me.

"This place is a fucking nightmare," I tell him.

He agrees.

"When I leave here, I won't look back," he says. "Afghanistan I could go back to, but this place is so fucked up."

Lieutenant Colonel Franks rounds us up for a trip to the morgue. There are two such Mortuary Affairs companies in the army, he explains, or about three hundred people in total. It is all volunteer; the men and women in Mortuary Affairs serve only six-month tours, due to the stress and psychological trauma of their military occupation specialty, or MOS. There are eight collection posts for bodies throughout the country. This spot at Camp Victory is the main depot for the dead. The Iraqis are being trained how to take the lead in mortuary affairs, building their own facilities with help from the Coalition, so they don't have to rely on local hospitals or the Americans to process their dead.

We drive out in SUVs to a small white building. Lieutenant Colonel Franks points to an even smaller, rundown building where they had worked until they recently upgraded to the new facility. The Mortuary Affairs group is isolated, Franks explains, away from the rest of the base, hidden in the corner, out of the way.

We walk inside. A group of soldiers is hanging out in a small office. I am introduced to Staff Sergeant Cruz, the young man who worked on Andi. We get a tour. "Everyone is treated with dignity and respect," he says. They bring us out back, where there is a white morgue truck and a stack of silver metal caskets. The caskets are temperature controlled and identical, with a slip of white paper containing the personal details of the contents on the side. Andi is already in one, but they don't tell me which one.

I ask Lieutenant Colonel Franks if I can see her remains; he shakes his head no. He moves closer to me and says we will have a talk, man-to-man. The rest of the group leaves.

"I know who you are," he says. "I know about *Newsweek* and the trip to Paris"—he'd read about it in the *L.A. Times*—"I know you're the media. I've done my research. I've Googled you. You know, the media is always reporting the negative news. I'm glad this is finally a positive story."

I am slightly stunned. I am amused that the colonel, meeting a representative of the press, takes a shot at the liberal media, then suggests that Andi's death is a good news story. I don't say anything, but I assume he means the fact that she died for something she believed in, she died for her ideals, and that she was being treated as a hero.

He gives me the details.

Her body was found in the backseat. The body of the Hungarian security guard was found on top of hers. It appears he was trying to protect her from the flames, from the bullets and the explosions. The front seat was broken, knocked back, so he must have jumped in the backseat to cover her up.

"Twenty-five hundred degrees Fahrenheit, fire burns down," he says.

I don't know what this means.

"There has been comingling of the remains," he says.

It dawns on me why the Hungarian has to go back to Dover—so the morticians with better equipment in the States can separate what is Andi from what is her security guard.

"Can I see her?" I ask.

"There is no body," he says. "She is not what you think. What is left is not recognizable as man or woman. It is ugly. It is not her. Trust me, you don't want to see."

"Was the driver found in the car? I was told he may have run away," I say.

There were only two found in the car, he says.

I thank him and go back to the SUV.

A further investigation is being conducted by the CID, or the criminal investigation division of the military. What will the forensics say about the last moments? Will the body of her driver show burn marks—will there even be a body?—like he was escaping from the fire, or will it be full of bullets, like he just stopped the car and tried to run away? Or did he stagger out in a daze after something hit him, a bullet, shrapnel? How many bullet holes in the car will there be?

At least one of her guards did his job, I tell myself, tried to cover her, tried to protect her from the heat, from the flames, from the grenades rolled under the vehicle, under the gas tank, the dense smoke, 2500 degrees Fahrenheit, fire burns down. I hope her guard covered her five-foot-three frame. I hope she was comforted by this. I wish I had been the one to die on top of her. I wish I had been there to protect her.

There are still a few hours left before the ceremony. Lieutenant Colonel Franks offers to show us around. He suggests going to the PX on Camp Liberty, another base on the airport compound. On the drive over, I ask where the Crisp is located. The Crisp is the name of the yard at Liberty where destroyed vehicles are brought—vehicles that are burned up, burned out, burned to a crisp. The Crisp is where Andi's car was taken. It is the Crisp that gives me images of scraping scorched bones off the melted carcass of the car she was in.

It's over there, he says. From a distance, it looks like a junkyard or parking lot.

The PX on Liberty is one of the nicest in Iraq, due to its proximity to the airport. There is a Taco Bell and Green Bean, and the PX itself is the size of a Wal-Mart. Franks, Lou, Karen, the speechwriter, and I enter the store. Bright lights shine on row after row of Doritos, Tostitos, Right Guard, Crest toothpaste, Marlboro Lights and Reds, magazines, *Car and Driver, Ebony, Maxim,* new DVDs, new video games for the Xbox and PlayStation and even the handheld PSPs. There is a back room with televisions and air conditioners, satellite dishes. There is combat gear, holsters, boots, socks, sanitary napkins; there is a counter for ballistic eye protection. I pick up a pack of Marb Reds, and I also decide I need a new pair of sunglasses for the upcoming funeral and plane ride. The sunglasses I have been wearing are slightly bent. I ask to look at a pair of Ray-Bans, a black pair that I press to my face. I buy them. There is a fifteen-minute wait in the checkout line, which stretches back to the refrigerated pizzas, customer after customer, some in uniform, some in the jeans and tight T-shirts or push-up bras of contractors.

Outside on a small cement sidewalk surrounded by the gravel that covers up the mud on the base, I ask Lieutenant Colonel Franks and Karen which pair of sunglasses looks better, my old ones or my new ones. Karen declines to answer; Lieutenant Colonel Franks says the Ray-Bans, definitely, they fit your face.

CHAPTER 23

January 21, 2007

BAGHDAD, KUWAIT

There is no blue in the sky. Dark gray clouds press down on the long runway, rolling in to stay for the afternoon. The cargo bay door on the C-130 drops to the ground; a white van pulls up about 150 feet away. Two rows of men and women, most in desert fatigues, others in blazers and dresses, form a line from the tail of the aircraft to the van. There must be at least thirty of them. I am standing second in line on the left side of the plane's ramp. Ambassador Khalilzad stands to my left. I take off the Ray-Bans.

"I'm sorry for your loss," he says.

"Thank you, Mr. Ambassador, and thank you for coming out here today, I know Andi would have appreciated it. It means a lot."

I try to say something else, and he does as well, but it is lost in the wind, and we stand in silence.

The first casket is removed from the van. It is the Hungarian's casket, wrapped in a Hungarian flag. It is a new flag—Lou finally convinced the Hungarian NATO attaché to provide a flag that didn't smell like French fries. The soldiers carry the casket onto the plane.

There are salutes, military commands are yelled out, the van's ramp is lowered to the ground again, and there she is, covered in an American flag.

Six soldiers step forward, one foot measured in front of the other, carrying her silver casket. She moves slowly. I see tears in the eyes of a number of people standing across from me, her friends from the State Department.

237

Lieutenant Colonel Franks discreetly takes pictures, pictures that will have to be approved by CENTCOM before they are released. I see Karen with her camera, videotaping, following the casket as it makes its way to the plane.

The wind picks up, the worst wind all day, sweeping across the runway, strong enough to knock me off balance.

It would not have been right for there to be sun on such a day. It has been sunny since she was killed, but as she gets closer to leaving this place, this evil place, there are thick clouds, threats of rain in the desert, the sky dark. The coffin passes me, the closest I have been to Andi since I kissed her goodbye nine days earlier, her head resting on my shoulder, fitting there, perfectly, such a rare thing.

The six men set the casket down inside the C-130's cargo bay.

Another military command is shouted, and the two lines of men and women move into the plane. There is no light inside the cargo bay; words fade without echoes. Ambassador Khalilzad speaks; the head of NDI's Baghdad Program speaks; the head of Unity Resources Group speaks; then I speak.

"When things like this happen, the first question one asks is why . . . In this case, the second question is why would she want to be with a jerk like me?"

I don't think the joke works.

"What I'm saying, what I'm trying to get at, is what an amazing person she is . . . Yesterday, when I was going through her personal effects, I found a piece of paper . . ."

> Dear Angels dear God dear Universe
> Please let me get the job at NDI.
> The NDI job will work out fine.
> I am protected by light and love
> I am protected by light and love

My hand shakes as I put the paper back in my pocket.

The army chaplain says a prayer.

A series of hugs, handshakes, goodbyes, be strong, and the people file out of the plane.

"You're gonna get these guys who did this," I say to the ambassador as he walks away. "No doubt about it," he responds.

I sit down in the seat closest to her casket at the back of the cargo bay, pulling on my body armor, putting on my sunglasses, and strapping myself in. Karen sits across from me. About fifteen other passengers come in the front entrance of the plane, so as not to walk past the two caskets strapped in the back. The ramp on the cargo bay closes; it's chilly in here.

The aircrew gives instructions—the bathroom, air sickness bags, what to do in case of emergency. They recommend we keep our body armor on. A Black Hawk helicopter was shot out of the sky the day before, killing thirteen, and there was speculation in the press and among the military about whether the insurgents had a supply of new missiles.

The plane starts to move, its engines roaring. There are no windows on the C-130, and you quickly lose sense of what altitude you are at, or even if you're still on the ground. I lean back in my seat and feel an urge to reach out and touch her casket, to touch the flag. Maybe I think it will be warm to the touch, maybe I think it will bring me closer to her. But I worry that if it is cold to my touch, I will not like that. I am wearing my sunglasses, tearing up so much there is now a layer of dried salt on the inside of the lenses. The other passengers are not looking or talking; they are staring straight ahead. Finally, I reach out and touch the corner of the casket, caressing her and the flag.

It is neither warm nor cold.

The plane lands, a faster flight than expected. We are in Kuwait.

A master sergeant enters the plane.

"We have two angels on board today, so please join me for a prayer."

Angels, I think, angels, not knowing at that point that the U.S. military calls all the fallen "angels." Planes with the dead are called "angel flights."

Another honor guard comes on; a sergeant is giving instructions. I stand next to him. I have a picture of Andi in my blazer pocket, a crumpled picture, and he talks in what seems to me like a casual manner.

It isn't his fault he is doing his job. I say to him: "This is Andi, this is who is in that casket." He says, "Really, I'm sorry," and they carry her off into another white van, to hold her in the morgue while we wait for the next flight to Germany.

In Kuwait, we wait at another PAX terminal. I watch CNN until three other soldiers show up, "escorts" as they call them. "Escort" is the word for friends who are allowed to accompany the dead on flights out of Baghdad. I am an escort, but I am a rarity because I have permission to travel with the casket all the way back to Dover. These three escorts just arrived on a flight from Baghdad; they are friends with the pilots who were killed in the Black Hawk crash yesterday. I talk to the soldiers. They tell me they were granted permission to escort their friends' bodies to Kuwait, but then they have to go back to Baghdad. I ask one if what I heard was true—if they think the Black Hawk was shot down by a missile. One of the soldiers tells me he thinks that is what happened.

There were only two caskets on my flight from Baghdad—Andi and the Hungarian—but in Kuwait the other war dead catch up to us. Thirty-five American soldiers have been killed in the past five days. On our next flight, to Germany, an army chaplain tells me, Andi will be joined by the caskets of twenty-four of the soldiers who have been killed since January 17, 2007, including those in the Black Hawk crash.

It is around 8 P.M.

Karen and I talk. It is really our only real conversation in the forty-eight hours we spend together.

She explains that NDI had such a good relationship with the IIP, such a good relationship. I do not say a word. She says there are people at very senior levels of NDI considering whether or not they should continue working with the IIP. I try not to say anything, but I am greatly disturbed by what she says. They had assumed a level of trust with these men, a fatal mistake when operating in that environment. I wish they had not trusted them so fully; I wish they had played it safe and had the meeting at the Green Zone, where the IIP members go regularly, or told them to visit the NDI compound instead.

I don't know if it is naïveté or incompetence on NDI's part, but either way, I am angry. I can't speak to Karen about my anger of course; I can't speak to her about Andi. I can see that she doesn't want to know about Andi, not really; she cannot bear to hear it. They never had the chance to know each other; I can see her struggle with her own feelings of guilt, as she was Andi's supervisor, one of those who had signed off on the trip to the IIP that led to Andi's death.

"I just remember she was so bright and beaming that morning," says Karen. "And in December we took one look at her résumé, and said of course we want this person; of course we want her to be part of the program. She was self-motivated; she had a plan for what she wanted to do, and she presented it to me, and I was like, go for it."

After talking to Karen, I realize there was no conversation that morning, no security briefing with Andi, no talk about what signs of danger to look for. There did not even seem to be much talk about the purpose of the trip, except as a meet and greet. I knew Andi would never refuse to go on a trip. It is the job of the field worker to want to push boundaries, to do as much as you can, and the job of the supervisors and private security team to temper that desire, to say, look, that is a big risk: Is it worth it? Can you accomplish your work without a visit? Can you meet them in the Green Zone or perhaps they can come here? These are the questions that should always be asked in Baghdad, especially in January 2007, when there was open fighting in the streets and kidnappings were a common occurrence. Were none of these most basic questions asked?

Karen tells me her information about the attack is from one of the PSDs who survived the attack, the man in the first car.

According to him, the first car drives out of the compound and down the street; his radio crackles with the word "contact." The driver, an Iraqi man, pulls a U-turn, and something gets in the way—an Iraqi family or something. Karen says the Iraqi driver then gets nervous, like something is wrong, maybe the family was trying to slow them down. By the time the first car goes back down the street, they think Andi's car has escaped, because there is so much smoke they couldn't see it. So then the first car pulls back into the IIP compound. A second team of NDI PSDs is dispatched and is on the way. The guard in the first car gets out and moves onto the street on foot; he sees about four or five insurgents try-ing to drag the body of the PSD team leader who had been killed after he left the tail car. He opens fire on the insurgents, hitting a few perhaps, and they run off. He then takes cover, and a gunfight ensues. The second NDI team arrives about twenty minutes later; they are also in heavy contact with the insurgents. Around forty minutes later, Coalition forces arrive, and—unusually, says Karen—they find the PSDs all still there. In most cases, the private security teams involved in gunfights leave the scene of an incident as quickly as possible.

It is a forty-five-minute-long gun battle, with bullets flying over the smoking remains of Andi's car. Karen says the PSDs were considering going back that night to find the killers, but they didn't do that—that was a bad idea, it was the anger talking, the desire for revenge, and besides, they probably wouldn't be able to find them.

This the last sequence of events I get for months. It is basically accu-rate, but a more complete description emerges in the coming year. I con-tact the American unit that arrived after the attack; I contact Andi's coworkers at NDI; I talk to Unity Resources Group, as well as my con-tacts in the security industry.

After months of asking NDI and URG for a full briefing, I finally get one in August 2007. I learn that the incident happened at 12:07 P.M. I learn that a local Iraqi car, believed to belong to the insurgents, got in front of Andi's car to slow it down. At that point, the car was attacked and disabled with machine-gun fire. The attackers rushed the car, shooting, tried to open the doors, and threw a grenade under it. After the explosion, the third car sped ahead into the smoke, crashing into Andi's car. That's what Jacob crashed into, the crash he couldn't talk to me about. One of the security guards in the third car got out and was killed; the other two, Jacob and the Iraqi driver, ran into a building for cover. The insurgents then rolled a grenade under the third car and it exploded. The first car returned to the incident, but it was too late. Twenty minutes later, they were joined by NDI's reinforcements.

NDI and URG tell me that they followed all of their normal security procedures. The procedures had never failed before; Andi is the first client

URG has lost, and the first NDI staffer to be killed in Iraq. NDI spent over $20 million a year on security for their Iraq program. However, NDI closed down its operation in Baghdad in the month following Andi's death, moved its Western staff to Amman and Kurdistan, and has not reopened it.

CHAPTER 24

January 21, 2007

KUWAIT

Karen and I wait for our flight in the television lounge at the Kuwait passenger terminal. It is late, past midnight, and we have not heard from our military contacts who are supposed to let us know what time we are leaving. Karen is asleep. I am getting nervous—I have little faith in the miracle of military travel. It has been five days since Andi was killed. I've been told that in Dover there might be up to a week's delay, as the U.S. military finishes the final identification of her remains. I am anxious to get out of Kuwait and into Germany for the last leg of the flight.

I ask the retired air force colonel, now hired as a private contractor, at the desk, "How's our flight?"

"The flight has been canceled," she says. "Mechanical problems."

"That's no good. So what flight are we on then?"

"You'll be on the flight with the other caskets from the Black Hawk crash," she explains.

"And what about our flight from Germany to Dover?"

"Right now, you're on a flight that takes off Tuesday morning from Germany."

"Tuesday morning? That's almost forty-eight hours later than when we were supposed to arrive. We need to get on the earliest flight possible from Germany to Dover. I can't believe there's not an earlier flight."

She nods, and says she will see what she can do.

I wake Karen. "Karen, there's an issue."

I hear the air force colonel on the radio. She is facing resistance. They don't want to move the flight in Germany up.

I make a call to *Newsweek,* and explain that we are being held up—they aren't giving us the flight that was promised. I tell them that I suspect what is happening is that with all the other dead over the weekend—a total now of twenty-four—they are trying to economize and put all of them on the same flight to Dover. I understand, I say, but Andi died first, she should have priority. *Newsweek* is going to make calls, to try to put pressure on the right people to get us an earlier flight. I say I will work it from my end to see what will happen.

I wait by the desk; the colonel says the problem is fixed. She arranged, in less than fifteen minutes, for the mission to be the earliest possible flight from Germany to Dover, which turns out to be leaving at 5 P.M. German time, arriving in Dover around 8 P.M. Eastern Standard Time.

It is still unclear when we will be leaving Kuwait, however.

I ask the Mortuary Affairs sergeant if I can come over to the terminal.

"Hi, Sergeant, I have a question for you, if you have a second, thanks. When are we going to get out to the flight line?"

"Sir, the HRs are going to be loaded in an hour, so you can go out in like fifteen minutes," he says.

"HRs? What does that mean?"

"Sorry, sir, HRs, uh, human remains."

"You know, Sergeant, in most organizations, HR stands for human resources, but hey, what are you going to do."

He laughs.

A van arrives to bring Karen and me out to the flight line. This time we are on a C-5. I climb inside, and it is the largest military aircraft I have ever been on. There are bright lights and an arenalike area for cargo that is currently empty. There are two levels, and the second floor is a passenger section of the plane that resembles the economy class of a commercial jet—it's up a wobbly set of folding stairs. We place our luggage on those seats, climb back down the stairs, and wait.

There will be another ceremony, I'm told. This time, it will take much longer, possibly up to an hour. There is only one honor guard detachment and there are twenty-five HRs that need to be loaded. They'll do it in two sets, the first twelve, then a brief break, then the second set.

I go smoke on the runway with members of the crew.

We are called back after twenty minutes.

It is 3 A.M. There is a glow of electric red light over the Kuwaiti base, blinking towers, high-intensity spotlights, vehicles scurrying across the runway. The war is getting farther away. The fear one feels instinctively in Baghdad fades. You can stand outside without thinking that a mortar or rocket could end your day. The loud noises aren't soldiers shooting or clearing their rifles, accidental discharges, warning shots, ambushes, death squads killing someone in the night—the loud noises are just noises. Most Americans posted to Iraq, all the living and all the dead, pass through Kuwait. We wait in the bright lights of the C-5 cargo bay, two rows of soldiers in air force gear, another chaplain, another prayer, another ceremony, standing and watching.

The ramp opens; another plain white delivery truck pulls up to it, revealing caskets resting inside. The caskets come in, one after the other, and after about five are loaded it all blends together, your legs start to get numb, and you start to shift your weight from one foot to the other. You can't sit down although you want to. You must respect them, the fallen soldiers, the angels, the lost, the mourned, the wasted, the sacrificed. You wait while one after the other is set down carefully, with precision, in two single-file rows. "Flag draped" is an inaccurate description. The flag does not drape, it is tightly tied down. The flag is much nicer than a black rubber body bag, it gives meaning to what is inside, the HRs, the human remains, the mutilated bodies, the bodies not mutilated, the bodies wrapped in plastic inside silver, the bodies whose organs are no more, the bodies without enough for a good DNA sample and bodies that are preserved, bodies with flesh and the bodies whose flesh has been burned away.

Andi's remains.

I am losing my shit.

I am numb. The twelfth casket is laid down on the floor of the plane.

There is a break in the ceremony; each casket takes about three minutes to load. The honor guard needs a break, as do those watching in silence.

"Which one is Andi?" I ask the master sergeant.

I want to make sure she is on the plane. I have asked this question a number of times, and have yet to get an answer. It is hard to say, they all look the same, and the only way is to check the papers on the side of the casket. The master sergeant goes and has words with the Mortuary Affairs sergeant. When he returns, he points to her casket.

The sixth one loaded on. I go up to it, and tap it.

She is here with me again.

The ceremony begins again.

The last thirteen caskets are loaded on. This time I am prepared for the time to pass slowly.

It is 4 A.M.

I notice Karen is on a cell phone.

When the ceremony is over, I ask Karen what's going on.

The Hungarian, Yonni, they didn't put the Hungarian on.

I look at her. I am too tired to try to get the Hungarian on. My responsibility is Andi, and Andi is on the plane. Her responsibility is the Hungarian, and he is not on, and she cannot get him on—something to do with orders. I realize this might delay things further in Dover—because of the "comingling of remains" they want to make sure Andi is separated properly from the Hungarian, and that can take time. But I don't have it in me to address the problem, and Karen doesn't seem to understand how it can be fixed. I don't have the strength to explain to her how to operate in this environment, that you must never take anything for granted, that you must be persistent, you must verify, you must keep on them, because things just don't happen. You can't be complacent and doze off in the TV lounge if you have to get things done. But I don't say any of this. We have been traveling now for almost twenty-four hours, I have not slept, and instead I go smoke another cigarette. The chaplain gives me a rosary and a quarter-sized gold angel coin, which I put in the top pocket of my blazer.

The C-5 takes off. Karen and I sit in separate rows on the second level, the whole compartment to ourselves. We are the only escorts, the only passengers on the flight. I wrap myself in three blankets; it is very cold up there. I sleep for four hours. When I wake up we are an hour away from Germany.

CHAPTER 25

January 22, 2007

RAMSTEIN AFB, DOVER

Ramstein Air Force Base Germany, near Frankfurt. Civilization is immediately apparent. There is a passenger terminal, a real one, without plywood and sandbags, but with clean glass and monitors that actually show what time flights arrive and depart. There are ticket counters and security checkpoints without M-4 rifles and grenades, where the soldiers meeting us are dressed nicely and know what is going on. There is no confusion once you get to Ramstein. This is an operation that moves cargo and people, and it runs smoothly—the airbase's motto, written on the map we are given when we land, is "Supporting the World!" We check into the hotel on base, a hotel like a Holiday Inn. I take a warm shower and change shirts and think about resting my eyes, but don't, and before I know it, I am back in the airport, getting my passport stamped at customs, and back on another plane. This one is a C-17. The caskets are already loaded up and strapped in place—no more ceremonies. There are two pairs of caskets in the first two rows, and then each row has three caskets. Each casket has about half a dozen clips on the side, which are strapped down on the floor with belts and metal buckles. At this stage of the trip, the war now on another continent, it is cargo to be carried.

The C-17 is smaller than the C-5, and the cargo bay is filled up with the caskets. They are close together in two rows, going back to the ramp and up to the cockpit. There is no passenger compartment for travelers; there is a long bench on the side of the cargo bay. I sit toward the front, and Karen sits next to me. We are the first passengers aboard the flight, the VIPs. I keep my sunglasses on. Other passengers file onto the plane, contractors and civilians who live in Germany and are catching a flight back to the States, to Charleston, with a stopover in Dover. There are men and women and families, toddlers and babies, about twenty people in all. They walk past me, being careful not to trip over the caskets, and sit down. I wonder if they got a warning—you can take this flight, even bring the kids, but be prepared, there are twenty-five caskets on board. Or you can take the next flight which leaves in four hours. Who wants a four-hour delay? The aircrew hands out earplugs and blankets, boxed lunches and soda.

The flight takes off.

I am hungry and thirsty and I need caffeine. I drink the Diet Pepsi and eat the sandwich in the box lunch. Other passengers do the same; some have brought their own meals for the flight.

The aircrew member lays down two sleeping bags on the floor, and asks if we want to sleep. Karen takes her up on the offer and lies down. I don't want to. The sleeping bags are lying parallel to the caskets, and I am not that tired. I prefer to sit back and close my eyes, perhaps pass out, perhaps not.

It is nine hours to Dover.

Some aircrew members work during the flight; some rest; others listen to iPods. A mother with two small children walks by me, carrying a baby, on the way to the restroom at the front of the plane.

I take out my iPod and listen to music. The songs Andi chose. I have figured out that her casket is toward the back of the plane, third row in.

I lean my head back.

One song after the other. I am beyond sobbing. I sit and grieve. I grieve for everything, for Andi and me, for Iraq, for my own stupid reasons for being there, for all of it, for this fucking travesty. Andi and two dozen soldiers, all with families dotted across America who are going through something like what I am going through right now, who received the message at the front door from the man in the uniform, who received the phone call with the terrible news, who dreaded this happening, it couldn't happen to them yet fuck if it didn't. And here I am, in this cargo bay, high above the ocean that keeps America away from the rest of the world, with air sickness bags nearby and boxed lunches with soda and military service families heading home for vacation and I feel the tremor of the plane and I close my eyes but I can still see the rows of caskets in front of me. My eyes are shut tight and I can see Andi perfectly in the third row and I know exactly what it would look like if we began the spiral down, if this plane crashed, if the cargo bay burst open right now and shot its cargo out, tearing off the metal clasps, the force of the catastrophic failure jettisoning each silver casket, twirling and spinning, mad batons, temperature-controlled containers though probably not too aerodynamic, flags ripping away from them, not at all like parachutes but like magnificent streamers, the twenty-five caskets falling in a beautiful burst, a grand finale, until finally they hit the ocean's surface one by one, an honorable splash, each making its own powerful ripple but one that will never make it to shore. The war is so far away now. Baghdad is now eight hours ahead, as I move back to the time zone of the United States, and half the passengers on this plane are still dead.

January 17, 2007

Andi sits in the back of the car. She is satisfied that the meeting went well. Nothing concrete, no progress, but more meetings lined up, the ball in motion. This is Iraq after all. What's progress? She feels cold for a moment. She had left her blue blazer back on her chair in her office. She has her folder, her work phone, her badges. Her body armor is on, snugly. The car is running; Yonni, from Hungary, gets in the front seat. An Iraqi man is behind the wheel. The day is still sunny, though it's not warm. It's January 17, 2007. Still winter in Iraq, or what passes for it. The sun comes in through the windshield, warming the inside of the car, the stale air.

She watches the first car leave the compound, out of view down the narrow street.

A minute or so passes. Her car goes forward. The guards at the Iraqi Islamic Party do not acknowledge them as her car passes through the gate.

The street is empty.

Or so it seems for a moment.

A car pulls in front of her vehicle; her driver has to stop. The noise begins. It takes only a second to know the noise is gunfire. The bullets hit the car. The driver cries out. The bullets hit the engine; her car jerks forward; the tires seem to explode; Yonni yells

Get down, get down, get down.

She inhales. She moves down in her seat. She hears yelling. The words are not clear. She looks out the window. Men are rushing toward her; they are wearing bandannas tied around their faces and pointing AK-47s at the car. She is down in her seat now. Does she scream? Does

255

she cry out? The men have grabbed the door handle and are yanking it, yelling; the noise has not stopped, not yet. They are pointing and waving the guns and trying to open the doors. The car is not moving. Why isn't the car moving?

She is now an observer. She is watching. It is all very clear to her.

This does not seem real. Why is it when things do not seem real, that's when they get real? When it is real it becomes unreal. She knows she will be safe. She knows that. No matter what happens.

It is happening so fast. It is so chaotic.

The men cannot get the doors open. They cannot get into the car. They cannot get her. They are like insane panhandlers in a traffic jam, in a nightmare, faces pressed against the glass. Distorted, excited, screaming. They decide to blow the car open.

The grenade doesn't make a sound when is it is dropped. The men run.

The explosion. In less then a second, the gas tank will catch fire.

Yonni sees the grenade. He somehow—he doesn't know how, he just does—he throws himself in the backseat. He covers her up, protects her from the blast.

Andi doesn't make a sound. She sees her guard do this; she sees him move to the backseat and cover her. The seat actually breaks as he climbs back. Crack. She is calm. She is looking at nothing now. She closes her eyes.

She sees her life. It all comes at once.

In her front yard, her mother calling. Her dad watching in the bleachers at a softball field in Perry, Ohio. She crashes against the center-field wall. The room she stayed in during summers with her grandmother. The red dress she wore at her sister's wedding. Chasing her two younger brothers around the couch.

There is more noise; there is a loud noise.

What is faster, sound or memories?

Her two nieces hugging her on the front porch, her sister snapping a digital picture. Her sister's husband serving swordfish just for her. A field of pine trees, snow covered, rows of white candles.

The flames are hot. It is so hot now.

What burns faster, memories or flames?

Ice skating. Raising her hand in a high school classroom. Graduation day. First day of college. Crossing the state line in a Ford. Moving into an apartment in Boston. At her desk in the governor's office, late at night, busy. An apartment in New York; a view of Central Park. Turning to tell her best friend the most recent crisis in her new office. She sees her friends; she sees her stones and her angels.

It is all there, it is coming.

There is her boyfriend, her significant other, the man she will marry. Seeing him that first night. Standing on the Charles Bridge in Prague. Standing at a glass counter looking at diamonds. Holding hands over the ocean, in a plane, through turbulence. Squeezing, twice for love. Staring into each other's eyes. Falling asleep, together.

She sees what happens.

Her father on a reclining chair in the living room crying, holding a picture of her, inconsolable. She sees her mother shaking softly in church, looking at her face, framed in a picture. She sees her sister on a bitter cold night alone in a snow-covered field screaming why, why, into the wind. She hears her niece ask where's Andi? She hears her brothers, playing music, loud, very loud, for her. She watches her fiancé writing with tears in his eyes.

It is almost over now.

She sees the rest of her life. She sees the ring. She sees a pure white wedding dress and an aisle. She sees her parents and brothers and sisters and friends smiling proudly. She sees the children and the house. She sees the reunions in Ohio; she feels the warmth and hears the laughter and feels the love for her.

The noise continues, but she is gone.

Afterword

I'm standing in the gravel yard of an American outpost in Afghanistan, eight miles from the Pakistani border. The outpost looks like a ski lodge without the snow. A comfortable stone building houses twenty-five soldiers, surrounded by three small mountains. The soldiers are loading up huge armored trucks—crates of eight-ounce cans of citrus-flavored Rippit energy drinks, plastic water bottles, a .50-caliber machine gun, a Mark II grenade launcher, flares, shoulder-fired rockets, boxes of ammunition, and seventy-two hours' worth of food. They're preparing for an overnight trip to a border checkpoint that gets attacked by the Taliban a few times a month.

It's 9 A.M., sunny, and I'm talking on my mobile phone. I don't remember who I'm talking to—a friend? An editor?—but I look at the phone before putting it back in my pocket. It's the same T-Mobile I had in Iraq, four years old, out of date, ancient. There's a crack in its plastic face, a piece of the silver coating ripped off. I should get a new one, one that has a battery that stays charged longer. I know why I haven't. It's an old phone, yes, and it has the memory capacity for only thirty text messages. Buried in the bottom of the inbox, text messages one, two, three, four, and five are some of the last that Andi sent me. It's October 15, 2008, nineteen months after her murder, and I haven't deleted them.

merry christmas mog. 12/25/06.
love you in red zone. 12/25/06.
Mog? 12/28/06.
did you hear from jeff? 12/29/06.

259

I put the phone back in my pocket.

There's a loud explosion. A funnel of white smoke shoots up behind a blast wall seventy-five feet away.

"Oh my god, we've been hit by a suicide bomber," screams the nineteen-year-old solider sitting in the guard tower.

The soldiers stop packing up the trucks and start to move, throwing their body armor and helmets on and sprinting toward the guard tower. There's gunfire from an AK-47, though it's impossible to see where it's directed. The Afghan guards, who live with the Americans at the outpost, come stumbling through the gate, carrying one of their own, a teenager, who looks like he's dying. They carry an older Afghan man, too, a police officer whose blood is running down his face. The American medic, Doc Allen, tells them to put the two men down and he gets to work, removing their clothes, trying to find out where all the blood is coming from. The kid has about forty or fifty small holes in him, made by the ball bearings that exploded out of the suicide vest. Doc Allen takes off the kid's pants to make sure he hasn't been hit in the groin and the kid's lying there naked and bleeding on a slab of concrete outside the motor pool, a white bandage pressed over his penis. One of his friends kneels next to him, holding his hand.

Outside the gate, Sergeant Joseph Biggs is making sure no one else is hit. Biggs is a twenty-four-year-old from Florida. He has over a dozen tattoos. One on his left arm says "WAR" and one on his right says "KILL," and another on his biceps spells out the Arabic word for "infidel." He points to a live grenade on the ground, near one of the severed legs of the bomber. "He was about to throw that," he says.

For forty-five minutes, Doc Allen keeps the kid alive, and then a Black Hawk helicopter arrives, stirring up a dust storm, and the two men are loaded on. After they leave, several of the soldiers meet in the tactical operations center inside the outpost, where the unit's captain, Terry Hilt, tries to piece together what happened. Hilt determines that the suicide bomber approached through the valley between the two hills. A group of five or six Afghan boys ran up and surrounded him as he got close. The children are eight or nine years old and are regulars at the base. They come over most days after school and the Americans give them chores to do, like filling sandbags or gathering up golf balls that have been hit into the valley. Most of the guys here like having them around.

The base's security cameras captured the attack. The footage shows the bomber approach the gate (the kids, at this point, have run away, taking a seat on the dirt-filled Hesco barriers that have been set up as backstops out on the firing range). The bomber stops outside the barbed-wire fence, and the young guard stands up and orders him to stay where he is and wait to be searched. On camera, the guard moves across the screen from right to left. Off-screen the suicide bomber has pulled out a grenade. The guard stops and backs up, cocking his AK-47 and lifting it up to fire, and that's when the suicide vest explodes. Smoke fills the screen and the guard disappears, then reappears, staggering backward and screaming, before falling to the ground. "We're going to need to clean that whole yard," Hilt says now. "Once everyone is inside, I'll talk to everyone real quick. We're going to try to HIIDE him [identify using a retinal or fingerprint scan], if we can find the head. Hey, Sergeant Biggs."

"Hooah," Biggs says.

"You said the head was out there?"

"No, just the scalp, just the hair."

"The flesh out there," another soldier adds, "it's everywhere."

"I guess we don't bring them kids back no more," Biggs says. "I always said with the kids around, there's going to be some shit like that. The kids are the ones who brought him over here, the little terrorist bastards."

The rest of the soldiers gather in the living room (or the Moral Welfare and Recreation area, as it's called), where at night they watch DVDs and play the video game *Rockstar*. "Everyone knows what just happened," Hilt says to the group. "The mission to the border is going to be off. Hey, what typically happens after one bomber?"

"Another one," the soldiers answer in chorus.

That night, the wild dogs that the Americans tried to scare off earlier in the week are back, barking and fighting over the bits of flesh that flew so far from the base they were missed during the cleanup.

This was my second visit to a conflict zone since Andi's death. The first was a trip back to Baghdad in April 2007.

There was no good excuse for me to be back in Afghanistan or Iraq, except that I told myself it was my job, covering America's two wars. But maybe that isn't entirely honest. Was part of me looking to get killed, too? To even the scales, neatly tie up my love for her, to complete the narrative. Two lovers, both dead. How tragic. Maybe there was part of me that didn't want to die just yet, wanting to say, "Fuck you war, you can't destroy me. I'm going to win this, on my terms." A delusion, of course, because war always wins. If I'm going to be completely honest, I have to admit that the empty prestige and the stupid glory—yes, the horrible rush, the deadly sense of importance that war brings to life— are hard illusions to shake off. Look at me, a war correspondent— seventy-five feet from a suicide bomber, still alive. I knew I wasn't going to learn anything fundamentally new in Afghanistan about the nature of war, the reason why I'd started to cover the conflicts in the first place. Andi's death was a brutal lesson, and I understood war on a level that I wished I didn't. I'd spent most of the time since she was killed trying to make sense of it.

Writing this book was a way for me to do that. I wrote most if it in a three-week period in February 2007, in my parent's attic in Vermont. It was as much a survival instinct as anything else. To cope, to not end my own life. It was to write or die. I needed to make sure Andi would not be forgotten; that her death wouldn't just be an uptick in statistics, another number in the more than 150,000 Iraqis and 4,500 Americans dead.

Over the next four months, from May to June, I took that first attic draft and made it into something people could read. On June 16, 2007, Andi's birthday, I traveled to Paris with her family and spread her ashes on the Seine. In September, I moved to Washington, D.C., where I spent the next year covering the U.S. presidential campaigns. After the primaries ended, I quit my job at *Newsweek*. I wrote a story for *GQ* about the elections, and then they put me on assignment to write a piece about Afghanistan. I had loved my time at *Newsweek,* for the most part. But after writing the book, I wanted to keep writing in my own voice. *GQ* would allow me to do that. I no longer cared as much about playing the career game, playing it safe, and climbing the corporate ladder. Life was too short to write things that I didn't fully believe in. The romanticism and excitement that had brought me to Baghdad were gone. Andi getting killed wasn't in the script. That's the thing with war, I guess, it follows its own script, and it's never what the authors have in mind.

By the time you read this, Andi will have been dead three years. She'll have lived with me as a memory twice as long as our relationship.

The memories never go away. Here are a few I didn't put in the book. Andi and I on long car rides, a handful of them, when she'd start talking and I would just sit and listen. Unself-conscious, opening up, she talked about her deepest beliefs and dreams. When she would call me while I was away and tell me that she had arranged her pillows on her bed to re-create the nook—that position where she placed her head on my chest and would drift off into sleep. When we would go out to dinner with friends (again, it will never have been often enough) and how she would retell the story of our first meeting at the Jerry Springer event, how I charged in the room, head down, note pad in hand; how I saw her, and pictured her as mine, as a girl I'd be happy to wait outside a movie theater for on a New York street, content, not questioning the possibilities of the sidewalk traffic, the other girls walking by, never making comparisons in my head.

The war left me with memories and grief and anger and a struggle to find hope, to find reasons to go on. It left me with this book, published in six different countries, with excerpts of the story in many more. In Perry, Ohio, Andi's hometown, a copy of the book sits in the library and in the local historical society.

The war left Mohammed, my translator, with a life in exile. He escaped Iraq with a Fulbright scholarship. In 2008, he received asylum in America. He now has a masters in journalism and is enrolled in a PhD program at the University of Indiana in Bloomington. Munib, our cook and houseboy, was fired in 2008 after he began making threats against the other staff members—his uncle, it turns out, was a commander in the Mehdi Army. The happy-go-lucky kid I had become friends with was subsumed by the sectarian forces unleashed in his country. Our Iraqi office manager fled Iraq and received asylum in Ireland; his brother, who also worked with us as a translator, was granted asylum in Houston, Texas. Last year, *Newsweek* shut down the house in the Green Zone, and in 2009, closed the magazine's permanent Baghdad bureau. (As the war has winded down, *Newsweek,* along with many other new agencies, has scaled back its presence in Iraq.)

The war has affected my family in other ways. It left my younger brother, Jeff, with a bronze star. He served a full fifteen-month tour. Three of his close friends weren't so fortunate. His best friend and roommate, Lieutenant Ferris Butler, lost both his feet in an IED attack in December 2007. (This is what the text that Andi sent me—*did you hear from Jeff?*—referred to. After Ferris got hurt, their unit had been subjected to a communications blackout to prevent news from reaching home before the families of the injured had been notified.) His other good friend, Captain Scott Quilty, lost his right arm and right leg below the knee. Jeff's next roommate, and another dear friend, Lieutenant Greg Cartier, was hit in April 2007, losing an eye. Two years out, they're all doing okay—Jeff is on his way to medical school; Ferris works in the senate office of John McCain; Scott is an executive at the Survivors Corps, a land-mine victim advocacy group; and Greg is a year into a law degree.

The war left Andi's family without a daughter and sister. Proceeds from this book helped establish the Andi Foundation. The foundation has awarded four scholarships and helped fund a fellowship program with the National Democratic Institute. The first Andi Parhamovich Memorial Fellowship was given to an Iraqi woman who worked this past year in Washington, D.C. She was able to visit Perry and spent Christmas 2008 with the Parhamovich family.

"On the day my life changed forever—when it was shattered by the grenade that killed my daughter—I knew that I would never be the same," Andi's father, Andre, emailed me last year:

I knew that every remaining day of my life would be filled with sadness and pain. I wish that I could say, two years later, that I'm learning to accept Andi's death. But I can't and never will. What I am learning, however, is how to find small comforts that soften the sadness in my soul. . . . I look at my children as my legacy to society and future generations. My legacy which was in Andrea would have been passed to her children. Now, that rite of passage has been closed. Whatever Andi had to share from her personal inheritance from me, can only now be accomplished by me acting on her behalf. Andi will remain alive in my thoughts and memories. She can still make a difference in society. Maybe if others can see me act in positive and compassionate ways, then Andi's spirit has "lived on" to help mold the future. And maybe the door to the rite of passage has been opened again.

"You know," Andre told me, "you could have named the book *We Lost Our Love in Baghdad*."

We lose our love, and it hurts to find it again. I think we can only ask ourselves, What else really matters?
—M.H.
June 17, 2009

Note on Names, Security Procedures, Sources

Due to the deadly nature of working in Iraq, I've changed or used only the first names of the Iraqi security guards and interpreters employed by *Newsweek*. The exception is Mohammed—his full name is Mohammed Heydar Sideq, and he is currently studying in the United States on a Fulbright scholarship. I have changed the names of the men and women working for NDI and URG. The name of the Mortuary Affairs officer has been changed. The names of the Western security managers working for *Newsweek* have been changed. Also, Tony is not the real first name of Crazy Tony the German.

I have slightly altered one aspect of a *Newsweek* security procedure described in the book: the color of cars we drive in Iraq. The cars are currently in use, and I do not wish to put anyone's life at greater risk by giving out those details.

There are a number of books I've read that have served as a source for inspiration. In chapter 1, the actual quote from Kapuściński's *Imperium* is: "But experience has taught that whenever people are taking me on a hazardous, uncertain improbable expedition, it is inappropriate to ask questions. If you ask, it means you don't trust them; you are uncertain; you are afraid. But you said you wanted to do this. Make up your mind—are you ready for anything or not? Besides—there is no time! It is too late for indecision, for hesitation, for alternatives." Other books: *Once Upon a Distant War* by William Prochnau, *If I Die in a Combat Zone* by Tim O'Brien, *Slightly Out of Focus* by Robert Capa, *Born on the Fourth of July* by Ron Kovic, Neal Sheehan's *A Bright and Shining Lie,*

Bernard Fall: Memories of a Soldier-Scholar, a memoir by his wife Dorothy Fall, and Timothy Findley, *The Wars.*

The events recounted in this book are largely drawn from my own notes, observations, and conversations over a two-year period, from August 2005 when I first arrived in Iraq to August 2007 when I completed the reporting for this book. But I also relied on day-to-day news accounts. For this, I am indebted to the excellent work of the Baghdad press corps—*The New York Times, The Washington Post,* the *L.A. Times, The Wall Street Journal,* AP, AFP, Reuters, *Newsweek, Time, The New Yorker,* CNN, and the other networks. I also found the Brookings Institute's Iraq Index website very helpful for chapter 14, as well as the Iraq Coalition Casualties website. The scenes describing my relationship with Andi are how I remembered them. The emails, text messages, and instant messages are all real. The scene that the book opens with—and the one it closes with, that of Andi's death—is what I imagined happened, based on the reporting I was able to collect.

Acknowledgments

There are many people I'd like to thank for support for me and for this book. First, I'd like to thank my editor Nan Graham at Scribner for her incredible insights, her amazing guidance, and her uncompromising standards. To my agent Sarah Chalfant at the Wylie Agency for her calming voice, her friendship, and for believing in this from the beginning. I am especially grateful for the support of *Newsweek* magazine. It has been a privilege for me to work for, and learn from, Jon Meacham, Fareed Zakaria, and Dan Klaidman. I would also like to thank Lally Weymouth, Don Graham, and Rick Smith, for treating me like a member of the family. To Scott Johnson, Babak Dehghanpisheh, and Rod Nordland for teaching me how to report in Iraq. To my editors at the magazine, Nisid Hajari, Jeff Bartholet, Andrew Nagorksi, and Sam Seibert, who week after week always asked the right questions. To Jon Darman for being a great friend willing to hear me vent. To my other editors and colleagues at the magazine (former and current) who I learned so much from over the years: Tony Emerson, Fred Guterl, John Wojno, Susan Greenberg, Christian Caryl, Jack Livings, David Kammerman, Christopher Dickey, Mark Whitaker, Alexis Gelber, Michael Hirsh, Dave Friedman, Cathy Ruggiero, Sharon Sullivan, Jamie Cunningham, Nancy Cooper, Ranya Khadri, Mark Miller, Marcus Mabry, Malcolm Beith, Michael Meyer, Sarah Childress, Stryker McGuire, Silvia Spring, Will Dobson, Richard Ernsberger, Dan Ephron, Kevin Peraino, Joanna Chen, Nuha Musla, Debra Rosenburg, Deidre Depke, Arlene Getz, and Carl Sullivan (for putting my stories up on the website, no matter the hour). I also need to thank my translators in Iraq, especially Mohammed Heydar Sideq, and

ACKNOWLEDGMENTS

I hope one day I can give you all the credit you deserve. I owe a debt of gratitude to the staff at the U.S. embassy in Baghdad: Lou Fintor, Nicole Sanders, John Sullivan, John Roberts, Clinton Carter, Armand Cucinello, and Ambassador Zalmay Khalilzad. For the *Newsweek* security managers I can't name—thanks as well. To my friends from the Baghdad press corps: Louise Rouge, Solomon Moore, Phillip Shiskin, Larry Kaplow, Borzou Dargahi, and Ned Parker. To Lucian Read for keeping me company with the 172nd and beyond. To all the U.S. soldiers and marines I met—there are too many to name, and I thank them for keeping me safe and letting me ride along. Captain Brad Velotta, LTC John Norris, LTC Steven Duke, LTC Barry Johnson, Captain John Grauer, Captain Gregory Hirschey, Staff Sergeant Jason DeMoss, Lance Corporal Andrew Gladue, Sergeant Brian Patton, and all the men of the 172nd Stryker Brigade. To Joel Lovell for getting me to the finish line with excellent editorial skill. To Edward Orloff at the Wylie Agency for his always good advice and willingness to listen to me ramble. To Lauretta Charlton at Scribner for making sure I got all the right pages at the right time. To my friends Sanjay Reddy, Raja Reddy, Michal Hanuka, and Nick Braccia. Thanks to Pat and Charlie Bresnahan and Suzie and Wendell Cook for the hospitality, and room with a view. To Sarah Raimo and Keri Bertolino. To Matt Hiltzik and Al Franken for keeping Andi's memory alive. To Jaime Horn for her friendship and love of Andi. To my family, Brent, Molly, Jeff, Jon, Margaret, and Ruthgram. To Joe, Marci, Kayla, and Abby Zampini. To Cory and Chris Parhamovich. And to Vicki and Andre Parhamovich for your love, your strength, and for bringing Andi into this world.

Index

NOTE: Andi refers to Andi Parhamovich; MH refers to Michael Hastings.

ABC, MH interview about Andi's death
 with, 218–19
Abu Ghraib prison, 118, 187
"abyss quote," 121–22, 123
acronyms, 41–43
Afghanistan, 134, 147, 214, 233, 259
Ahmed (airport friend), 167–68
Ahmer (Iraqi staff member), 24, 25, 187
Air America, 30, 31, 32, 101, 129, 133
Airport, Baghdad International
 ceremony for casualties returning
  home at, 229, 230–34, 235,
  237–39
 checkpoints at, 65–66
 conditions at, 65–66
 MH first trip between Baghdad and,
  6–9, 12–13
 MH flights out of, 63, 64–66, 167–68
 MH stuck at, 167–68
AKE security company, 29
Al Qaeda, 52, 114, 118, 202, 215, 219
al-Hakim, Abdel Aziz, 142, 143
Al-Hakimiya prison, 114–18
al-Sadr, Moqtada, 200–201, 220
Al-Zawra TV, 185–86
Alaska
 Rumsfeld trip to, 157
 as Stryker Brigade home base, 148,
  149, 150, 157
Albright, Madeleine, 133
Ali (Iraqi staff member), 24

Alias Restaurant (New York City), 34,
 39
Allegro (Prague restaurant), 125
American Colony Hotel, 172
Ammad (security guard), 186
Amman, Jordan
 Andi at IRI conference in, 162–63
 Andi and MH in, 172–73
 MH in, 78
 NDI moves to, 243
Amnesty International, 178
Anbar Province, insurgency in, 52
Andi
 Baghdad "home" of, 164–65
 birthdays of, 33, 35, 37, 134
 character of, 33
 childhood and youth of, 76
 early days in Baghdad of, 161–67,
  170–71
 fright of, 203–4
 and IRI, 133–34, 145–46, 162–63,
  170–71
 job change by, 133–34
 last day in Baghdad of, 1–3, 255–57
 and Live 8 concert in England, 32, 37
 personal and professional background of, 33, 75, 133
 security equipment for, 163, 255
 security guards/procedures for, 164,
  165, 170, 173, 194, 242–43,
  255, 256

Andi (*cont.*)
views about Bush of, 32–33
at wedding, 56, 60, 61–62
See also Andi and MH; Andi—death
of; *specific topic*
Andi and MH
and Andi's feelings about MH in
Iraq, 127
and Andi's reaction to MH permanent assignment in Iraq, 132–33
and Andi's ring, 161, 162–63, 167,
169, 204, 209, 219, 257
"breakups" between, 71–72, 130–31
emails/instant messages between,
79–84, 99–108, 259
engagement of, 132, 219
first meetings and dates of, 29–35,
37–40
future plans of, 171, 204
gifts between, 39, 67, 213, 223
"goodbyes" between, 40, 78
holidays of, 71–78, 173–74, 223
in Jerusalem, 172, 189
in Jordan, 172–73
"The March 6 Agreement" between,
125–26
and MH commitment to work,
127–28
and MH decision to stay in Iraq, 61–62
and MH in Fallujah, 56, 60–62
and MH first byline from Iraq, 27
and MH initial deployment to Iraq,
31, 32, 38, 39, 40
and MH jealousy, 163
and MH return to New York, 65, 67,
68–69
and MH worries about Andi's safety,
171–72
in Ohio, 73–77
in Prague, 125–28, 257
in Puerto Rico, 134
Vermont visit of, 77–78, 223
Vienna meeting of, 107, 109–10,
112, 123–24, 126, 128, 223, 224

Andi—death of
Baghdad Airport ceremony for, 223,
229, 230–34, 237–39
belongings of, 213, 223–25, 230
blame for, 216–17, 220, 221
body of, 213–14, 215, 221, 234
burned car in, 235
CID investigation of, 234–35
details of, 209, 217, 219, 225–27,
234–35, 241–42, 255–57
embassy report about, 219
FBI investigation of, 217, 231
flight home from Baghdad of, 223,
229, 230–36, 237–43, 245–49,
251–53
funeral for, 229
as good news story, 234
Islamic jihadists as responsible for,
215, 219
Jacob's story about, 225–27
and Kuwait ceremony, 239–40, 246–48
and lack of security briefing for Andi,
241
MH accompanies body, 223
MH initial reactions to, 208–12,
213–22
MH inquiry about, 217, 242
MH learns of, 207–12
MH media interviews about, 217–19
MH permission to accompany body
of, 214–15, 229
MH views about, 227
as setup, 209, 216, 219
Andi Foundation, 264
Anfal Province, genocide campaign in,
177, 178
anthrax, 12
anti-Americanism, 110, 163, 187,
200–201
Armstrong Williams Radio Show, 194
Army, Iraqi
avoidance of, 176
and clearing of Ghazaliya, 152, 154,
155, 156

clothing for, 202
Duke's views about, 198
and Haifa Street battle, 193, 197
as undermanned and underequipped, 198
Asian Games (2006), 136
Associated Press, 218
Aziz, Khalid, 56–57, 58

Badr Brigade, 142
Baghdad Bomb Squad, 47–52
Baghdad Country Club, 162, 174
Baghdad Headhunters, 50
Baghdad, Iraq
Andi applies for job in, 133–34
Andi's early days in, 161–67, 170–71
Andi's "home" in, 164–65
Andi's last day in, 1–3, 255–57
bombing of (2003), 166
challenges of having relationships in, 164, 199
Christmas and New Year's in, 173–74
clearing of neighborhoods in, 147–60
curfew in, 201
daily life for MH in, 135–41
journalists' feelings about, 24
MH arrival in, 5–6
MH early days in, 15–17
MH first views of, 13
MH "home" in, 22–23
number of checkpoints in, 113
tourist attractions in, 19
walls around neighborhoods in, 184
women in, 163
See also specific person or topic
Balkans, refugees from, 113
Battle of Baghdad, 147–60
BBC, 140, 180
Berg, Nicholas, 18
Biggs, Joseph, 260, 261
The Big Lebowski (film), 11

Black Hawk helicopter, shooting down of, 239, 240, 245
Blackwater security guards, 18, 20, 164, 165
Blue Star (Baghdad restaurant), 146, 161–62, 163, 166, 167, 225
Bohne, Jeff, 51
Bomb Garden, 47, 48
"Bombs Over Baghdad" (Outkast), 11
bribes, 64, 114, 116
Bring Them Home concert, 129
Brooklyn Diner (New York City), 32
Buffalo (armored vehicle), 44, 45
Burns, John, 112
Bush, George H. W., 10, 33
Bush, George W.
and "abyss quote," 122
Andi's views about, 33
criticisms of, 160
and elections of 2000, 11
and elections of 2004, 33
and Hurricane Katrina, 52
and Hussein's execution, 182
Iraqi Islamic Party visit with, 219
and Stryker Brigade, 150, 160
Vietnam visit of, 170
Byron, Robert, 137

Cairo, Egypt, as MH base, 132, 169
Caldwell, William, 113, 182
Camp Cropper, 177
Camp Justice, 181
Camp Liberty, 123, 151, 235
Camp Striker, 148, 151, 156, 158
Camp Victory, 47–52, 64, 121, 122, 191, 221, 233
Capa, Robert, 77
car bombs, 6, 21, 22, 46–47, 171, 184, 186. See also type of bomb
Carroll, Jill, 216
Carter, Jimmy, 134
Casey, George, 103, 150, 191
CASH (Combat Army Support Hospital), 159, 214

casualties
    aid worker, 196
    American, 141, 174, 183, 195, 198,
        239, 240
    Blackwater employees as, 18
    civilian contractors, 196
    and denial of civil war, 123
    of insurgents, 193
    Iraqi, 141, 174, 193, 195, 198
    journalists as, 25, 196, 216
    and Karma patrols, 58
    odds for becoming, 59
    See also specific person
CBS, MH interview about Andi's death
    with, 217–18
cell phones, 138–39, 194
Central Criminal Court of Iraq, 101–3
Chambersburg, Pennsylvania, Green
    interview in, 130
checkpoints
    at Baghdad Airport, 65–66
    executions and kidnappings at, 113
    around Green Zone, 19
    guards at, 17, 19, 20
    illegal, 113, 176
    kidnappings at, 176
    and MH visit with Andi at NDI,
        176
    number of Baghdad, 113
    and rules for moving around Green
        Zone, 16
Cheney, Dick, 11
Chiarelli, Peter, 191, 192
Chicago Tribune, 117–18
Christmas
    in Baghdad, 173
    in Vermont, 77–78, 223
CIA (Central Intelligence Agency),
    174
civil war, Iraqi
    and attacks on mosques, 119
    and Battle of Baghdad, 147
    beginning of, 109–12
    debate about existence of, 112–14
    and definition of civil war, 113–14

denial of existence of, 110, 113–14,
    121–22, 123
as "low-intensity ethnic conflict," 113
MH first story about, 114
and "sectarian violence," 112–13
U.S. efforts to stop, 147
"clear, hold, build" strategy, 147
Clinton, Bill, 11, 170
CNN, 109, 140, 149, 212, 240
Coalition of the Willing, 17, 230–31,
    233, 242
C.O.B.R.A., 12
combat patrols, MH first with, 44–47
Combined Press Information Center
    (CPIC), 182–85
conspiracies, Iraqi beliefs in, 202
contractors, civilian/defense, 19, 196.
    See also specific contractor
Convention Center, Iraqi
    Andi's work at, 165
    car bombs/assassination attempt at,
        171
    and Hussein's trial and execution,
        178, 179
    MH first visit to, 16–17
    See also parliament, Iraqi
convoys, military, and trip between
    Baghdad and airport, 6, 9
"corkscrew landings," 6
Crazy Tony the German, 21
CRG Logistics, 19
The Crisp, 235
Crossed Swords monument, 19, 158,
    159, 179
Cruz, Staff Sergeant, 233
CTU security firm, 176
curfews
    and beginning of civil war, 110, 111,
        112
    and MH flight to Vienna, 124
    and state of emergency, 123

"A Daily Dance with Death" (MH), 59
Dana (Slav woman), 125
Danny (bomb squad tech), 48

INDEX

DBIED (donkey-borne improvised explosive device), 46
death squads
  and clearing of Ghazaliya, 152, 155, 156
  Duke's comments about, 198
  ethnic cleansing by, 18
  first Shiite, 142
  formation of, 18, 142
  joke about, 140–41
  MH interview with, 118
  ordinariness of, 118
  police as, 117–18
  Sadr's Mehdi, 220
  U.S. capture of first, 117–18
Defense Department, U.S.
  casualty reports by, 198
  and JIEDD program, 131
  and MH travel orders to accompany Andi's body, 229, 230
  and military public relations, 183
  and Stryker Brigade extension, 150
defense/civilian contractors, 19, 196. See also specific corporation
Dehghanpisheh, Babak, 186, 187, 199, 211
Democratic Party, 133–34
Desert Rogues, 44–47
Desert Storm, 9–11, 49
Diana (psychic), 224
Diefenbaker, John, 33
displacement camps, 143
Dover Air Force Base, 229–30, 245, 246, 248, 252–53
Drudge Report, 180
DSN (defense switched network), 214
Dubai, 66–68, 167–68, 169, 209, 216
Dujaili massacre, 177
Duke, Steven, 196–99, 201
DynCorp, 19

Edinburgh Risk, 15, 22
EFP (explosively formed projectile or penetrator), 46, 186
82nd Airborne Division, 184, 195

elections, Iraqi, 63–64
elections, U.S., 11, 33, 153
email
  Andi-MH, 101, 104–7
  Andi's access to MH, 224
embassy, U.S.
  and Andi's death, 214, 218
  and ceremony for Andi at airport, 230–31
  and Christmas in Baghdad, 173
  description of, 20–21
  guards for, 20
  and MH permission to accompany Andi's body home, 214–15
  and MH-ABC interview about Andi's death, 218
  public relations for, 182
  See also Green Bean
embeds
  equipment for, 43–44
  and first combat patrol for MH, 44–47
  on MH first trip to Iraq, 41–61
  and MH loss of weight, 68
  of MH in Mosul, 63–64
  and movement of journalists in Iraq, 17
  and rules of reporting, 24
  See also specific embed
Emirates Airlines, 68
EOD (explosives ordnance disposal), 47–52
Es-Vee-Bid. See SVBIED (suicide vehicle-borne improvised explosive device)
ethnic cleansing, 18, 197–98
execution(s)
  of Saddam Hussein, 178–82
  and "sectarian violence," 113
exit visas, 64–65, 66

Fallujah, Iraq
  battle of, 159
  casualties in, 52
  and early days of journalists in Iraq, 17

INDEX

Fallujah, Iraq (*cont.*)
    MH embed in Karma and, 52–62, 194
    murder of Blackwater employees in, 18
families, military, strains on, 150, 157
Fatah, 172
FBI (Federal Bureau of Investigation), 217, 231
Fintor, Lou, 214–15, 230, 231, 233, 235, 237
1st Battalion 64th Armor Regiment, 44–47
"flag-draped" caskets, 247
flags, of the Coalition of the Willing, 230–31
flashbangs, 58
Fleur, 19
FOB Rustamiyah, combat patrols from, 44–47
"FOBBIT," 42
Fort Lewis (Alaska), 148, 157
Fort Richardson (Alaska), 148
Forward Operating Base Prosperity, 196
Four Seasons Hotel (Amman, Jordan), Andi-MH stay at, 172, 224
Four Seasons Hotel (New York City), Andi-MH stay at, 134
4th Infantry Division, 156
4-23 Tomahawk battalion, 148, 149, 150–59
Fox News, MH interview on, 122, 131–32
Franks, John, 232–34, 235, 236, 238
Freeman, Robert "Freebase," 54, 55

games, video, during soldiers' free time, 48, 55–56, 77, 78, 80
Garden of Shame, 47–48
Gates, Bill, 170
Gaza Strip, 170, 171
Georgian soldiers, 19
Germany. *See* Ramstein Air Force Base
Ghazaliya (Baghdad neighborhood), clearing of, 151–59, 220
Gladue, Andrew, 60

Glass House (Sather Airfield), 232–33
Global Security, 66
Golden Mosque (Samarra), bombing of, 109, 110, 111, 113, 118, 119, 122, 148
government, Iraqi
    MH views about, 220–21
    See also parliament, Iraqi
Grauer, John, 149–50, 157
Green, Steven, 130
Green Bean coffee shop (Baghdad), 20, 179, 235
Green Zone
    and Andi and MH meetings, 187, 199
    barriers around, 16
    checkpoints around, 12–13, 19
    culture in, 19–20
    daily life in, 18–19
    Duke's concerns about security in, 198
    identity badges for, 15, 21, 142–43, 187
    IRI location in, 146
    lack of women in, 163
    life for journalists in, 21–24
    lock down of, 171
    population of, 18
    rules for moving around in, 16
    and Saddam's trial and execution, 174, 177, 179, 181
    shelling in, 23, 165–66, 200
    Stryker Brigade convoy in, 158–59
    See also specific location
Green Zone Café, 162
Greene, Graham, 137, 169
Gurkhas, 17, 19–20

Hadi, Ma'an, 117
Haditha massacre, 129–30, 159
Haifa Street battle, 193, 196–99, 200, 201, 216
Hakki (Iraqi staff member), 26–27
Halliburton. *See* KBR

Halo 2 (game), 48
Hamas, 170
Hammond, Major, 149
Hamra Hotel (Baghdad), 17, 22, 24
Hamza, Omar, 102
Hashemi, Tarek al-, 219
Hastings, Brent (father), 10, 11, 77, 158, 210, 223
Hastings, Jeff (brother), 77, 158, 202, 213, 218, 264
Hastings, Jon (brother), 77
Hastings, Michael
    in Afghanistan, 260–62
    Baghdad "home" of, 22–23
    birthday of, 107
    and blame for Andi's death, 216
    body armor/equipment of, 43–44, 194–95, 232, 239
    childhood and youth of, 10–11, 67
    commitment to work of, 127–28
    desire to go to Iraq of, 29–30
    effects of Iraq on, 73
    as freelance reporter, 30–31
    grieving of, 253
    hometown of, 119
    ID photographs of, 142–43
    job at *GQ*, 263
    planned Iraq trip of, 31, 32, 38, 39, 40
    security training for, 29, 31
    See also specific person or topic
Hastings, Molly (mother), 77, 122, 158, 210, 211, 213
Hilt, Terry, 260, 261
Hirschey, Gregory, 48, 49
Ho Chi Minh, 170
"honor of the troops," 59
Horn, Jaime, 210–11
hotspots, naming of, 42
human rights, 103, 114
Humvees
    Al-Zawra broadcasts about, 185
    armor on, 151, 176, 197
Hungarian Airlines, 67
Hurricane Katrina, 49–52

Hussam (Iraqi staff member), 24
Hussein, Saddam, 10, 177–82, 200
Hyatt Regency Hotel (Dubai), 68

identity badges, 15, 17, 21, 142–43, 146, 187
IEDs (improvised explosive devices)
    Al-Zawra broadcasts about, 185, 186
    casualties from, 43, 121, 122, 123
    and cell phone network, 138
    and clearing of Ghazaliya, 155, 156, 159, 220
    Fox-MH interview about, 131
    and Grauer as "combat chaplain," 149
    and Haditha massacre, 130
    and Karma patrols, 58
    as most feared among soldiers, 18
    and "route security" patrols, 54–55
    and Stryker Brigade, 149, 150, 155, 156, 159
    as trash, 45
    See also specific type of IED
If I Die in a Combat Zone (O'Brien), 137
IIP. *See* Iraqi Islamic Party
insurgents, Iraqi
    Al-Zawra broadcasts about, 186
    and Andi's death, 216, 217, 219, 242
    and Battle of Baghdad, 147
    and Black Hawk helicopter crash, 239
    casualties among, 193
    and civil war, 114
    and clearing of Ghazaliya, 152, 154–55
    and Haifa Street battle, 197, 201
    IIP ties to, 220
    increase in strength of, 142
    press releases of, 185
    U.S. base attacked by, 166
International Republican Institute (IRI), 133–34, 145–46, 162–63, 170–71

INDEX

International Zone. *See* Green Zone
interrogation cells, 115, 118
Iran, 46, 185
Iran-Iraq War, land mines in Iraq from, 49
Iraq
  Andi's feelings about MH in, 127
  Andi's preparations for job in, 146–47
  constitution for, 63–64
  effects on MH of, 73
  elections in, 63–64
  films about, 11
  Kuwait invasion by, 136
  MH decision to stay in, 61–62
  MH desire to go to, 29–30, 129–30
  MH offered job of permanent correspondent in, 132–33
  MH return to, 78, 79–84, 135
  MH views about, 81, 219, 221
  political parties in, 220
  U.S. invasion of, 11–12
Iraqi Islamic Party (IIP), 2–3, 156, 216, 217, 219–20, 226, 227, 240–41, 255
Iraqi leaders, homes of, 19
Iraqi staff (*Newsweek*)
  characteristics of, 25
  and daily life in Baghdad, 138
  location of, 25
  members of, 24–25
  risks for, 23, 143
  as sources for stories, 24
  See also specific member
Iraqis
  anti-Americanism of, 110, 163, 187, 200–201
  grievances of Baghdad, 143
  names for, 42
  as refugees, 143
  soldiers' shooting of, 45–46
  See also specific person
Iraqna, 138, 158, 194, 203, 204, 207, 208
IRI. *See* International Republican Institute
Islamic State of Iraq, 215, 219

Israel
  and Andi-MH plans for future, 204
  MH trip to, 169, 170–72

Jabouri, Mishaan al-, 185
Jacob (security guard), 225–27, 242
Jadriya Bunker (Iraqi police base), 103
Jereza, Phillip, 153
Jerusalem
  Andi-MH in, 172, 189
  and Andi-MH plans for future, 204
Johnson, Scott
  asks MH to come to Iraq, 31–32
  and Christmas in Baghdad, 173
  and daily life in Baghdad, 135, 136, 137, 140
  and Hussein's trial and execution, 179
  and MH decision to stay in Iraq, 61
  and MH early days in Baghdad, 15, 17
  and MH first embed, 43, 44
  and MH Karma patrols, 55, 56
  and MH visit with Andi at NDI, 187
  and military media stories, 182
  professional background of, 15–16
  relief of, 186
  and rotation schedule, 169
  and rules of reporting, 24
Joint IED Defeat Task Force, 131
Jordan, Alexander, 159
Jordan
  Andi-MH in, 172
  See also Amman, Jordan
journalists
  casualties among, 25, 196, 216
  Green Zone life of, 21–24
  manual for, 22
  rotating schedule of, 167
  rules of reporting for, 24
  views about Baghdad of, 24
  See also specific person
Jupiter Air, 67
justice system, Iraqi, 101–7, 177–82

Kaplow, Larry, 177
Kapuściński, Ryszard, 9

Karen (NDI employee), 229, 231–32, 235, 236, 238–42, 245–46, 248, 249, 252

Karkh Children's Teaching Hospital, 200–201

Karma, Iraq, MH embed in, 55–60

KBR (Kellogg Brown and Root), 19, 21, 123

Khadri, Ranya, 214

Khalilzad, Zalmay, 112, 215, 223, 237, 238, 239

Khan Younis (Palestinian town), 171

kidnappings, 113, 120, 152, 176

Knight Ridder, 218

"knock and talk," 57–58

Kurdistan, 162, 243

Kurds, 177, 202

Kuwait
    ceremony for casualties flying home in, 246–48
    and flight home, 229, 239–40, 245–49
    Iraqi invasion of, 136
    Stryker Brigade in, 149

land mines
    Al-Zawra broadcasts about, 186
    in Iraq, 49

Latin Americans, 19

lawyers, Iraqi, 114

Lincoln Group, 19

"Little Venice" (Baghdad neighborhood), 19

Live 8 concert (England), 32, 37

Los Angeles Times, 8, 22, 215, 234

Louisiana National Guard, 49–52

love, MH views about, 80

Lynch, Rick, 123

Mabry, Marcus, 29

McCain, John, 133

Mad Max Highway (Amman to Baghdad), 8

Mahmoud (prison officer), 114

Mahon, Ruth (MH's grandmother), 210

Maliki, Nouri al-, 141, 180, 196–97, 207

Maliki, Saadi al-, 90–92

Mansour (Baghdad neighborhood), 21

"The March 6 Agreement," 125–26

marines, U.S., 42, 56, 130

martial law, 110

Martin, James, 54–55

Mason, Johnny, 49

Massedy, Ali al-, 180

Massen (Jordanian driver), 7–8

Matt (intel officer), 46–47

MCI, 138

media
    and Andi's death, 212
    banning from parliament of, 165
    and Battle of Baghdad, 147
    Franks's views about, 234
    IIP strategy toward, 3
    MH interviews about Andi's death, 215, 217–19
    NDI strategy toward, 215–16
    See also specific organization

Mehdi Army, 200, 202, 220

military bases, naming of, 42

military, U.S.
    and details of Andi's death, 217
    and Hussein's trial and execution, 181
    IIP request for security from, 220
    investigation of Andi's death by, 234–35
    Iraqi relations with, 196–99
    MH fascination with, 11
    public relations for, 182–85
    and Shiite government interference, 196–97
    shortages of forces in, 147–48
    strains on, 150
    uniforms and equipment of soldiers in, 153
    views about U.S. policy of, 191–92
    See also soldiers, U.S.; specific person

militias, Shiite, 114, 142, 147, 152, 156, 198

Ministry of Information, 19, 25

Ministry of Interior, Iraq, 103, 114, 142, 198
Miramax, 133
Mohammed (Iraqi staff member), 24, 25, 101, 106, 142–43, 263–64
Mohanid (Iraqi staff member), 24, 25
Mortuary Affairs, 233, 246, 248
mosques
    attacks on, 123
    and clearing of Ghazaliya, 155–56
    snapshots of, 119–21, 123
    See also Golden Mosque
Mosul, Iraq, 63–64, 148, 149, 194
Mott, Specialist, 150
MSNBC, MH interview with, 180
Munib (cook and houseboy), 110–12, 135, 140, 173, 264

Nablus (West Bank), 172
Nagy, Benjamin "Ox," 150
Najaf, Iraq, MH in, 194
Nasser, Abdul, 172
National Democratic Institute (NDI)
    and Andi's death, 208, 213–14, 215–16, 217, 219, 225–27
    Andi's employment with, 1–3, 171–72, 173, 199–200, 224, 238, 255–57
    background about, 133–34
    and Baghdad Airport ceremony, 229, 231–32, 238
    Baghdad location of, 173, 175
    closing of Baghdad operation by, 243
    IIP relationship with, 240–41
    media strategy of, 215–16
    MH briefing from, 242–43
    and MH reactions to Andi's death, 216
    MH views about, 240–41
    MH visit with Andi at, 175–77, 186–91, 192
    security for, 216, 223, 227, 241–42, 243
    See also specific person

National Guard, Iraqi (ING), 117
NATO (North Atlantic Treaty Organization), 231, 237
NBC, MH interviews about Andi's death with, 217, 218
Nepalese. See Gurkhas
New Year's Eve, in Baghdad, 173–74
New York City
    Andi leaves, 147
    Andi-MH in, 128–34
    and MH return from Iraq, 68–69
    MH views about being based in, 129–30, 132
    See also specific person or organization
The New York Times, 171, 215, 220
news, MH childhood interest in, 10
Newsweek
    Baghdad headquarters of, 8, 15, 21–22, 264
    car bombs at Baghdad headquarters of, 21
    and dangers of Yarmouk neighborhood, 220
    interviews as way to promote, 131
    Iraqi staff for, 23, 24–25, 138, 143
    and MH delay in Kuwait, 246
    MH departure from, 263
    MH early work with, 11
    and MH "Editor's Note" about Andi's death, 218
    MH first byline from Iraq in, 25–27
    MH offered job as Iraq permanent correspondent for, 132
    risks of Iraqis working for, 23, 143
    rotating schedules for Baghdad personnel with, 167, 169
    security procedures at, 173, 175–76
    See also specific person
Nile Sat, 185
Norris, John "RPG Magnet," 148–49, 151–52, 159, 160
Nuha (Palestinian fixer), 172, 190

Obama, Barack, 205
O'Brien, Tim, 137

Ocean Cliffs, 182
Omar (Iraqi staff member), 24, 25
Omar (prison warden), 116–17
On the Record with Greta Van Susteren (Fox News), 122
Operation Together Forward Phase II, 139, 147–48. *See also* Battle of Baghdad
Orascom Telecommunications, 138
Ordierno, Ray, 191

Packer, George, 199–200
Palestinians/Palestinian territories, 170, 171, 172, 204, 223
Parhamovich, Andi. *See* Andi; Andi and MH; Andi—death of
Parhamovich, Andre (Andi's father), 73, 75–77, 256, 257, 265
Parhamovich, Chris (Andi's brother), 73, 76, 256, 257
Parhamovich, Cory (Andi's brother), 73, 76, 256, 257
Parhamovich, Vicki (Andi's mother), 73, 75, 76–77, 146, 211, 256, 257
Parhamovich family
  and Andi's acceptance of IRI job, 146
  and Andi's death, 209, 210, 211, 213, 223, 229
Paris, France, Andi-MH plans for vacation in, 190–91, 204, 205, 209, 234
parliament, Iraqi, 16–17, 24, 141, 165, 171, 220. *See also* Convention Center, Iraqi
Patton, Brian, 153–54
Pearl Harbor, 184
Peraino, Kevin, 169
Periscope, 24
Perry, Ohio, Andi-MH trip to, 73–77
Peruvians, 19
Peterson, Joseph, 117–18
Pettingkill, Robert, 51
Polar Bears, 184
police, Iraqi
  avoidance of, 176
  and clearing of Ghazaliya, 152, 154, 155, 156
  at Convention Center, 17
  as "death squads," 117–18
  Duke's views about, 198
  and Haifa Street battle, 197
  and kidnapping of Ghazaliya men, 152
  in Mosul, 148
  prisoners of, 114–17
  risk for disobeying, 176
  during Saddam's rule, 26
  as Shiite, 114
  training of, 103
  U.S. raid on Jadriya Bunker of, 103
political parties, Iraqi, 220
politicians, Iraqi, IRI conference for, 162–63
post-traumatic stress disorder, 47, 226
Powell, Colin, 12
Prague, Czechoslovakia, Andi-MH in, 125–28, 257
prisons, 114, 116, 117. *See also* Abu Ghraib prison; Al-Hakimiya prison
private security guards. *See* Gurkhas; security guards; *specific person or security company*
public relations, U.S. military, 182–84
Puerto Rico, Andi-MH vacation in, 134

Quarghuli Village, Polar Bears in, 184
The Quiet American (Greene), 137, 169

Ragas, Jason, 50–51
Ramadan, 65
Ramadi, Iraq, 17, 52
Ramal Hotel (Baghdad), 1, 173, 188
Ramallah, 172
Ramsay, Tom, 207–9, 211, 231
Ramstein Air Force Base, 245–46, 249, 251–52
Ranya (Amman fixer), 136
Rasheed Hotel (Baghdad), 17, 21, 24, 170

INDEX

Read, Lucian, 159
Reagan, Ronald, 133
Red Cross letters, 149
Red Zone, 24, 170, 171, 173, 186, 188
refugees, 113, 143
Republican Party, 153
roadside bombs. *See* IEDs
Rod (*Newsweek* bureau chief), 139
Roosevelt, Theodore, 191, 192
Rosa Mexicano restaurant (New York City), 30
rotation schedules, 167, 169
"route security" patrols, 54–55
routes, naming of, 42
Royal Jordanian flights, 214, 232
RTI, 19
Rubaie, Mowfak, 180
rules of engagement (ROE), 43, 57
Rumsfeld, Donald, 150, 154, 157, 160
Russell, David O., 11
Ruzicka, Marla, 6
Rwanda, 113

Sadoon, General, 114, 115–16
Sadr City, and early days of journalists in Iraq, 17
Saif (Iraqi teenager), 155
Samarra, bombing of Golden Mosque in, 109, 110, 111, 113, 118, 119, 122, 148
Sarah (magazine correspondent), 140–41
Sather Airfield (Glass House), 232–33
Schwarzkopf, Norman, 10
SCIRI (Supreme Council for Islamic Revolution in Iraq), 142, 220
security forces, Iraqi
    Iraqi views about, 187
    and kidnapping of Ghazaliya men, 152
    and shortage of U.S. military forces, 147
    training and funding of, 103, 135
    See also Army, Iraqi; police, Iraqi

security guards
    for Andi, 2, 3, 164, 170, 173, 194, 255, 256
    at checkpoints, 17, 19, 20
    and Christmas in Baghdad, 173
    demand for, 175–76
    killing of Andi's, 209, 215, 217, 225–27, 229, 234, 235, 237, 241–43, 255–56
    NDI, 223, 227, 241–42
    number of, 20
    quality of, 175–76
    and rules for moving around in Green Zone, 16
    sources for private, 19–20
    and trip between airport and Baghdad, 6, 7
    See also Gurkhas; *specific person or company*
security training, MH receives, 29, 31
Senegalese, 20
September 11, 2001, 11
shape charge. *See* EFP
Shelley's restaurant (New York City), 37
Shiites
    Al-Zawra broadcasts about, 185, 186
    Hussein's massacre of, 177
    as Iraqi staff members, 24
    power in Iraq of, 24
    See also civil war, Iraqi; *specific person*
Shula (Baghdad neighborhood), 152
Simpson, Xeon, 200, 201
SITE institute, 215
smoking, 65
soccer, 136–37
soldiers, U.S.
    free time of, 48, 55–56, 77, 78, 80
    questions asked MH by, 41
    uniforms and equipment of, 153
Springer, Jerry, interview with, 30, 31, 37
State Department, U.S.
    and Baghdad Airport ceremony, 229, 237

denial of existence of civil war by, 121–22

and Hussein's trial and execution, 178

Iraqi employees of, 134

and IRI and NDI, 133

issues MH travel orders to accompany Andi's body, 229

and land mines in Iraq, 49

report about conditions in Baghdad by, 141–42

report about refugees and displaced Iraqis by, 143

rotation of officials with, 167

travel advisories of, 6, 172

Stone, Greg, 119–21, 123

stress, 47, 59–60, 226

Stryker armored vehicles, 63, 151–52, 153, 157, 158, 159

Stryker Brigade, 172nd, MH embed with, 63–64, 148–59, 220

Sudan, prisoners from, 116, 117

suicide car bomb. *See* car bombs

Sunnis

in Anbar Province, 52

as Iraqi staff members, 24

power in Iraq of, 24

See also civil war, Iraqi; *specific person*

surge, military, 196. *See also* Operation Together Forward Phase II

SVBIED (suicide vehicle-borne improvised explosive device). *See* car bombs

Swift, Jane, 75

Tapes, Jack, 5, 6, 7–9, 43, 44, 112, 176

Tavern on the Green (New York City), 72–73

10th Mountain Division, 26, 119–23, 158

Terrazas, Miguel, 130

terrorists

and clearing of Ghazaliya, 154–55

trials concerning, 101–3

Thompson, Hunter S., 39

Three Kings (film), 11

Thuraya satellite network, 208

Time magazine, 129

TOA (transfer of authority ceremony), 191

TOCroach, 42

Tomb of the Unknown Soldier (Baghdad), 16

torture, 102, 103, 104, 106, 107, 114–15, 116, 117, 187, 199, 219

trash, 44–45

Triple Canopy, 19–20

trust, Mohammed's concerns about, 143

Twain, Mark, 107

Uday (Iraqi security guard), 64, 186

United Nations, 26, 103, 114, 167, 196, 198

Unity Resources Group (URG), 216, 229, 238, 242–43

UXO (unexploded ordnance), 49

Velotta, Brad, 156, 157, 158, 159

Vermont, Andi-MH visit to, 77–78, 223

Vienna, Austria, Andi-MH meeting in, 107, 109–10, 112, 123–24, 126, 128, 223, 224

Vietnam, 24, 137, 169–70, 198

violence

Al-Zawra broadcasts about, 185

and Battle of Baghdad, 147, 148

and daily life in Baghdad, 137

in Green Zone, 165–66

increase in, 191

and military public relations, 182–84

in Mosul, 148

"sectarian," 112–13, 141, 142, 147, 183, 185

and shortage of U.S. forces, 147

State Department report about, 141–42

INDEX

violence (*cont.*)
  talk about ending, 185
  See also casualties; *specific event*

Wall Street Journal, 8, 22, 26
"war junkies," 67
Ware, Michael, 113
Weinstein, Harvey, 133
West Bank, 172, 223
The Wire (TV), 203
Wolfowitz, Paul, 170
women
  fraternizing with Iraqi, 163
  in Green Zone, 163
  in Iraq, 146
  raping of Iraqi, 219
World War II, land mines in Iraq from, 49

X (security manager)
  and Andi's death, 209–10, 211
  and Hussein's trial and execution, 179–80
  and Jacob-MH meeting about ambush, 225, 227

  and MH departure to accompany Andi's body home, 230, 232
  and MH visit with Andi at NDI, 175–77, 186–87, 188, 189, 191
  and search for Andi's body, 214

Yarmouk (Baghdad neighborhood), 2–3, 216, 220
"Yellow Pages," 57–58
Yonni (Andi's Hungarian guard), 225–26, 229, 231, 234, 237, 240, 248, 255, 256
Yusafiya, Iraq, raping in, 130

Zakaria, Fareed, 201
Zampini, Abby (Andi's niece), 73, 74–75, 223, 256, 257
Zampini, Kayla (Andi's niece), 73, 74–75, 223, 256, 257
Zampini, Marci (Andi's sister), 73, 74, 76, 211, 256, 257
Zeena, trial of, 104–6
Ziad, trial of, 104–6

I Lost My Love in Baghdad

DISCUSSION QUESTION

1. One of the themes of *I Lost My Love in Baghdad* is how people can be driven by their passions—the author, Andi, soldiers, and even the insurgents. What brings Hastings and his fiancée to Iraq? How are they different than many of the American soldiers? How does Hastings compare the motivations of the Americans in the book with those of the Iraqis?

2. Hastings describes the Green Zone as having a "bastardized Disneyland quality" to it. What does he mean?

3. How does the author strive to paint a human face on those taking part in the war? Do you think he succeeds?

4. How do the soldiers depicted in the book view their job? How does this contrast with the American public's view of their job? How does it compare with your own expectations?

5. What role does technology play in the events of the book? How does it affect the soldiers? How does it affect the author?

6. Hastings makes references to Robert Byron and his travels in the Middle East, as well as writings about the French and American experiences in Vietnam. How has war and war reporting changed in the twenty-first century? Why do you think the

Bush administration allowed reporters to embed themselves with units of soldiers?

7. President George W. Bush: "They looked into the abyss and did not like what they saw." Michael Hastings: "They looked into the abyss and they learned a valuable lesson." (See page 122.) What does Hastings mean by revising Bush's statement?

8. Hastings and his interpreter, Mohammed, often joke about the phrase "It's your country, my friend." Explain the significance—and the irony—of the phrase.

9. How did Hastings deal with the pressures from *Newsweek* and the military to print the "good news"?

10. From the moment Hastings learns of Andi's death, the tone of the book changes. How?

11. At the end of the book, do you view Andi's death as waste or sacrifice?

12. Has reading *I Lost My Love in Baghdad* influenced your view of the war in any way? If so, how?

13. How do you think Hastings's view of the war in Iraq affected the way he grieved over Andi's death?

14. Read the new afterword that Hastings wrote for the paperback edition of the book. Are you surprised that he chose to return to a war zone—this time Afghanistan—to report on it? Do you think his views have changed since the time he first wrote the book?